WOMEN'S VOICES

By the same author

Women Novelists Today
Women Writing Worldwide
Women Writers Talk
The Writer's Imagination
800 Years of Women's Letters

WOMEN'S VOICES

THEIR LIVES AND LOVES THROUGH
TWO THOUSAND YEARS OF LETTERS

Olga Kenyon

Foreword by Gavin Ewart

Constable · London

Special Edition for

PAST TIMES®

Oxford, England

First published in this format in Great Britain 1997
by Constable and Company Limited
3 The Lanchesters, 162 Fulham Palace Road
London W6 9ER
Copyright © Olga Kenyon 1995
The right of Olga Kenyon to be identified as the author
of this work has been asserted by her in accordance with
the Copyright, Designs and Patents Act 1988
ISBN 0 09 477210 X
Printed in Great Britain by
St Edmundsbury Press Ltd
Bury St Edmunds, Suffolk

A CIP catalogue record for this book
is available from the British Library

Illustrations reproduced by kind permission
of the National Portrait Gallery, London

Letters remind us that history was once real life

Lincoln Schuster

CONTENTS

ILLUSTRATIONS

FOREWORD

Increasingly, in literature of all kinds, and in our attitudes to it, the importance of work by women is becoming obvious. Throughout the centuries many educated women, who never published a book of any kind, nevertheless wrote letters. It is these letters, to their families, their friends and their lovers, which give us a truthful, uncensored view of their lives – and from this a clear picture of the age in which they lived. Letters are more nearly spontaneous than the formal means of communication, and nearer to speech itself; they are seldom 'planned', like a novel or a poem or a play.

It is this freshness and spontaneity that Olga Kenyon has captured in this book, covering the experience of women from the everyday details of running a household or a hospital (Florence Nightingale) to the dangers and delights of exploration (Freya Stark).

GAVIN EWART

INTRODUCTION

A letter can be as dramatic as theatre, as structured as a short story and as lyrical as poetry. Yet women's letters were not defined as a literary form until I began researching them and discovered that women had been writing impressively and skilfully for over 2,000 years. Letters tell us more about other people's feelings and activities than all but the best biographies and social histories. Of all historical documents, they speak most directly to us. As readers, we are like voyeurs, looking directly into other people's lives.

When writing to women friends, many adopted conversational modes, capable of sensitive psychological analysis, which should no longer be downgraded as 'gossip'. In these post-colonial days we stress the value of oral tradition. Our first speech is learned orally from our mother: a vernacular 'mother-tongue' often scorned later by a 'father language' – such as Latin – until recently taught in school but omitted from most girls' educations.

These letters show the ability of women to use a far greater range of discourse, or types of language, than generally realized. They include the intuitive, the sensitive, the caring, which may be termed 'feminine' qualities. They also deploy rational, philosophical, and political dis- courses, termed 'patriarchal' since too frequently the preserve of middle- class males in power, in the law, the church and government. Many women developed skill to persuade and reason, from abbesses and queens to nineteenth- and twentieth-century social reformers.

Women have traditionally been thought of as biologically determined, and associated with instinct rather than reason, and a passive rather than active attitude to life. These women letter-writers, however, frequently rise above such polarities through their skill in both patriarchal discourse (and strategies for subverting male power) and in the 'female' areas of sharing, of feelings, of improving daily life.

The oldest letter written by a woman dates from 200 B.C. (see page

48). Significantly it deals with difficulties over money and marriage. It is only recently that feminist historians have uncovered such documents, and shown us a wealth of female writing that hitherto had been ignored. Few letters have survived from the time of the barbarian invasions, after the fall of the Roman Empire, but I managed to find one from the Anglo-Saxon Queen Emma.

By the twelfth century, once life became a little more settled, a few women gained public prominence, among them the visionary Hildegard of Bingen (1098–1179). Her mystic prose poems and her sermons reached the notice of abbots, kings and popes, who wrote to her for advice. Her mother-tongue was German, yet her letters are in Latin, which she taught herself. Until recently her Latin has been considered inadequate, simplistic, repetitive. Now the force of her direct language is being revalued, like the spoken discourse of the abused black child Celie in Alice Walker's *The Color Purple*. Both these writers, in very distinct ways, show the power of female letters to gain an audience for young women hitherto considered of no consequence.

This book proves that from the time of the Roman Empire onwards many were able to express themselves forcefully on a breadth of subjects. There is correspondence here from the second century B.C. on child-rearing, that sounds astonishingly contemporary. There are letters which show that Anglo-Saxon women received greater respect than we had realized. Women emerge as powerful administrators: they managed large institutions, such as convents, or the castle, while the lord was absent, as shown in the recently re-edited *Lisle Letters*.

In the *Paston letters*, written during the Wars of the Roses (and only republished in 1980), Margaret Paston gives us invaluable knowledge of the running of a large medieval household in her detailed, forceful, affectionate letters to her husband. Before then letters were mostly official. It is women who were foremost in using letters to communicate feelings, and thus teach us more about this essential element in our psyche. While doing so they extended our ability to use language, one of our vital tools in communication. This female role in our culture has been underestimated since the Stone Age, when men hunted, while women cultivated seeds, children and conversation.

Far more is now available from the twelfth century onwards, thanks chiefly to feminist historians: The best known is probably Héloïse (pre-viously translated by Dorothy L. Sayers) who writes in the scholastic language she had learnt in her uncle's house, as she pleads for a letter from her adored Abelard. It is significant that the first professional writer was a widow, Christine de Pisan, who supported herself, and orphaned children in fourteenth-century Paris. She explicitly offered role models in *The City of Ladies* (1405), the first book written in praise of women, and forgotten till the last decade. Late medieval England produced fascinating collections of letters, such as the Plumpton, Lisle and Paston ones. The women in these families, all highly literate, are among the first people to write in English rather than Latin. By Tudor times queens were well educated, setting an encouraging example. From the seventeenth century women rebel more overtly against restrictions. To counteract their subversion, the eighteenth century produced many middle-class writers (usually men) expounding on female duties. These attitudes were often interiorized by women who wrote letters, both real and fictitious, often to daughters, on topics such as duty towards husbands, female education, and proper behaviour. From the 1740s we see greater attempts to define women's roles and determine sexual ethics. Sadly, there is *less* radicalism after the demise of Mary Wollstonecraft (author of *Vindication of the Rights of Women*). Mary Astell (1700) wrote on wifely submission, but with irony; whereas Hannah More (1799) stressed obedience, while advocating education ('industry and humility are worth more than splendour'). Lady Pennington (1761) advised 'discreet improvement' of indifferent males, and education of daughters.

After the French Revolution far more schools were set up: for private boarders, like the Brontë sisters, dame schools for the lower middle class, ragged schools for the urban poor, Sunday schools and a few schools attached to factories. Little writing came from the schools for working-class children, as the standards were low. The Education Act of 1873 imposed primary education, though parents had to pay a penny a week, and classes were made up of sixty to seventy children. At last literacy was being offered to most, however inadequately.

FRIENDSHIP

Female friendship, like motherhood, is one of the great untold stories of history. Until recently relegated as gossips, cronies, sexual rivals, women friends show themselves, over centuries, as supportive. Their letters reveal deep affections and shared interests, and offer mutual advice on managing work, husbands, children, and illness. Their supportiveness might serve as a model for communitarianism.

The private letter implicitly transgresses the male order of

rule-governed forms. Ironically it was the one area of writing allowed
women, because, according to Virginia Woolf, it appeared non-
threatening. In the attempts to define the female self through language,
these letters can be viewed as 'anti-nodels' to help friends face the
restrictions of male cultural conditioning.

My research has uncovered the sharing of a wealth of ideas on topics
from gardening and cookery to aspects of science and medicine. For her
nuns (and local women) Hildegard of Bingen wrote a book on herbal
medicine, with recipes and psychological advice. (Some of her sensible
diets and curative herbal remedies have helped me, 800 years later.)

The importance of friendship in women's lives and their ability to
sustain lifelong relationships are shown between many well-known sisters, such as Jane Austen and Cassandra. The word sisterhood is now
as evocative as 'brotherhood' – which had excluded women, without men
seeming to notice, neither during the French Revolution nor in Trade
Union meetings. We have few written records till the eighteenth century
when Lady Mary Wortley Montagu and her sister shared their ideas and
feelings with other wealthy intellectuals. These well-educated women,
named 'blue stockings' by Dr Johnson, displayed both social commitment
and the ability to work together on many philosophical, social and educational issues. This blossomed into effective social reform in the nineteenth century.

At the same time more intimate friendships flourished: sisters sharing
beds in Tudor times, friends later using the language of romance without
arousing social reprobation, in phrases such as 'she is my passion'; 'I
dream of her all night' (Mrs Carter's *Letters*, vol. 1, p. 2). 'Romantic
friendship', a term used to describe lesbianism, evokes shared interests
and devotion, free from the social hostility still too apparent today.

TRAVEL WRITING

Women have been travelling ever since nature and wars forced them to
move. Yet we hear little of them till the sixteenth century, when Teresa
of Avila toured Spain to reform convents and re-organize religious life.
By the second half of the seventeenth century the open-minded Lady
Fanshawe visited Spain with her ambassador husband and found the food
and conditions in general far better than in Commonwealth England.
A French contemporary, Madame d'Aulnoy, wrote virtually the first
well-known travel book, based on letters from her exiled mother: *Travels*

into Spain in 1691, which became a bestseller, but is seldom mentioned by male academics. The first travel-writer in English is Celia Fiennes (1662–1741). She kept a lively journal for her family, describing her extensive tours – the first comprehensive survey of change in the English countryside.

Travel letters were initiated by the witty Lady Mary Wortley Montagu. She married a man of far less intellect than herself and relied on the fellowship of the pen to keep in touch with her women friends. When Lord Montagu was appointed ambassador to Turkey, she shocked English society by following him, on her own. Of the travel writers to the East until our century she is unique in imposing few preconceptions of her own about exoticism and sensuality. She learned about smallpox vaccination, seventy years before it was developed in Britain by Jenner, and asked for her small children to be vaccinated, showing a striking respect for alien culture and learning.

In the nineteenth century letter-writers such as Emily Eden and Lucie Duff Gordon discovered that they had the gift to interest a wide audience back in Britain, before the days of the foreign correspondent – or photographs. To travel is to put oneself at risk, physically and emotionally. Few male travel writers have to contend with fear of rape, or ostracism by fundamentalist cultures.

Women also express the need for escape and evasion, and range from those who dressed as men to become soldiers, to Victorian girls wishing to flee the repression of chaperone and spinsterhood.

Travel imagery sometimes echoes sexual metaphors, with descriptions of 'exploits' and 'conquests'. Some found love, including Isabelle Eberhardt, Lady Jane Digby and Isabella Bird, whose 'Jim' was a native of the Rocky Mountains. Perhaps fewer women have a 'wilderness' in them, more are torn between desire for travel, and a longing to return home. This makes their travel writing more complex than men's since they dwell less on externals, and include intimate reflections. Mary Wollstonecraft, the radical social reformer, bemoans the absence of her baby daughter and incorporates her emotional reactions to impressive landscape in the letters she wrote to earn money for her husband. Female letters, like 'gothic' novels, serve both to analyse inner landscapes and conventional society, a dialogue between what they feel and what they observe.

Today we are revaluing the achievements of the intrepid Victorian ladies who travelled through Africa and the East at a time when few men welcomed the many hardships. Some, such as Isabel Burton, who idolized her explorer-writer husband Richard, did it for love. Others travelled for their health, like Isabella Bird and Lucie Duff Gordon, author of *Letters from Egypt*. Her tone is so friendly, her responses to people so acute that I have included a number of extracts from her correspondence. Alexandra David-Néel became a Buddhist and learned Tibetan so fluently that she passed as a native, the first Western woman to enter the Forbidden City. Her mysticism helped her to survive frost on the open mountains, and confirms the continuing spirituality – and enterprise – of women over the centuries.

I have managed to obtain some working-class letters, mainly from the nineteenth century, though primary education was still so inadequate. They provide new information about how this large, underrepresented group lived and thought. The Imperial War Museum, London, now has a moving collection of writing from all classes made during the First and Second World Wars.

THE EPISTOLARY NOVEL

The epistolary novel grew out of women's letter-writing. Until the last decade we were taught that Defoe and Richardson were the creators of the English novel. But almost a century before them, two *women*, Aphra Behn and the Duchess of Newcastle, first realized ways of unifying their epistles with a semblance of narrative. In *Sociable Letters* (1664) Margaret Cavendish, Duchess of Newcastle, proffered moral advice to daughters 'who are but branches which by marriage are broken off from the root'. Behn, the first professional woman playwright, supported herself and sometimes her lover, with her pen. Her *Love Letters between a Nobleman and his Sister* was probably published as early as 1683. Based on a real scandal, this novel responds to a desire, equally evident today, for news reports and contemporary sexual scandal. More importantly, Behn realized that letters deal with emotional problems and responses between personalities in ways that can be developed into the pattern-making and character analysis of fiction. Women's epistolary novels are among the first examples of the novel (from the Latin *novellus*, meaning 'new').

Unlike other forms of female writing, letters had the advantage of (a) male acceptance, (b) flexibility and (c) popularity. Soon they widened to include travel reports, so enabling the heroine to widen her experience, a strategy developed further in 'gothic' novels. They inspired tales of adventure in distant countries, when some newspapers were little more than letters.

A fair number of women published in the eighteenth century. Eliza Haywood established the popularity of the epistolary novel, extending the structure while putting the heroine through a moral test. Her works can be seen as a document of the development of the genre, from *Love in Excess* (1719) to *The History of Betsy Thoughtless* (1751), in four volumes. Increasing criticism by males led Eliza Haywood to impose moral endings on her work, to avoid the view that professional women were sexually immoral. Her plots which rewarded 'good' heroines with marriage or equated tragic endings with loss of a desired male fitted social conventions. Letters were an acceptable mode in a Protestant culture that advocated introspection and conscience-searching, rather than Catholic confession. To sell to the rising middle class, epistolary novels had to be both religious and easy to read. The then popular *Letters Moral and Entertaining* (1729) by Elizabeth Rowe is fiction based on sermons to young ladies, recommended for their moral education. It is a worthy precursor of Richardson's *Pamela*.

By 1773 the *Monthly Review* stated that fiction was almost entirely the domain of women. By then the novel was not only commenting on morals and offering guides to manners, it offered entertainment to a wide readership. The Austen family were 'great novel readers and not ashamed of being so'. Indeed Jane Austen's first experiments with novel-writing, as a young adolescent, were epistolary: a charming, brief four-page novelette (p. 45).

The nineteenth century gave enforced leisure to middle-class women, who enjoyed longer novels, to read to the family, or on their own. Only a few writers continued with the epistolary form, notably the Irish Lady Morgan (1776–1859), daughter of Owenson, an impoverished actor. To help feed her family she began writing young. As her *Poems by a Young Lady Between the Ages of 12 & 14* did not sell well she turned to the novel, gaining a reputation as a regional novelist with *The Wild Irish Girl: A National Tale* (1805). Like George Eliot she used the novel to present social issues, though her passionate defence of the Irish Cause led to ostracism by some English aristocrats. Nevertheless, she was the first woman to be granted a literary pension – of £300 a year.

By the late twentieth century, after decades of neglect, experimental women novelists are turning to epistles. Fay Weldon in *Letters to Alice* (1981) continues the potential to offer advice; Gillian Hanscombe in *Between Friends* (1983) stresses the powers of female directness; Alice

Walker in *The Color Purple* (1983) demonstrates the vigour of black women's discourse, and American Lee Smith, an oral historian, in *Fair and Gentle Ladies* (1989) displays the strength of hitherto despised working-class speech. The oral rhythms of letters are once again revaluing and shaping women's experience.

THE STRUCTURE OF THIS BOOK

The structure of this book takes the form of a woman's life, from birth, through loving and childrearing, middle age and widowhood, to dying. This structure shapes most women's lives, not unlike the way they shape their reactions through their writing. The opening chapters can be read like biography, tracing real lives, from childbirth, through childhood to adolescence.

I have divided adult life into a number of categories that cover relationships, daily life, managing money, managing the household, work, travel, illness, growing old, facing death. The letters are from contrasting periods which offer valuable historical insights, both explicit facts and implicit evidence of differing cultural attitudes. Furthermore, the discourses of different centuries provide unusual comparisons, and primary source material for literary criticism.

The original inspiration for this book was an interest in women's lives, thoughts, preoccupations and occupations. Soon I became fascinated by the astonishing diversity of writing, much of which had never been studied. This shaping of experience through letters frequently becomes as readable as fiction, which is the shaping of imaginative experience. As Edith Wharton, the great American novelist and letter-writer said: 'we can enjoy the breathless first reading, the slow lingering over each phrase, the taking possession of the one that will be carried in one's thought all day'.

CONCLUSION

The book ends with letters that face up to illness, old age and death, an admirable chronicle of bravery, and resourcefulness. Madame de Sévigné and Fanny Burney devise helpful physical and spiritual exercises; George Sand's vitality and love for grandchildren are contrasted with the carping of her friend Gustave Flaubert. The women whom I have selected attempt to come to terms with some of the most difficult and lonely aspects of life. They offer us advice and consolation about topics that still worry the majority of people. Through their correspondence on subjects like death, which are difficult for many to discuss, they provide comfort, sometimes hope. Some even manage to do this with humour! And truth is better than sedatives, as Fay Weldon is fond of pointing out. These letters demonstrate women's capacity to make a great deal out of the little space which society allotted, and to create a remarkable chronicle out of their lives by reflecting on experience through their letter-writing.

PART ONE

The beginning of life – Childhood –
Education – Religious teaching – Growing up

THE BEGINNING OF LIFE

We have few letters celebrating the birth of a daughter. Until the twentieth century the yearly child, and frequent deaths in many families, led men like Montaigne to remark that the deaths of his children had scant effect on him. Small children seem to have been little valued until Tudor times, when effigies of dead offspring begin to appear on tombs, alongside praying parents. By the seventeenth century we see paintings of family groups, and by the eighteenth century the baby has become a sexy cherub and the small child a symbol of beauty and innocence – or dressed as an adult.

There were different attitudes to the birth of a daughter, as these two nineteenth-century letters show.

29 Oct. 1843

At a quarter before nine a little girl was born. I was beside myself when I saw her and heard her loud crying. It is bewildering to see a human being, one's own child, where just before there was nothing, and I cried out alternately, 'My child, thank God, my child, thank God, thank God'.

CAROLINE CLIVE
(1801–1873, a British novelist and vicar's wife)

1849

Ask a French peasant about his family, he will reply, 'I have no children, sir; I have only daughters.' The Breton farmer whose wife has brought a daughter into the world still says to this day, 'My wife has had a miscarriage.'

ERNEST LEGOUVE

MILLICENT GARRETT FAWCETT (1847–1929) describes a demanding baby daughter. She married the M.P., Henry Fawcett, in 1867. He worked hard with her for women's rights, together helping to found Newnham College. Their daughter Philippa was born in 1868. Philippa was able to benefit from her intelligent care. This note was written to help a friend.

1876

About your baby, I think I may perhaps be able to console you a little, because I always say that Philippa screamed incessantly for many months in her baby hood. Probably it was something to do with health, and may be modified by hitting upon just the right sort of feeding; but I think it also has to do with nervous organisation, a highly strung nervous body being the victim of it, while a stupid one does nothing but digest, sleep and grow fat. That is where my consolation comes in – it may be a sign of nascent mental activity, and you are nursing into life and strength someone who will leave an impression on the history of the world. So cheer up, dear C. and try to 'bear with patience'. Make your husband hold the baby sometimes while you write me a letter to say how you are.

Bringing up a baby daughter was a joy for Mary and Robert Abell, who lived in the eastern United States in the second half of the nineteenth century. He was a Methodist preacher who moved to Illinois in 1868.

Dec. 12, 1866, New York

Baby Nettie is well and just as sweet and pretty as ever. She has on a little grey sack and she looks so cunning. Just now Mary is trotting her, saying, 'This is the way the ladies ride, the ladies ride, the ladies ride, etc.' which seems to suit Baby Nettie a good deal.
ROBERT ABELL to Mary's sister Kate.
(Nettie is five months old.)

Jan. 18, 1869, Illinois

It is now 1 o'clock p.m. Baby [Eddie] is taking his nap and Nettie is also sleeping. She is quite sick today. Has vomited six times this a.m. We thought she was troubled with worms and gave her a new kind of medicine yesterday which does not seem to agree with her. It tastes just like McLeam's Vermifuge – I have been opposed to her taking it all of the time – but Robert thought it would be good for her. I'll not give her any more of the miserable stuff. She has slept most all day. Is very pale and sick to her stomach all the time. I don't know what to do for her. She has been quite fretful for several days past – has been teasing to 'go home' as usual. I told her not to do something the other day and she looked at me and said 'they sant buse 'ittle Nettie – Nettie Grandma going to send Nettie something *nice*' – so she has not forgot her Grandma's humoring her you see. Expect if she could *go home* – she would be the happiest little thing ever was. I should not be able to do any thing with her. She has been very much interested about learning the letters in 'Aunt Katie's Book' for a week or so past. She has learned the names of quite a number.

MARY ABELL to her sister Kate.
(Nettie is two and a half.)

April 4, 1869, Illinois

Thought I had finished your letter but I must tell you what Nettie has just been about. I told her to put the old cat out of doors – she and Eddie went into the back room with her and presently I heard Nettie laughing and Eddie saying 'burn burn' – and guess what the little rogues had been doing – well Nettie had put the cat into the stove (one we use washing days) and had shut and was holding the door. There did not happen to be any fire in the stove which was lucky for the cat – if it had been washing day – poor puss might have fried hard. As it was she only came out considerably sooted up, the cat is maltese, yellow and white spotted or mottled, but a good deal of white on her. I am going to make an 'Indian pudding' today and do some other cookings so goodbye.

MARY ABELL to her sister Kate.

CHILDHOOD

ST TERESA of Avila was born to a devout Catholic family. Her childhood games inspired her later life, founding convents.

1645

If I had not been so wicked it would have been a help to me that I had parents who were virtuous and feared God, and also that the Lord granted me His favour to make me good. My father was fond of reading good books and had some in Spanish so that his children might read them too. These books, together with the care which my mother took to make us say our prayers and to lead us to be devoted to Our Lady and to certain saints, began to awaken good desires in me when I was, I suppose, about six or seven years old. It was a help to me that I never saw my parents inclined to anything but virtue. They themselves had many virtues. My father was a man of great charity towards the poor, who was good to the sick and also to his servants – so much so that he could never be brought to keep slaves, because of his compassion for them. On one occasion, when he had a slave of a brother of his in the house, he was as good to her as to his own children. He used to say that it caused him intolerable distress that she was not free. He was strictly truthful: nobody ever heard him swear or speak evil. He was a man of the most rigid chastity.

My mother, too, was a very virtuous woman, who endured a life of great infirmity: she was also particularly chaste. Though extremely beautiful, she was never known to give any reason for supposing that she made the slightest account of her beauty; and, though she died at thirty-three, her dress was already that of a person advanced in years. She was a very tranquil woman, of great intelligence. Throughout her life she endured great trials and her death was most Christian.

We were three sisters and nine brothers: all of them, by the goodness of God, resembled their parents in virtue, except myself, though I was my father's favourite. And, before I began to offend God, I think there was some reason for this, for it grieves me whenever I remember what good inclinations the Lord had given me and how little I profited by them. My brothers and sisters never hindered me from serving God in any way.

I had one brother almost of my own age. It was he whom I most loved, though I had a great affection for them all, as had they for me. We used to read the lives of saints together; and, when I read of the martyrdoms suffered by saintly women for God's sake, I used to think they had purchased the fruition of God very cheaply; and I had a keen desire to die as they had done, not out of any love for God of which I was conscious, but in order to attain as quickly as possible to the fruition of the great blessings which, as I read, were laid up in Heaven. I used to discuss with this brother of mine how we could become martyrs. We agreed to go off to the country of the Moors, begging our bread for the love of God, so that they might behead us there; and, even at so tender an age, I believe the Lord had given us sufficient courage for this, if we could have found a way to do it; but our greatest hindrance seemed to be that we had a father and a mother. It used to cause us great astonishment when we were told that both pain and glory would last for ever. We would spend long periods talking about this and we liked to repeat again and again, 'For ever – ever – ever!' Through our frequent repetition of these words, it pleased the Lord that in my earliest years I should receive a lasting impression of the way of truth.

When I saw that it was impossible for me to go to any place where they would put me to death for God's sake, we decided to become hermits, and we used to build hermitages, as well as we could, in an orchard which we had at home. We would make heaps of small stones, but they at once fell down again, so we found no way of accomplishing our desires. But even now it gives me a feeling of devotion to remember how early God granted me what I lost by my own fault.

I gave alms as I could, which was but little. I tried to be alone when I said my prayers, and there were many such, in particular the rosary, to which my mother had a great devotion, and this made us devoted to them too. Whenever I played with other little girls, I used to love building convents.

The Brontë family is remembered for its writing, and poverty. Though their mother died after the birth of her seventh child, the girls got on extremely well. They enjoyed sharing the work in the kitchen, and all wrote novels together.
Here CHARLOTTE BRONTË is thirteen.

March 1829

While I write this I am in the kitchen of the Parsonage, Haworth; Tabby, the servant, is washing up the breakfast things, and Anne, my youngest sister, (Maria was my eldest) is kneeling on a chair, looking at some cakes which Tabby had been baking for us. Emily is in the parlour, brushing the carpet. Papa and Branwell are gone to Keighley. Aunt is upstairs in her room, and I am sitting by the table writing this in the kitchen. Keighley is a small town four miles from here. Papa and Branwell are gone for the newspaper, the Leeds Intelligence, a most Tory newspaper, edited by Mr. Wood, and the proprietor, Mr. Henneman. We take two and see three newspapers a week.

Charlotte and Emily shared a tiny bedroom, and composed plays together in bed.

Emily's and my Bed Plays were established the 1st December 1827; the others March 1828. Bed Plays mean secret plays; they are very nice ones. All our plays are very strange ones. Their nature I need not write on paper, for I think I shall always remember them.

QUEEN VICTORIA remembers her childhood.

1872

We lived in a very simple plain manner; breakfast was at half past eight, luncheon at half past one, dinner at seven – to which I came generally (when it was no large dinner party) – eating my bread and milk out of a small silver basin. Tea was only allowed as a great treat in later years. I was brought up very simply – never had a room to myself till I was nearly grown up – always slept in my Mother's room till I came to the Throne. At Claremont, and in the small houses at the bathing-places, I sat and took my lessons in my Governess's bedroom. I was not fond

of learning as a little child – and baffled every attempt to teach me my
letters up to 5 years old – when I consented to learn them by their being
written down before me.

In the year 26 (I think) George IV asked my Mother, my sister and
me down to Windsor for the first time; he had been on bad terms with
my poor father when he died, and took hardly any notice of the poor
widow and little fatherless girls who were so poor at the time of his
[the Duke of Kent's] death that they could not have travelled back to
Kensington Palace had it not been for the kind assistance of my dear
Uncle, Prince Leopold.

When we arrived at the Royal Lodge the King took me by the hand
saying 'Give me your little paw'. He was large and gouty but with a
wonderful dignity and charm of manner. He wore the wig which was
so much worn in those days. Then he said he would give me something
to wear and that was his picture set in diamonds, which was worn by
the Princesses as an order to a blue ribbon on the left shoulder. . . .
I went with him in a pony carriage with my governess to Sandpit Gate
where the King had a Menagerie – with wapitis, gazelles, chamois etc.
We drove round the nicest part of Virginia Water and stopped at the
Fishing Temple. Here there was a large barge and everyone went on
board and fished while a band played in another!
VICTORIA R.

Some children had no time to play at all. Child labour in English mines was
considered acceptable until the 1850s. This is an extract from a Parliamentary
paper. If these girls had been taught to write, this first-hand account would
have been more widely available, to shock the reading public.

1842

I hurry with my brother. It tires me a great deal, and tires my back and
arms. I go sometimes at half past four and sometimes five; it's dark
when I go; it often rains and we get wet, but we take off our top clothes
when we get in the pit. They never lace or ill-use me in the pit. I can't
read; I have never been to school. I do nought on Sundays. I have had
no shoes to go in to school. I don't know where I shall go if I am a bad
girl when I die. I think God made the world, but I don't know where
God is. I never heard of Jesus Christ.
ELIZA COATS eleven years old

EDUCATION

Most children did not go to school until universal primary education was introduced in the 1870s. Before the nineteenth century children were often considered little adults, whose psyche and imagination were of no intrinsic interest; therefore we have virtually no writing from them. The concept of childhood is, to a certain extent, an invention of the Victorians, explored in novels such as *David Copperfield* and *Jane Eyre*.

These letters come from rich and poor, from early to late adolescence. The letters of Queen Elizabeth I at eleven and Queen Victoria at eighteen show the high standards demanded of pupils when they were fortunate enough to have tutors. There are extracts from eighteenth-century letters, hoping to improve the education of the daughters of the wealthy, and a rare passage from the French feminist Flora Tristan, on one of the few working-class schools which she found in London in the 1830s.

The letters from an epistolary novel show the delights of growing up and discovering London at sixteen, in Fanny Burney's *Evelina*. These probably reflect her own joy at being in London as an adolescent. Like many clever daughters of ambitious men, she was forcefully directed by her famous musicologist father, in whose home she showed herself as far shyer than these letters suggest. Dale Spender in *Mothers of the Novel* (1988) describes this phenomenon as fairly frequent; there are instances of men signing the work of daughters and wives, even in the twentieth century, as happened to Colette.

Until universal primary education, introduced by European governments in the nineteenth century, few girls received much schooling. Education can be defined as a leading-out of the child's innate abilities, *or* a putting-in of knowledge. The Church tended to 'put in' many hours of theology, and Greek and Latin – subjects not taught girls. Until Virginia Woolf's time, women have written of their frustration at not being allowed to learn this privileged discourse of men. Nuns were among the few women to receive education, though in some cases this proved scanty. Hildegard of Bingen in the twelfth century, and Dame Julian of Norwich, like many aristocratic women, dictated their letters.

It still remains a mystery how Hildegard learned Latin and theology: perhaps from listening to sermons very attentively, as so many girls had to do if they were to pick up an education. Heloïse, in twelfth-century Paris, educated by a scholastic uncle, used the same discourse as her ambitious churchman-lover, Abelard. She learned the ability to manipulate *their* language, as did Christine de Pisan, the first woman to earn her living by writing. The late middle ages in England produced correspondence of literate women in collections such as the Stonor, Lisle and Paston letters (extracts from some of these are given later in this book).

By Tudor times daughters of the rich were often well educated, though not always for the child's sake, but to improve their marriage prospects and consequently the family. Early in childhood Lady Jane Grey suffered 'nips and beatings' from her ambitious parents. Henry VIII's last wife, Catherine Parr, chose one of the best tutors of the time (and unusually also a governess for Elizabeth) for all her stepchildren. By the late eighteenth century the upper middle class were employing underpaid women from poorer homes to 'improve' their girls.

The following are the views of young queens of their education. Here the future QUEEN ELIZABETH I when only eleven writes to her stepmother Catherine Parr. Elizabeth had been given an excellent tutor, Roger Ascham, and learned Latin and Greek at the age of five.

To Queen Catherine (Parr)   31 December 1544
To Our most Noble and Virtuous Queen Catherine, Elizabeth, her humble daughter, wisheth perpetual felicity and everlasting joy.

Not only knowing the affectuous will and fervent zeal, the which your Highness hath towards all godly learning, as also my duty towards you (most Gracious and Sovereign Princess), but knowing also, that pusillanimity and idleness are repugnant unto a reasonable creature, and that even as an instrument of iron soon waxeth rusty, unless it be continually occupied, even so the wit of a man *or a woman* wax dull and unapt to do or even to understand any thing perfectly, unless it be always occupied in some manner of study. And therefore, have I translated this little book out of French rhyme into English, combining the sentences together as well as the capacity of wit and small learning could extend themselves, which book is entitled *The Mirror, or Glass of the Sinful Soul*, wherein is contained, how she (beholding what she is) doth perceive how, of herself, she can do nothing that good is, unless it be through the grace of God.

Although I know that, any part I have wrought in it, is nothing done as it should be, nor else worthy in your Grace's hands, but rather all imperfect, yet do I trust also that the file of your excellent wit, in the reading of it, shall rub out, polish and mend.

Praying God Almighty, the Maker and Creator of all things, to grant unto your Highness the same New Year's day, a lucky and a prosperous year, with prosperous issue, and continuance of many years in good health and continual joy, and all to His honour, praise and glory.

From Ashridge, the last day of the year of our Lord God, 1544.
Sent with Elizabeth's translation of 'The Mirror of the Sinful Soul'.

A letter from the PRINCESS VICTORIA *to the King of the Belgians*
                                                 19th November 1834.
My dearest uncle – It is impossible for me to express how happy you have made me by writing so soon again to me, and how pleased I am to see by your very kind letter that you intend to write to me often. I am much obliged to you, dear Uncle, for the extract about Queen Anne, but must beg you, as you have sent me to show what a Queen *ought not* to be, that you will send me what a Queen *ought to be*. [King Leopold had sent the Princess an extract from a French Memoir, containing a severe criticism of the political character of Queen Anne.]

I like reading different authors, of different opinions, by which means I learn not to lean on one particular side. Besides my lessons, I read [Sir John Thomas] Jones' account of the [Peninsular] wars in Spain, Portugal, and the South of France, from the year 1808 till 1814. It is well done, I think, and amuses me very much. In French, I am now in *La Rivalité de la France et de l'Espagne*, par [Gabriel Henri] Gaillard, which is very interesting. I have also begun [*Histoire Ancienne*] Rollin [Charles]. I am very fond of making tables of the Kings and Queens, as I go on, and I have lately finished one of the English Sovereigns and their consorts, as, of course, the history of my own country is one of my first duties. I should be fearful of tiring you with so long an account of myself, were I not sure you take so great an interest in my welfare.

Pray give my most affectionate love to *dearest* Aunt Louisa, and please say to the Queen of the French and the two Princesses how grateful I am for their kind remembrance of me.

Believe me always, my dearest Uncle, your very affectionate, very dutiful, and most attached Niece,
VICTORIA.

An adolescent girl attempts to rule. In 1553, at the age of eleven, LADY JANE GREY was proclaimed queen of England. She wrote to Lieutenants of the English Counties, anxious to gain their support.

Jane the quene.   July 1553

Right trustie and right wellbeloved Cousen, we grete you well, advertising the same that where yt hath pleased Almighty God to call to his mercie out of this lief our derest Cousen the King your late Sovereigne Lorde, by reason wherof ande suche Ordenances as the said late King did establishe in his lief tyme for the securitie and welthe of this Realme, we are entrerid into our rightfull possession of this Kingdome, as by the last Will of our said derest Cousen, our late progenitor, and other severall instruments to that effect signed with his own hande and sealed with the grete Seale of this Realme in his own presence, wherunto the Nobles of this realme for the most parte and all our Counsaill and Judges, with the Mayor and Aldermen of our Cytie of London, and dyvers other grave personages of this our Realme of England, have also subscribed there names, as by the same Will and Instrument it maye more evidently and plainly apere; We therefore doo You to understand, that by th'ordenance and sufferaunce of the hevenly Lord and King, and by th'assent and consent of our said Nobles and Counsellors, and others before specifyed, We doo this daye make our enterye into our Towre of London as rightfull Quene of this realme; and have accordingly sett furthe our proclamacions to all our loving subjects gyvenge them therby to understande their duties and allegeaunce which they now of right owe unto us as more amplie by the same you shall briefly perceyve and understand; nothing doubting, right trustie and right welbeloued cosen, but that you will indever yourself in all things to the uttermost of your powre, not only to defend our just title, but also assist us in our rightfull possession of this kingdome, and to disturbe, repell, and resist the fayned and untrue clayme of the Lady Mary basterd daughter to our grete uncle Henry the Eight of famous memory.

Henry VIII had passed an Act of Parliament, declaring the issue of his first two marriages illegitimate. On 19 July 1553, a few days after this earnest missive, an army marched against her. She was imprisoned but not executed till 12 February 1554.

LADY MARY WORTLEY MONTAGU (1689–1762) wrote to give advice for her daughter on the education and attitudes that an aristocratic woman in the eighteenth century needed to face life – and marriage.

1753

It is a saying of Thucydides, that ignorance is bold, and knowledge reserved. Indeed it is impossible to be far advanced in it, without being more humbled by a conviction of human ignorance, than elated by learning. At the same time I recommend books, I neither exclude work nor drawing. I think it as scandalous for a woman not to know how to use a needle, as for a man not to know how to use a sword. I was once extremely fond of my pencil, and it was a great mortification to me when my father turned off my master, having made a considerable progress for the short time I learnt. My over eagerness in the pursuit of it had brought a weakness in my eyes, that made it necessary to leave off; and all the advantage I got was the improvement of my hand. I see, by hers, that practice will make her a ready writer; she may attain it by serving you for a secretary, when your health or affairs make it troublesome to you to write yourself; and custom will make it an agreeable amusement to her. She cannot have too many for that station of life which will probably be her fate. The ultimate end of your education was to make you a good wife (and I have the comfort to hear that you are one): hers ought to be, to make her happy in a virgin state. I will not say it is happier; but it is undoubtedly safer than any marriage. In a lottery, where there is (at the lowest computation) ten thousand blanks to a prize, it is the most prudent choice, not to venture. I have always been so thoroughly persuaded of this truth, that, notwithstanding the flattering views I had for you (as I never intended you a sacrifice to my vanity), I thought I owed you the justice to lay before you all the hazards attending matrimony: you may recollect I did so in the strongest manner. Perhaps you may have more success in the instructing your daughter.

Views of two eighteenth-century mothers on educating daughters.

1770

It is necessary for you to be perfect in the four first rules of Arithmetic
– more you can never have occasion for, and the mind should not be
burthen'd with needless application.

The management of all domestic affairs is certainly the proper
business of woman – and, unfashionably rustic as such an assertion
may be thought, it is not beneath the dignity of any lady, however high
her rank, to know how to educate her children, to govern her
servants. . . . Make yourself, therefore, so thoroughly acquainted with
the most proper method of conducting a family, and with the necessary
expense which every article.

LADY PENNINGTON, to her daughters

1790

. . . Confine not the education of your daughters to what is regarded
as the ornamental parts of it, nor deny the graces to your sons. Suffer
no prejudices to prevail on you to weaken Nature, in order to render
her more beautiful; take measures for the virtue and the harmony of
your family, by uniting their young minds early in the soft bonds of
friendship. Let your children be brought up together; let their sports
and studies be the same; let them enjoy, in the constant presence of
those who are set over them, all that freedom which innocence renders
harmless, and in which Nature rejoices.

. . . I have given similar rules for male and female education, on the
following grounds of reasoning.

First, that there is but one rule of right for the conduct of all rational
beings; consequently that true virtue in one sex must be equally so in
the other, whenever a proper opportunity calls for its exertion; and,
vice versa, what is vice in one sex, cannot have a different property when
found in the other.

Secondly, that true wisdom, which is never found at variance with
rectitude, is as useful to women as to men; because it is necessary to
the highest degree of happiness, which can never exist with ignorance.

Lastly, that as on our first entrance into another world, our state of
happiness may possibly depend on the degree of perfection we have
attained in this, we cannot justly lessen, in one sex or the other, the
means by which perfection, that is another word for wisdom, is acquired.

CATHERINE MACAULAY

As eldest daughter of an ambitious writer, who had been three times widowed, MARIA EDGEWORTH (1768–1849) helped bring up his increasing family. When they moved to his estate in Ireland, she collaborated with him in writing *Practical Education* (1798) and enlightened reading schemes. She soon became popular in her own right, with novels such as *Castle Rackrent* (1800). Her *Letters to Literary Ladies* (1795) proclaims the dignity and equality of women, here put into the mouth of a man:

From a Gentleman to his friend on the birth of a Daughter

I congratulate you, my dear Sir, upon the birth of your Daughter; and I wish that some of the Fairies of ancient times were at hand to endow the damsel with health, wealth, wit, and beauty – Wit? – I should make a long pause before I accepted this gift for a daughter.

As I know it to be your opinion, that it is in the power of education more certainly than it was ever believed to be in the power of Fairies, to bestow all mental gifts; and as I have heard you say that education should begin as early as possible, I offer my sentiments:

Allowing that women are equal to our sex in natural abilities, from their situation in society, from their domestic duties, their love of romance, poetry and all the lighter parts of literature, their time must be so fully occupied that they could never have the leisure even supposing they had inclination, for that severe application to which our sex submit. Now calculate the time which is wasted by the fair sex, and tell me how much the start of us they ought to have in the beginning of the race, if they are to reach the goal before us? It is not possible that women should ever be our equals in knowledge, unless you assert that they are far our superiors in natural capacity. . . .

You will, in a few years, have educated your daughter; and if the world be not educated exactly at the right time to judge of her perfections, to admire and love them, you will have wasted your labour, and you will have sacrificed your daughter's happiness: that happiness, analyse it as a man of the world or as a philosopher, must depend on friendship. Love the exercise of her virtues, the just performance of all the duties of life, and the self-approbation arising from the consciousness of good conduct.

I am, my dear friend, Yours sincerely.

JANE AUSTEN at the age of seventeen shows the love of an aunt for her baby niece. Unfortunately we do not know what the 'morsels' consisted of, but can guess they contained moral advice. The letter is addressed To Miss Jane Anna Elizabeth Austen.

My dear Neice [*sic*],
Though you are at this period not many degrees removed from Infancy, Yet trusting that you will in time be older, and that through the care of your excellent Parents, you will one day or another be able to read written hand, I dedicate to You the following Miscellanious Morsels, convinced that if you seriously attend to them, you will derive from them very important Instructions, with regard to your Conduct in Life. – If such My hopes hereafter be realised, never shall I regret the Days and Nights that have been spent in composing these Treatises for your Benefit.
I am my dear Neice,
Your very Affectionate Aunt
THE AUTHOR
2 June 1793

It was rare for the daughters of working-class Londoners to be sent to school before 1870. FLORA TRISTAN, an early French feminist, visited London in the 1830s. In letters home, which she turned into her *London Journal 1842*, she describes the only school she found.

1842
At last after many wrong turnings and vain inquiries our guide made us stop at the mouth of an alley even dirtier than the rest. There we had to leave our cab as it could never have got through the way we had to follow: the school was in an interminable lane with several sharp turnings, and every so often we came upon ponds in which rain-water was carefully saved for washing clothes. This lane, a positive sewer, is dangerous enough for a fully grown person and must be even worse for children as they make their way to school. It was only after great care and many tribulations that we reached the house. It had rained that morning and what with the sticky mud and the soapy water we nearly fell into the pond twenty times over.
    A young woman of between twenty and twenty-five was in charge of

the school: she was of decent appearance, had a soft voice and courteous manner, and seemed well-bred. She was somewhat embarrassed at our visit and no sooner had we entered than she began to tell us how badly the house was situated; the spot was marshy and the laundries all around made it a very unhealthy place to live in. 'The kind lady who founded the school,' she went on, 'is a good friend of the poor, but she is far from wealthy; this house is all she has, and however shabby and inconvenient it may be, her charity is no less admirable for that! What is more, she goes without the barest necessities of life in order to pay me twenty pounds a year to look after the girls, and the same to my father to look after the boys.' I agreed that such generosity was indeed very noble, and I wondered if anywhere in the three kingdoms there was a rich man capable of such an action.

The school consisted of two rooms, each far too small for the number of children (there were eighty in all) and so low-pitched that the windows had to be kept open in all weathers to let in some air. The boys were on the ground floor and the girls above; there was access from one room to the other by means of a wooden ladder, and children of two were climbing up and down holding on to a rope.

This establishment, judged by its situation, accommodation and furnishings was indeed very poor, but such considerations disappeared in the presence of the affectionate and intelligent spirit of charity which guided it. The children were very clean and so were their clothes, with not a hole to be seen. The girls were particularly neat and tidy; the big ones were making clothes for them all; each one was addressed as *mother* and had charge of two little ones whom she washed, combed and instructed in habits of cleanliness and self-control. The young teacher told me that the children had Miss Doyle to thank for their clothes as well; this respectable lady spent her time in going to all the grand houses asking for charity and used the money she was given to buy material for the children's clothes.

MRS GASKELL (1810–65), who combined writing and motherhood, wrote on her daughter's education to Anne Robson.

                                        1 September 1851
It is delightful to see what good it has done Marianne, sending her to school; & is a proof of how evil works out good. She is such a 'law

unto herself' now, such a sense of duty, and obeys her sense. For
instance she invariably gave the little ones 2 hours of patient steady
teaching in the holidays. If there was to be any long excursion for the
day she got up earlier, that was all; & they did too, influenced by her
example. She also fixed on 9 o'clock for her own bed-time, & kept to
it through all temptations. These are but small instances but you will
understand their force. She grew strong, & fat, & ruddy in the holidays,
& I could not find out any reason for the paleness on first coming
home. She seemed well, had plenty and good food to eat; plenty of
rest & exercise, and was evidently very happy at school, & with reason,
for Meta (who staid one night with her while we were in London, &
was strongly prejudiced against the school before going,) said every
one was so kind, such good dinners, such a pretty garden, & a bathroom
to every bed-room, all which thing took my second little lady's fancy
very much. MA looks at nothing from an intellectual point of view; &
will never care for reading, – teaching music, & domestic activity,
especially about children, will be her forte.

Meta is untidy, dreamy, and absent; but so brim-full of I don't know
what to call it, for it is something deeper & less showy than talent. Music
she is getting so fond of, which we never expected; and I'll tell you a
remark of hers the other day, which will explain a little of what I mean.
She had a piece by Mendelsohn to learn called The Rivulet. When
she was playing it to me she said towards the end 'Now Mama I
transpose this into the minor key, for I think the rivulet is wandering
away and lost in the distance, & then you know brooks have such a sad
wailing sound'. Now it's a great deal of trouble to transpose a piece,
but she had done it perfectly & played it so. Then her drawings are
equally thoughtful & good. She has not lessons, for Miss Fox said
lessons from any drawing master here would spoil her, but she reads
on the principles of composition, & does so well. She is quite able to
appreciate *any* book I am reading!

She talks very little except to people she knows well; is inclined to
be over-critical & fastidious with everybody & everything, so that I
have to clutch up her drawings before she burns them, & she would
be angry if she could read this note, praising her.

STEVIE SMITH (1902–71), the poet, recalls her childhood and education,
in an extract from a letter to her friend Anna Browne.

I remember my early childhood as a golden age, a time untouched by war, a dream of innocent quiet happenings, a dream in which people go quietly about their blameless business, bringing their garden marrows to the Harvest Festival, believing in God, believing in peace, believing in Progress (which of course is always progress in the right direction), believing in the catechism.

Here's a poem of myself as censorious baby:

> I sat upright in my baby carriage
> and wished mama hadn't made such a foolish marriage.
> I tried to hide it, but it showed in my eyes unfortunately
> And a fortnight later papa ran away to sea.

When I went to North London Collegiate, the stiff curriculum and long journey exhausted me, and as I would rather have been thought naughty than stupid, I rebelled. It was certainly at that school, my first grand second school after I had left behind my dear kindergarten, that I first learnt to be bored and to be sick with boredom, and to resist both the good with the bad, and resist and be of low moral tone and non-co-operative, with 'Could do better' for ever upon my report and the whole of schoolgirl strength going into this business of resistance, this Noli-me-tangere, this Come near and I shoot.

RELIGIOUS TEACHING

CHARLOTTE BRONTË was brought up by a strict Calvinist aunt. When she was nineteen she wrote to her friend Ellen Nussey about her religious beliefs.

More books were sold and read on religion than on any other topic in the nineteenth century. The educated and uneducated received religious instruction, as this and the following extract testify.

1836

My eyes fill with tears when I contrast the bliss of a saintly life . . . with the melancholy state I now live in; uncertain that I have ever felt true contrition, wandering in thought and deed, longing for holiness which I shall never, never attain, smitten at times to the heart with the conviction that —'s ghastly Calvinistic doctrines are true, darkened, in short, by the very shadows of spiritual Death! If Christian perfection be necessary to Salvation, I shall never be saved. . . .

. . . I keep trying to do right, checking wrong feelings, repressing wrong thoughts – but still . . . I find myself going astray. I have a constant tendency to scorn people who are far better than I am, a horror at the idea of becoming one of a certain set – a dread lest, if I made the slightest profession, I should sink at once into Phariseeism, merge wholly into the ranks of the self-righteous. In writing at this moment I feel an irksome disgust at the idea of using a single phrase that sounds like religious cant. . . . If the Doctrine of Calvin be true I am already an outcast. . . .

As slaves were not taught to write, I include a verbal account of intense religious experience.

I was born in Huntsville, Alabama, during slavery time. When the war broke out I was married and had one child.

My mother was a good old time Christian woman. Me and my sister used to lay in the bed at night and listen to her and my aunt talk about what God had done for them. From this I began to feel like I wanted to be a Christian. I got so that I tried to pray like I heard them pray. I didn't know what it meant. I hardly know what I said half the time. I just said something with the Lord's name in it and asked Him to have mercy on me.

The first time I heard God's voice I was in the blackberry patch. It seemed like I was all heavy and burdened down more than common. I had got so I prayed a lot and more I prayed it look like the worse off I got. So while I was picking blackberries I said, 'Lord, what have I done; I feel so sinful.' A voice said, 'You have prayed to God and He will bring you out, a conqueror. You are born of God. You have been chosen out of the world and hell can't hold you.' The law is written in my heart and I don't need no book. He told me to ask through faith and He would grant it in grace.

GROWING UP

An adolescent girl taken to London for the first time is described by
FANNY BURNEY (1752–1840), who began writing fairly young, once she
had taught herself to read in her father's library. At sixteen she destroyed
most of her writing in a puritanical rejection of fiction, but the imagination of this shy woman needed an outlet and she took up writing again
at seventeen. In secret she composed a novel out of letters: *Evelina*
(1778). Her brother took it to a publisher, who promptly accepted it –
for a low fee. It was reprinted three times in its first year, since it
was both lively *and* moral, and won the praise of many leading figures,
such as Dr Johnson. In these two letters the orphan Evelina is taken to
London and discovers Garrick (with similar enthusiasm to Burney's
own).

Saturday Night
O my dear Sir, in what raptures am I returned! Well may Mr. Garrick
be so celebrated, so universally admired – I had not any idea of so great
a performer.

Such ease! such vivacity in his manner! such grace in his motions!
such fire and meaning in his eyes! – I could hardly believe he had
studied a written part, for every word seemed spoke from the impulse
of the moment.

His action – at once so graceful and so free! – his voice – so clear,
so melodious, yet so wonderfully various in its tones – such animation!
– every look *speaks!*

I would have given the world to have had the whole play acted over
again. And when he danced – O how I envied Clarinda. I almost
wished to have jumped on the stage and joined them.

I am afraid you will think me mad, so I won't say any more; yet I
really believe Mr. Garrick would make you mad too, if you could see
him. I intend to ask Mrs. Mirvan to go to the play every night while

we stay in town. She is extremely kind to me, and Maria, her charming daughter, is the sweetest girl in the world.

I shall write to you every evening all that passes in the day, and that in the same manner as, if I could see, I should tell you.

Monday

We are to go this evening to a private ball, given by Mrs. Stanley, a very fashionable lady of Mrs. Mirvan's acquaintance.

We have been *a shopping*, as Mrs. Mirvan calls it, all this morning, to buy silks, caps, gauzes, and so forth.

The shops are really very entertaining, especially the mercers; there seem to be six or seven men belonging to each shop, and every one took care, by bowing and smirking, to be noticed; we were conducted from one to another, and carried from room to room, with so much ceremony, that at first I was almost afraid to follow.

I thought I should never have chosen a silk, for they produced so many, I knew not which to fix upon, and they recommended them all so strongly, that I fancy they thought I only wanted persuasion to buy every thing they shewed me. And, indeed, they took so much trouble, that I was almost ashamed I could not.

At the milliners, the ladies we met were so much dressed, that I should rather have imagined they were making visits than purchases. But what most diverted me was, that we were more frequently served by men than by women; and such men! so finical, so affected! they seemed to understand every part of a woman's dress better than we do ourselves; and they recommended caps and ribbands with an air of so much importance, that I wished to ask them how long they had left off wearing them!

The dispatch with which they work in these great shops is amazing, for they have promised me a compleat suit of linen against the evening.

I have just had my hair dressed. You can't think how oddly my head feels; full of powder and black pins, and a great *cushion* on the top of it. I believe you would hardly know me, for my face looks quite different to what it did before my hair was dressed. When I shall be able to make use of a comb for myself I cannot tell, for my hair is so much entangled, *frizled* they call it, that I fear it will be very difficult.

I am half afraid of this ball to-night, for, you know, I have never danced but at school; however, Miss Mirvan says there is nothing in it. Yet I wish it was over.

Adieu, my dear Sir; pray excuse the wretched stuff I write, perhaps

I may improve by being in this town, and then my letters will be less
unworthy your reading. Mean time I am,
Your dutiful and affectionate,
though unpolished,
EVELINA

The subject of a girl's first period is aired in this letter from MARY
WILDER to her daughter Mabel Loomis Todd, a writer and lecturer in
Amherst, Massachusetts. Here she proffers heavy-handed advice on the
menarche. She shows just how forceful a grandmother could sound and
how the whole family watched a girl's puberty. The daughter Millicent
was thirteen when this occurred.

1893

You can never do a wiser thing than to *leave all your work* – and take
that dear precious child away to Bermuda – or anywhere else – to give
her a great change – and you will *always* be glad you did it! Do not
delay! You need not let her see your motive – only say you both – need
a change! for *months* before this change came *to you*, your Father, G'ma
and I watched you daily. Especially just before the time the menses came
– we planned walks in the Catholic grounds – Rock creek – Etc. Your
father became your *companion* – talked in the liveliest manner – and
kept your spirits even and happy – we saw to it that your studies did
not depress you. You were so tenderly watched all through this dangerous
crisis – that it came to you very naturally – and without any special
sickness – Our great sorrow over our dear Eliza's death [Mary Loomis's
sister] – made us very careful. She died at eighteen – and *slipped away*
from us making no sign! She *loved* her books and studies so that she
kept her distress away from us – until *too late*! She was never regular
– and became more and more *irregular* until her death. When at last
Dr Wesselhoeft came he told us it was too late – and she lived only a
few months – there was not *then* vitality enough to work on –
    I waited until your book was ready for the press before writing you
– but *everyone* who comes to our room sees the framed photograph [of
Millicent] and all exclaim, 'How very sad and depressed the dear child
looks!'

Mabel Todd was editing the poems of Emily Dickinson.

PART TWO

Courtship – Proposals, engagements, dowries and doubts – Being
in love – Love affairs – Lesbian love

COURTSHIP

Since the invention of the Pill, courting is out of fashion. Courting began in the courts of France, in the late Middle Ages. While the lord of the castle was away, fighting the Crusades, the troubadour had to sing for his supper. It was wise to praise the lady of the manor, thus worship of women's charms was initiated, reaching England by Tudor times. But even then only a few very rich maidens were courted. The majority of girls, working all day as labourers or servants, were deemed unworthy. Yet the comedies of Shakespeare show that the idea was percolating down.

A letter from Henry VIII's sixth wife, Catherine Parr, proves that even Queens had little leisure to be wooed. The letters from the sparkling Dorothy Osborne were penned over seven years, during the Civil War, waiting for her fiancé, on the other side. The situation became slightly easier in France, once Louis XIV had centralized his warring barons at Versailles.

By the nineteenth century some middle-class girls were allowed a little time and space for wooing. This was an advantage when it gave them greater freedom, but could leave them unprotected, as the rise in illegitimacy rates indicates. Marriage was such an important event in a woman's life that the choice of which suitor to marry was often hazardous. The French were more sensible, making public enquiries about dowries. Interestingly, one of our first extant letters is about problems over a Greek dowry. These letters range from passionate to realistic. They show women taking considerable initiative, towards men, and in the final letter, to another woman.

When Henry VIII died his sixth wife, Catherine Parr, was immediately courted by her former love, Sir Thomas Seymour. Did he want her hand in order to gain power, or did he still care for her? She obviously loves him but had to be circumspect. Seymour prevailed, and she agreed to marry him in secret. Soon she succeeded in obtaining the permission of young King Edward VI for her marriage, so was able to retain the title of Dowager.

My lord,
As I gather by your letter, delivered to my brother Herbert, ye are in some fear how to frame my lord your brother to speak in your favour; the denial of your request shall make his folly more manifest to the world, which will more grieve me than the want of his speaking. I would not wish you to importune for his good will, if it come not frankly at the first; it shall be sufficient once to require it, and then to cease. I would desire you might obtain the king's letters in your favour, and also the aid and furtherance of the most notable of the council, such as ye shall think convenient; which thing obtained, shall be no small shame to your brother and loving sister, in case they do not the like.

My lord, whereas ye charge me with a promise, written with mine own hand, to change the two years into two months, I think ye have no such plain sentence written with my hand. I know not whether ye be a paraphraser or not. If ye be learned in that science, it is possible ye may of one word make a whole sentence, and yet not at all times after the true meaning of the writer; as it appeareth by this your exposition upon my writing.

When it shall be your pleasure to repair hither, ye must take some pain to come early in the morning, that ye may be gone again by seven o'clock; and so I suppose ye may come without suspect. I pray you let me have knowledge over-night at what hour ye will come, that your portress may wait at the gate to the fields for you. And thus, with my most humble and hearty commendations, I take my leave of you for this time, giving you like thanks for your coming to court when I was there. – From Chelsea.

P.S. – I will keep in store till I speak with you my lord's large offer for Fausterne, at which time I shall be glad to know your further pleasure therein.

By her that is and shall be your humble, true, and loving wife during her life,
KATERYN THE QUENE, K.P.

Mary Queen of Scots was married in her teens to the Dauphin of France, and enjoyed her brief time at the French court. She had to return to Scotland when he died, and attempted to rule, in spite of the opposition of John Knox and the Puritanical Scots Kirk. Her unfortunate loves and marriages are fairly well known. When imprisoned by Elizabeth, she was incriminated partly by evidence of letters, said to be in her handwriting (the 'Casket Letters'). It is still uncertain whether they were actually written by her, but this one sounds genuine in its description of a suitor's declaration of love for her. She was celebrated for her good looks and great height, unusual at that time. I have simplified the original spelling slightly.

1568

Being gon from the place where I had left my harte [heart], it may be easily judged what my countenance was . . . I went my waye to supper, this be[a]rer shall tell you of my arrival. He prayed me to com agayne, which I did and he told me his grefe [grief] and that he would make no testament [will] but leave all unto me, and that I was the cause of his sicknes for the sorrow he had that I was so strange unto him.

'And' (said he) 'you asked me what I ment in my lettre to speake of cruelty: it was of your cruelty who will not accepte my offres and repentance: I avowe that I have don amisse, but not that I have always disavowed: and so have many other of your subjectes don, and you have well perdonid them, I am yong. You will saye that you have also perdonid me many tymes, but that I returne to my faultes. May not a man of my age for want of counsell, fayle twise or thrise, and mysse of promes, and at the last repent and rebuke him selfe by his experience? Yf I may obtayn this perdon, I protest I will never make faulte agayne, and I aske nothing but that we may be at bed and at table together as husband and wife. And if you will not, I will never rise from this bed. I pray you tell me your resolution heerof; God knowith that I am punished to have made my God of you, and had no other mynd but of you: and when I offende you som tyme, you are cause thereof. For if I thought whan any body doth any wrong to [me] that I might for my refuge make my mone therof unto you, I wold open it to no other. But whan I heare any thing, being not familiar with you, I must keepe it in my mynde, and that troublith my wittes for anger.' I did still answear him, but that shall be to long.

The contemporary English copy of this long (second) casket letter was made by the clerk at the Westminster Conference, December 1568. [*Calendar of Scottish Papers*, Vol. 2].

QUEEN ELIZABETH I writes a skilful letter of comfort to her young friend, the Earl of Essex.

In the summer of 1597 another English expedition against the Spaniards was prepared, but the weather was very bad throughout July and August. The fleet set out from Plymouth on 10 July, but was caught in a violent storm and scattered. Though no ships were lost, much repair was necessary. This letter was written when the Queen heard of Essex's disappointment.

July 8, 1597

Eyes of youth have sharp sight, but commonly not so deep as those of elder age, which makes me marvel less at rash attempts and headstrong counsels, which give not leisure to judgement's warning, nor heed advice, but make a laughter at the one, and despise with scorn the last. This have I not heard but seen, and thereof can witness bear; yet I cannot be so lewd of nature to suppose the scope was not good. Now, so the race was run, and do more condemn the granters than the offerer, for when I see the admirable work of the Eastern wind, so long to last beyond the custom of nature, I see, as in a crystal, the right figure of my folly, that ventured supernatural haps upon the point of frenetical imputation: but it pleaseth His goodness to strengthen our weakness, and warns us to use wit when we have it hereafter; foreseen haps breed no wonder, no more doth your short returned post before his time. But for answer; if your full fed men were not more fitted by your desired rate, that purse should not be thinned at the bottom, that daily by lightening is made too thin already; but if more heed were taken how, than haste what, we needed not such by reckonings. Kings have the honour to be titled earthly gods, and therefore breeds our shame, if we disgrace so much our name, as though too far short, yet some piece of proportion were not in us, not even to reward desert, by the rule of their merit, but bear with weakness, and help to lift from ground the wellnigh falling man. This, at this present, makes me like the lunatic man that keeps a smack of the remain of his frenzy's freak, helped well thereto by the influence of *Sol in Leone*, that makes me yield for company to a larger proportion than a wiser in my place would ever grant unto, with this caveat, that this lunatic goodness make you not bold to keep too many that you have, and much less taken in more to heap more errors to our mercy; also, that you trust not to the grace of your crazed vessel, that to the ocean may fortune be too humble; foresee and prevent it now in time, afore too late; you vex me too much with small regard of what I scape or did. Admit that by miracle it would do well, yet venture not such wonders where such approachful mischief might betide you. There remains that you, after your perilous first attempt, do not aggravate that danger with another in a farther off climate, which must cost blows of good store; let character serve your turn, and be content when you are well, which hath not ever been your property. Of this no more, but for all my moods I forget not my tenses, in which I see no leisure for aught but petitions, to fortify with best forwardness the wants of this army, and in the same include your safe return.

DOROTHY OSBORNE, daughter of a supporter of King Charles I, fell in love with William Temple, later to become Archbishop of Canterbury. Their engagement lasted for nearly twenty years, partly because of the Civil War. She wrote him many lively letters, which might easily have become the basis of a novel had she lived in a society that allowed women greater ambitions.

5 March 1653?

Sir,

Your last letter came like a pardon to one upon the block. I have given over the hopes on't, having received my letters by the other carrier, who uses always to be last. The loss put me hugely out of order, and you would both have pitied and laughed at me if you could have seen how woodenly I entertained the widow, who came hither the day before, and surprised me very much. Not being able to say anything, I got her to cards, and there with a great deal of patience lost my money to her – or rather I gave it as my ransom. In the midst of our play, in comes my blessed boy with your letter, and, in earnest, I was not able to disguise the joy it gave me, though one was by that is not much your friend, and took notice of a blush that for my life I could not keep back. I put up the letter in my pocket, and made what haste I could to lose the money I had left, that I might take occasion to go fetch some more; but I did not make such haste back again, I can assure you. I took time enough to have coined myself some money if I had had the art on't, and left my brother enough to make all his addresses to her if he were so disposed. I know not whether he was pleased or not, but I am sure I was. . . .

The following is a case of courtship rejected – even when paid for. HARRIETTE WILSON became a celebrated courtesan in the early nineteenth century. She came from a humble family with many sisters who also had to earn their living, as their father was often out of work. She took happily to the oldest profession and discovered many scandals involving the powerful men with whom she consorted. She decided to make her mark by writing witty, revelatory *Memoirs* – about which Wellington pronounced the famous 'Publish and be damned!' This letter from Lord Craven was written to her when she was only seventeen.

1803

A friend of mine has informed me of what has been going on at Brighton. This information, added to what I have seen with my own eyes, of your intimacy with Frederick Lamb, obliges me to declare that we must separate. Let me add, Harriette, that you might have done anything with me, with only a little more conduct. As it is, allow me to wish you happy; and further, pray inform me, if, in any way, à la distance, I can promote your welfare.

CRAVEN

This letter completed her dislike of Lord Craven, and she answered it immediately, as follows:

MY LORD,

Had I ever wished to deceive you, I have the wit to have done it successfully; but you are old enough to be a better judge of human nature than to have suspected me of guile or deception. In the plenitude of your condescension, you are pleased to add, that I 'might have done anything with you, with only a little more conduct', now I say, and from my heart, the Lord defend me from ever doing any thing with you again! Adieu.

HARRIETTE

How to get married after the briefest of courting is outlined in JANE AUSTEN's first novel, written in letter form, when she was in her early teens.

1778

AMELIA WEBSTER
an interesting & well written Tale
is dedicated by Permission
to
Mrs Austen
by
Her humble Servant
THE AUTHOR

Letter the first
TO MISS WEBSTER
MY DEAR AMELIA

You will rejoice to hear of the return of my amiable Brother from abroad. He arrived on thursday, & never did I see a finer form, save that of your sincere freind.

MATILDA HERVEY

Letter the 2^d
TO H. BEVERLEY ESQ
DEAR BEVERLEY

I arrived here last thursday & met with a hearty reception from my Father, Mother & Sisters. The latter are both fine Girls – particularly Maud, who I think would suit you as a Wife well enough. What say you to this? She will have two thousand Pounds & as much more as you can get. If you don't marry her you will mortally offend

GEORGE HERVEY

Letter the 3ᵈ

TO MISS HERVEY

DEAR MAUD

Believe me I'm happy to hear of your Brother's arrival. I have a thousand things to tell you, but my paper will only permit me to add that I am yʳ affecᵗ Freind

AMELIA WEBSTER

Letter the 4ᵗʰ

TO MISS S. HERVEY

DEAR SALLY

I have found a very convenient old hollow oak to put our Letters in; for you know we have long maintained a private Correspondence. It is about a mile from my House & seven from yours. You may perhaps imagine that I might have made choice of a tree which would have divided the Distance more equally – I was sensible of this at the time, but as I considered that the walk would be of benefit to you in your weak & uncertain state of Health, I preferred it to one nearer your House, & am yʳ faithfull

BENJAMIN BAR

Letter the 5ᵗʰ

TO MISS HERVEY

DEAR MAUD

I write now to inform you that I did not stop at your house in my way to Bath last Monday. – I have many things to inform you of besides; but my Paper reminds me of concluding; & beleive me yʳˢ ever &c.

AMELIA WEBSTER

Letter the 6ᵗʰ

TO MISS WEBSTER

MADAM   Saturday

An humble Admirer now addresses you. I saw you lovely Fair one as you passed on Monday last, before our House in your way to Bath. I saw you thro' a telescope, & was so struck by your Charms that from that time to this I have not tasted human food.

GEORGE HERVEY

Letter the 7ᵗʰ

TO JACK

As I was this morning at Breakfast the Newspaper was brought me, & in the list of Marriages I read the following.

"George Hervey Esqre to Miss Amelia Webster"
"Henry Beverley Esqre to Miss Hervey"
&
"Benjamin Bar Esqre to Miss Sarah Hervey".
yours, TOM

Being courted by a younger man is described in this letter from JANE AUSTEN to her sister Cassandra, about the probable love of her nephew, Tom Lefroy.

1807

You scold me so much in the nice long letter which I have at this moment received from you, that I am almost afraid to tell you how my Irish friend and I behaved. Imagine to yourself everything most profligate and shocking in the way of dancing and sitting down together. *That* would hold for my adviser. You, sister need not worry, need not scold me for being a fool at least. I *can* expose myself only *once more*, because he leaves the country soon after next Friday, on which day we *are* to have a dance at Ashe after all. I am disappointed that Charles Fowle has not come to last night's ball, because he would have given you some description of my friend, and I think you must be impatient to hear something about him. What is Tom like? Well, he is a very gentlemanlike, good-looking, pleasant young man, I assure you. But as to our having met, except at the three last balls, I cannot say much; for he is so excessively laughed at about me at Ashe, that he is ashamed to come to Steventon, and ran away when we called on Mrs. Lefroy a few days ago . . .

When Tom Lefroy calls with his cousin George, he is correct with Mrs Austen, and has but *one* fault, in that his morning coat is too light. Tom Lefroy admires Fielding's *Tom Jones*, and therefore wears the same coloured clothes, I imagine, which *he* did when he was wounded.

Tom was 'wounded' enough perhaps to be on the brink of declaring himself, and might have blurted out 'I love you' if his aunt had let him; he said in old age that he had been 'in love' with Jane Austen though it was only a boy's love.

PROPOSALS, ENGAGEMENTS, DOWRIES
AND DOUBTS

Throughout history, girls have been vulnerable economically and sexually. Mary Tudor at eleven allowed her father, Henry VIII, to use her in his power games. Mary Queen of Scots attempted some initiative, which brought her tragic unhappiness. By the following century the relative tranquillity of Louis XIV's court allowed Madame de Sévigné to play with the metaphor of 'surrender'. By the nineteenth century girls are openly balancing the financial offers of respective suitors. Three letters from France demonstrate how much more thought the French put into economic arrangements before marriage; the proposal had to be accompanied by the offer of a dowry. These detailed financial arrangements are compared to the *very* first letter we have from the hand of a woman, of the second century BC, complaining about the use made of her dowry.

The letters from Charlotte Brontë and Stéphanie Jullien show the seriousness with which many middle-class girls weighed proposals. The ideal of romantic love put pressure on women to marry, and roughly eighty-five per cent did so, according to available statistics. The consequences of remaining single were arduous financially, and spinsterhood usually meant hard work and considerable self-sacrifice, as revealed in Charlotte Brontë's comments on spending her evenings sewing rather than writing. Yet she preferred to remain single till she was thirty-nine, because like many at that time she felt that marriage should include emotional and intellectual satisfaction.

Problems over a dowry are described in this, one of the very first letters in the world from a woman. It dates from the second century BC.

To Ptolemaeus, state official, from Senesis daughter of Menelaus, one of the women living in Oxyrhyncha in the Polemon area. I lived with

Didymus son of Peteimouthes from the said village, on the terms of
an Egyptian alimentary silver contract for [   ] gold pieces in
accordance with the laws of the country, and for this money and my
maintenance he had pledged all his property, including a house in the
aforesaid village. But the accused wished to deprive me of this and
went round to one person after another in the said village and wanted
to alienate the house from me. But they did not go along with him
because I would not give my consent. After that he tried to give it as
collateral to the treasury for Heraclides the tax farmer, and accordingly
thinks he can exclude me from my rights.

    On account of this I beg and beseech you; do not allow me, a
defenceless woman, to be deprived of the property pledged for my
dowry because of the irresponsibility of the accused, but if you will,
order that a letter be written to Ptolemaeus the treasurer asking him
not to accept the house from Didymus as collateral. If this is done, I
shall have your assistance. Farewell.

MARY TUDOR's engagement: when Mary Tudor was only eleven years
old, her father, Henry VIII, arranged for her to marry the Hapsburg
Emperor, Charles. (In fact this never took place, much later she married
his son, Philip II of Spain.)
    But in April 1525, Mary sent Charles an emerald with a curious
message, showing that she was still taught to consider herself his
promised bride. The letter which accompanied the gift ran:

Her Grace hath devised this token, for a better knowledge to be had,
when God shall send them grace to be together, whether his Majesty
do keep himself as continent and chaste as with God's grace she woll,
whereby ye may say, his Majesty may see that her assured love towards
the same hath already such operation in her, that it is also confirmed
by jealousy, being one of the greatest signs and tokens of hearty love
and cordial affection.

After the victory of Pavia, Charles, no longer in fear of Francis, declared
openly that he owed nothing to the help of his allies, and released himself
from his pledges to Henry by the very extravagance of his demands. He
sent a commission to Wolsey requiring that Mary should be sent to

Spain at once, with a dowry of 400,000 ducats, and 200,000 crowns besides, to defray the expenses of the war with France.

Madame de Sévigné (1626–96) was loved by her cousin Bussy. Here he uses the courtly language of wooing to make up a quarrel. She replies with knightly metaphors, taken from medieval romance, sharing his courting joke.

31 August 1668

I have surrendered in the reply I sent you. I have sued for my life, and now you would kill me lying at your feet. That is rather inhuman. I never thought women could be so cruel except in love affairs. Come now, little savage, abandon your desire to strike a man who throws himself at your feet, confessing his fault and craving your pardon.

If you are not satisfied with what I have written, tell me what words you wish me to use, and I shall write you whatever kind of letter you wish for, signed with my hand, countersigned by my Secretary, and sealed with the seal bearing my arms. What more would you have?

And here is the lady's last word:

4 September 1668

Rise, Count! I would not kill you at my feet, or take up your sword to renew the combat. It is better that I should give you your life, and that we should live in peace. But you must always acknowledge the part you played in this affair. I ask nothing more than that. You will see that I am treating you generously, and you can no longer call me a little savage. . . .

Adieu, Count. Now that I have conquered you, I shall say that you are the bravest man in France, and whenever remarkable duels are spoken of I shall tell the story of ours.

A proposal from a 'peevish' suitor.

MISS STANHOPE TO M^{rs} . . .

My dear Fanny

I am the happiest creature in the World, for I have received an offer
of marriage from Mr Watts. It is the first I have ever had & I hardly
know how to value it enough. How I will triumph over the Duttons! I
do not intend to accept it, at least I beleive not, but as I am not quite
certain I gave him an equivocal answer & left him. And now my dear
Fanny I want your Advice whether I should accept his offer or not, but
that you may be able to judge of his merits & the situation of affairs I
will give you an account of them. He is quite an old Man, about two
& thirty, very plain, *so* plain that I cannot bear to look at him. He is
extremely disagreable & I hate him more than any body else in the world.
He has a large fortune & will make great Settlements on me; but then
he is very healthy. In short I do not know what to do. If I refuse him he
as good as told me that he should offer himself to Sophia and if *she*
refused him to Georgiana, & I could not bear to have either of them
married before me. If I accept him I know I shall be miserable all the
rest of my Life, for he is very ill tempered & peevish, extremely jealous,
& so stingy that there is no living in the house with him. He told me
he should mention the affair to Mama, but I insisted upon it that he did
not for very likely she would make me marry him whether I would or
no; however probably he *has* before now, for he never does anything he
is desired to do. I believe I shall have him. It will be such a triumph
to be married before Sophy, Georgiana & the Duttons; And he promised
to have a new Carriage on the occasion, but we almost quarrelled about
the colour, for I insisted upon its being blue spotted with silver, &
he declared it should be a plain Chocolate; & to provoke me more said
it should be just as low as his old one. I wont have him I declare. He
said he should come again tomorrow & take my final answer, so I
believe I must get him while I can. I know the Duttons will envy me &
I shall be able to chaprone Sophy & Georgiana to all the Winter Balls.
But then what will be the use of that when very likely he wont let me
go myself, for I know he hates dancing & [has a great idea of Womens
never going from home] what he hates himself he has no idea of any
other person's liking; & besides he talks a great deal of Women's always
staying at home & such stuff. I beleive I shant have him; I would
refuse him at once if I were certain that neither of my Sisters would
accept him, & that if they did not, he would not offer to the Duttons. I
cannot run such a risk, so, if he will promise to have the Carriage
ordered as I like, I will have him, if not he may ride in it by himself

for me. I hope you like my determination; I can think of nothing better;
And am your ever Affec^{te}
MARY STANHOPE

Man proposes, but the actress disposes: A proposal from the essayist
Charles Lamb to FANNY KELLY, actress, and her reply.

                                                            20 July 1819
Dear Miss Kelly, We had the pleasure, *pain* I might better call it, of
seeing you last night in the new Play. It was a most consummate piece
of Acting, but what a task for you to undergo! Would to God you were
released from this way of life; that you could bring your mind to consent
to take your lot with us and throw off for ever the whole burden of
your Profession. I neither expect nor wish you to take notice of this
in your present over occupied state. But think of it at your leisure. I
have quite income enough, if that were all, to justify me for making such
a proposal, with what I may call even a handsome provision for my
survivor. What you possess of your own would naturally be
appropriated to those for whose sakes chiefly you have made so many
hard sacrifices. I am not so foolish as not to know that I am a most
unworthy match for such a one as you – but you have for years been
the principal object of my mind. In many a sweet unassumed character
I have learned to love you, but simply as F.M. Kelly I love you better
than them all. Can you quit these shadows of existence, and come
and be a reality to us? can you leave off harassing yourself to please a
thankless multitude who know nothing of you, and begin at last to
live to yourself and your friends?
    As plainly and as frankly as I have seen you give or refuse assent in
some feigned scene, so frankly do me the justice to answer me. It is
impossible I should feel injured or aggrieved by your telling me at once
that the proposal does not suit you. It is impossible that I should ever
think of molesting you with idle importunity and persecution after your
mind once firmly spoken – but happier, far happier, could I have leave
to hope a time might come when our friends might be your friends;
our interests yours; our book-knowledge, if in that inconsiderable
particular we have any little advantage, might impart something to you,
which you would every day have it in your power ten thousand fold to
repay by the added cheerfulness and joy which you could not fail to

bring as a dowry into whatever family should have the honour and happiness of receiving you, the most welcome accession that could be made to it.

In haste, but with entire respect and deepest affection, I subscribe myself
C. LAMB.

July 20, 1819

An early and deep-rooted attachment has fixed my heart on one from whom no worldly prospect can well induce me to withdraw it but while I thus *frankly* and decidedly reject your proposal, believe me I am not insensible to the high honour which the preference of such a mind as yours confers upon me, let me however hope that all thought upon this subject will end with this letter, and that you will henceforth encourage no other sentiment towards me than esteem in my private character and a continuance of that approbation of my humble talents which you have already expressed so much and so often to my advantage and gratification. Believe me I feel proud to acknowledge myself your obliged friend,
F. M. KELLY.

The French middle class frequently drew up marriage contracts. But financial considerations were no more important than emotional for many girls. STÉPHANIE JULLIEN (1812–83) was born to a large family, the only girl among brothers. Her future happiness and security will depend not on ability to work, but on the choice of suitor. She writes to her father who is pressing her to get married.

20 Feb. 1836

I don't mean to say by all this that I don't have any faults. I have them, and I know they are very great. That is yet another reason why I hesitate to marry – for now it is time to talk about the matter at hand. I feel very keenly the urgent necessity of guaranteeing myself support. I have gone over and repeated to myself all the arguments that you have addressed to me. I know all the reasons why this party is so suitable and that it will be difficult, perhaps impossible, to find someone else as fitting. . . . That is why I hesitated for so long, that is why I did not say *no* three months ago. I have reflected a great deal, perhaps *too much* – although you appear to doubt it – and it is these reflections that make me irresolute.

I am asking for more time. It is not too much to want to see and know a man for ten months, even a year when it is a matter of passing one's life with him. There is no objection to make, you say. But the most serious and the most important presents itself: *I do not love him.* Don't think I am talking about a romantic and impossible passion or an ideal love, neither of which I ever hope to know. I am talking of a feeling that makes one want to see someone, that makes his absence painful and his return desirable, that makes one interested in what another is doing, that makes one want another's happiness almost in spite of oneself, that makes, finally, the duties of a woman toward her husband pleasures and not efforts. It is a feeling without which marriage would be hell, a feeling that cannot be born out of esteem, and which to me, however, seems to be the very basis of conjugal happiness. I can't feel these emotions immediately. Indeed, considering the bustle and bother that this affair has caused, it would not be surprising if I never felt them. Let me have some time. I want to love, not out of any sense of duty, but for myself and for the happiness of the one to whom I attach my life, who will suffer if he only encounters coldness in me, when he brings me love and devotion.

I am, you say, cold and not very hospitable. How else could I be with someone that I do not love, that I would marry for reason's sake, in order to give myself *a lot in life*, who would be imposed on me by a kind of necessity? How could I be sufficient to his happiness? How could I hold onto him, if I do not love him and desire him?

I hesitate, then. I wait for duty's sake, for reason's sake, for necessity's sake. I don't think I'm being a prude or a coquette. I don't mean to turn anyone's head or inspire ill-fated affection. I only want to make sure that I don't risk my happiness and my virtue. I want to be sure that I will be able to fulfill my duties. If I am cold and reserved, it is because I fear becoming involved. I fear giving hopes to someone that perhaps will not be realized.

CHARLOTTE BRONTË's ruminations about Willie Weightman, whom her sister Anne probably loved reflect an unmarried girl's thoughts on marriage.

15 May, 1840

To Ellen Nussey
I am fully convinced, Ellen, that he is a thorough maleflirt, his sighs
are deeper than ever and his treading on toes more assiduous. I find he
has scattered his impressions far and wide. Keighley has yielded him
a fruitful field of conquest, Sarah Sugden is quite smitten so is Caroline
Dury – she however has left – and his Reverence has not yet ceased
to idolize her memory – I find he is perfectly conscious of his
irresistibleness and is as vain as a peacock on the subject – I am not
at all surprised at this – it is perfectly natural – a handsome – clean
– prepossessing – good-humoured young man – will never want troops
of victims amongst young ladies – So long as you are not among the
number it is all right – He has not mentioned you to me, and I have
not mentioned you to him – I believe we fully understand each other
on the subject. I have seen little of him lately and talked precious little
to him . . . now that he has got his spirits up and found plenty of
acquaintances I don't care and he does not care either.
    There is no doubt he will get nobly through his examination, he is
a *clever* lad.
[   ]

'A Grandmother's Advice' to Ellen Nussey from Charlotte Brontë:

20 November, 1840
. . . no young lady should fall in love, till the offer has been made,
accepted – the marriage ceremony performed and the first half year
of wedded life has passed away – a woman may then begin to love, but
with great precaution – very coolly – very moderately – very rationally –
if she ever love so much that a harsh word or cold look from her
husband cuts her to the heart – she is a fool. . . .
    Did I not once tell you of an instance of a Relative of mine who
cared for a young lady till he began to suspect that she cared more
for him and then instantly conceived a sort of contempt for her? You
know to what I allude – never as you value your ears mention the
circumstance – but I have two studies – *you* are my study for the success,
the credit, and the respectability of a quiet, tranquil character. MARY
IS MY STUDY – FOR THE CONTEMPT, THE REMORSE, the misconstruction
which follow the development of feelings in themselves noble, warm –

generous – devoted and profound – but which being too freely revealed – too frankly bestowed – are not estimated at their real value.

The Brontës' biographer, Winifred Gérin, suggests that the man in the second letter is Branwell Brontë.

ELIZABETH GARRETT astonished her family by announcing her engagement to Mr Anderson when she was already thirty-three. She was making her name in medicine, and had been elected member of the London School Board. Here she explains her plans to her beloved sister, Millicent Garrett Fawcett, who helped found Newnham College, Cambridge.

Aldeburgh, Christmas Day 1870

On Friday night my horizon was suddenly changed by Mr. Anderson asking me to marry him. I do hope, my dear, that you will not think that I have meanly deserted my post. I think it need not prove to be so, and I believe that he would regret it as much as you or I would. I am sure that the woman question will never be solved in any complete way so long as marriage is thought to be incompatible with freedom and with an independent career, and I think there is a very good chance that we may be able to do something to discourage this notion. . . . Father was, I fancy, a little disappointed that I should marry at all. . . .

I hope you will like him and that Henry will too when you meet. I am very happy, dear Milly. I think we shall be married at Easter. There is nothing to wait for, as our joint income will be a good one, and we are both certainly old enough.

Whilst a proposal was often linked to a subtle enquiry about the dowry in nineteenth-century France, in this letter there is no mention of it. It is written to a well-to-do peasant family for the hand of CÉLINA GOUEVER, in her early twenties.

1889

M., Mme Gouever,

I am coming today to ask for the hand of your demoiselle.

My parents live in Savigny-sur-Braye and live on their income and

my father is in the guano business. There are two children, my brother
is married.

Since you are not acquainted with me I am taking the liberty of
quickly tackling a difficult question.

My parents will add 2,ooof to my present savings of 3,ooof.
Consequently I will then have 5,ooof.

Knowing that you want your *demoiselle* to stay with you, I would
accept that willingly.

I will furnish all the necessary information on my family background
as well as on my immediate family. As for me you could ask the priest
of St. Ouen and his mother who both know me, having known me at
M. Martellière's where I worked for six years. As for my family ask
M. Prudhomme. I write as quickly as possible now because our masters
are away for a month and I could visit more easily.

I hope that my letter will be well received and hoping to have a
response.
Paul Noulin, driver

Célina Gouever's uncle counsels her to reject Noulin's suit.

Your dark, handsome, beardless suitor, mounted on his black horse,
reminds me of two handsome beasts one mounted on top of the other.
That is the impression he made on me when I read his letter. But I
am wrong to speak like that because in truth the price he offers your
parents for you, 5,000 and a few hundred francs, is obviously what
you're worth, what do you think? Of course, I would not have offered
as much.

What you should say to him is that the price is not suitable, that he
should go to the fair; he seems to be a real horse trader.

BEING IN LOVE

The prudish sexual attitudes of the Victorians may make us forget the exuberance of many earlier periods, such as the Restoration, or Rabelaisian Paris. These letters prove that throughout history women have been far more sexually responsive in love than nineteenth-century medical textbooks would allow. From the time of Héloïse in twelfth-century Paris, there is a frankness about physical passion. Though our culture has associated female sexuality with child-bearing and marriage, these writers scarcely mention either; there appears less difference in male and female attitudes than Sigmund Freud and so many other male commentators on sexuality recognized.

HÉLOÏSE is celebrated for her passionate love of the priest Abélard. She bore him a child, but agreed not to marry him for the sake of his career in the Church.

Twelfth century
. . . You know, beloved, as the whole world knows, how much I have lost in you, how at one wretched stroke of fortune that supreme act of flagrant treachery robbed me of my very self in robbing me of you; and how my sorrow for my loss is nothing compared with what I feel for the manner in which I lost you. Surely the greater the cause for grief the greater the need for the help of consolation, and this no one can bring but you; you are the sole cause of my sorrow, and you alone can grant me the grace of consolation. You alone have the power to make me sad, to bring me happiness or comfort.

You yourself did not altogether forget this in the letter of consolation I have spoken of which you wrote to a friend; there you thought fit to set out some of the reasons I gave in trying to dissuade you from binding us together in an ill-starred marriage. But you kept silent about most of my arguments for preferring love to wedlock and freedom

to chains. God is my witness that if Augustus, Emperor of the whole
world, thought fit to honour me with marriage and conferred all the
earth on me to possess for ever, it would be dearer and more honourable
to me to be called not his Empress but your whore.

For a man's worth does not rest on his wealth or power; these depend
on fortune, but worth on his merits. And a woman should realize that
if she marries a rich man more readily than a poor one, and desires
her husband more for his possessions than for himself, she is offering
herself for sale. Certainly any woman who comes to marry through
desires of this kind deserves wages, not gratitude, for clearly her mind
is on the man's property, not himself, and she would be ready to
prostitute herself to a richer man, if she could. This is evident from the
argument put forward in the dialogue of Aeschines Socraticus by the
learned Aspasia to Xenophon and his wife. When she had expounded
it in an effort to bring about a reconciliation between them, she
ended with these words: 'Unless you come to believe that there is no
better man nor worthier woman on earth you will always still be looking
for what you judge the best thing of all – to be the husband of the best
of wives and the wife of the best of husbands.'

These are saintly words which are more than philosophic; indeed,
they deserve the name of wisdom, not philosophy. It is a holy error
and a blessed delusion between man and wife, when perfect love can
keep the ties of marriage unbroken not so much through bodily
continence as chastity of spirit. But what error permitted other women,
plain truth permitted me, and what they thought of their husbands, the
world in general believed, or rather, knew to be true of yourself; so
that my love for you was the more genuine for being further removed
from error. What king or philosopher could match your fame? What
district, town or village did not long to see you? When you appeared in
public, who did not hurry to catch a glimpse of you, or crane his neck
and strain his eyes to follow your departure? Every wife, every young
girl desired you in absence and was on fire in your presence; queens
and great ladies envied me my joys and my bed.
HÉLOÏSE

Here DOROTHY OSBORNE fears that her passionate love of her Royalist
suitor, William Temple, at the time of the Civil War, may bring their
destruction in the way it already had for the wretched Anne Blunt, who

had left her first husband, been disowned by Mr Blunt, with whom she ran away. Dorothy is concerned because she has received no letter from her fiancé.

20 Nov. 1653

Can I discern that it has made the trouble of your life, and cast a cloud upon mine, that will help to cover me in my grave? Can I know that it wrought so upon us both as to make neither of us friends to one another, but agree in running wildly to our own destructions, and that perhaps of some innocent persons who might live to curse our folly that gave them so miserable a being? Ah! if you love yourself or me, you must confess that I have reason to condemn this senseless passion; that wheresoe'er it comes destroys all that entertain it; nothing of judgment or discretion can live with it, and puts everything else out of order before it can find a place for itself. What has it not brought my poor Lady Anne Blunt to? She is the talk of all the footmen and boys in the street, and will be company for them shortly, who yet is so blinded by her passion as not at all to perceive the misery she has brought herself to; and this fond love of hers has so rooted all sense of nature out of her heart, that, they say, she is no more moved than a statue with the affliction of a father and mother that doted on her, and had placed the comfort of their lives in her preferment. With all this is it not manifest to the whole world that Mr. Blunt could not consider anything in this action but his own interest, and that he makes her a very ill return for all her kindness; if he had loved her truly he would have died rather than have been the occasion of this misfortune to her. My cousin Franklin (as you observe very well) may say fine things now she is warm in Moor Park, but she is very much altered in her opinions since her marriage, if these be her own. She left a gentleman, that I could name, whom she had much more of kindness for than ever she had for Mr. Franklin, because his estate was less; and upon the discovery of some letters that her mother intercepted, suffered herself to be persuaded that twenty-three hundred pound a year was better than twelve.

Having tired myself with thinking, I mean to tire you with reading and revenge myself that way for all the unquiet thoughts you have given me. Adieu

GERMAINE DE STAËL (1766–1817) could prove an importunate correspondent when rejected. Yet she was the most respected woman writer
at the time of the French Revolution, whose books exerted a powerful
influence on the Romantic movement in Europe. The novelist Benjamin
Constant fell in love with her and based his exquisite novel *Adolphe* on
their affair, among others. Some years before she had been in love with
a well born, unappreciative writer called De Pange. When he wrote that
he felt too ill to see her, this letter was her reply.

> Midnight, 11 September 1795
>
> I am so upset by your letter that I don't know how to express or how
> to contain a feeling which is capable of producing on you an effect
> so contrary to the desires of my soul. What expressions you are using!
> 'Breaking off a friendship – avoiding a commitment – not knowing
> when you will be able to come – believing me happy where I am.' Ah,
> Monsieur de Pange, has love taught you nothing except its injustice,
> its forgetfulness, its inconstancy? . . . You have no right to torture me.
> Remember what you said to me about friendship. What life there is
> left me depends on that friendship; for the past four months I owe
> everything to it and, what is worse, I need everything still. I have no
> intention of intruding on your independence. . . . But if to need you
> means to disturb you, then you have a right to be afraid of me. . . . You
> know as well as I do what is missing from my happiness here, but you
> cannot know as well as I know that you are perfection itself in the eyes
> of those who know you, that you are, to me, something even more
> desirable than perfection, and that I should find in your friendship
> all the happiness there is for me in this world, if only you removed that
> sword that hangs over my head.
>
> I beg you on my knees to come here or to meet me in Paris or at
> Passy for just one hour. . . . I refuse to give up what I have won; this
> friendship is to me a *necessity* – I do not care if it is not one for you.
> Give me what you can spare, and it will fill my life. . . .

Germaine begging on her knees could no more be resisted than an order
of the Emperor of Turkey. De Pange relented and met her, but the
thing that was missing from her happiness he did not give. A month
after her exile, in January 1796, he married Madame de Sérilly.

QUEEN VICTORIA's letter to Albert on the day of their marriage expresses
how much she is in love.

10 Feb 1840

Dearest, How are you today, and have you slept well? I have rested
very well, and feel very comfortable today. What weather! I believe,
however, the rain will cease.

Send me one word when you, my most dearly beloved bridegroom,
will be ready. Thy ever-faithful, Victoria R.

And her letter to her uncle, the King of the Belgians, the following day
reiterates that feeling.

Windsor Castle, 11th February 1840

My dearest Uncle, – I write to you from here, the happiest, happiest
Being that ever existed. Really, I do not think it *possible* for anyone in
the world to be *happier*, or as happy as I am. He is an Angel, and his
kindness and affection for me is really touching. To look in those dear
eyes, and that dear sunny face, is enough to make me adore him. What
I can do to make him happy will be my greatest delight. Independent of
my great personal happiness, the reception we both met with yesterday
was the most gratifying and enthusiastic I ever experienced; there was
no end of the crowds in London, and all along the road. I was a good
deal tired last night, but am quite well again to-day, and happy. . . .

My love to dear Louise. Ever your affectionate,
Victoria R.

By the nineteenth century, some women felt freer to express passion,
particularly in some middle-class groups in the USA. This letter is from
a young schoolteacher, BESSIE HUNTTING (1831–62) to her fiancé in
New York. They had become secretly engaged after a brief acquaintance.
Her expressions of devotion to God are even stronger than her words
of love to him.

26 Sept 1858

Were you *here*, at this lovely sunset hour, *kind friend*, I know your *heart*
would join in the anthem of praise, which meets my ear, and your
eyes would brighten, with the view of these golden clouds, so very *like*

those you were enjoying *last Sabbath eve.* Only the still, sacred quick of the country, enhanced by the cricket's low chirp give to the heart a holier, purer feeling of deep inward joy. *Sister* is playing and singing the sacred hymns *you so much* delight in, and I have stolen away, for a few brief *minutes,* to talk with one, who may wish to hear by this time of an absent spirit, and who *perchance,* may have allowed some thoughts to linger around her home – I almost regretted your absence, yesterday so charming was the *ride* I took, or more especially the sail across our beautiful bay. You, *hid* away among brick walls, and office books, knew not how beautifully the sun was gilding, mountain, hill & vale, the air clear & bracing, was surrounded by no clouds to mar its beauty, & I enjoyed it keenly. You too, it may be, felt an inward satisfaction with the past and entuned more engagedly into the *duties* of life – I wondered to myself whether you were *alone,* or if Mr. Carlton had recovered sufficiently, to be there? I hope so, for the sake of both. . . . I could not help wishing for you today! so holy seemed this blessed Sabbath, though I *felt* that you *intensely enjoyed* every *moment* of its blessedness. I *rejoice* when I think of your engagedness in the cause, of our dear Savior, and may our correspondence (if continued) be a bond of union, helping each other on, in the pathway to Heaven. I was thinking *this noon,* of your *beginning* the Christian course, for you have only just *entered upon its glorious* warfare; for truly it is a *warfare,* in which we had no hope to win, did not *Christ* sustain, & urge us on. I *pray* you may be calm decided & consistent. Let us remember *words are not actions*; profession is not possession. While I pray for you – I almost faint at my own short-comings and weakness. I know I ought not to say one word. I am so weak & erring – but I do *earnestly desire* to see you such a Christian as Paul was – Full of *zeal* and energy, tempered by Love, and restrained by calm, impassive holiness. May we both assist each other & *strive* to 'Live for Christ' and while the pleasures of life are to be enjoyed, we will not fail to perform its duties. . . .

Write me how this letter pleased thee.

ISABEL, a headstrong girl from a prosperous family, decided to marry an orientalist and writer. She had to wait nine years to overcome parental

opposition. The following letter is from Isabel to her mother, insisting
that she be allowed to marry the explorer Richard Burton.

1860

The moment I saw his brigand-dare-devil look I set him up as an idol
and determined that he was the only man I would ever marry. . . .
But when I came home one day in ecstasy and told you that I had
found the Man and the Life I longed for, and that nothing would
turn me, and that all other men were his inferiors, what did you answer
me? That he was the *only* man you would never consent to my marrying;
that you would rather see me in my coffin. Did you know that you were
flying in the face of God? Did you know it was my Destiny? . . . Look
at his military services – India and the Crimea! Look at his writings,
his travels, his poetry, his languages and dialects! Now Mezzofanti
[the great prelate and linguist] is dead, he stands first in Europe: he is
the best horseman, swordsman and pistol shot. . . . He has been
presented with the gold medal, and is a F.R.G.S., and you must see
in the newspapers of his glory and fame, and public thanks, where he
is called 'the Crichton of the day', 'one of the Paladins of the Age',
'the most interesting figure of the nineteenth century', . . . He is
lovable in every way . . . every thought, word or deed is that of a
thorough gentleman (I wish I could say the same for all our own
acquaintances or relations).

I believe that our proudest record will be our alliance with Richard
Burton . . . and I wonder you do not see the magnitude of the position
offered me. . . .

*I wish I were a man. If I were, I would be Richard Burton; but being only
a woman, I would be Richard Burton's wife.* You have said you do not know
who he is – that you do not meet him anywhere. I don't like to hear
you say the first, because it makes you out illiterate, and you know
how clever you are; but as to your not meeting him, considering the
particular sort of society whom you seek for your daughters, you are
not likely to meet there, because it bores him, and is quite out of his
line. He is a world-wide man, and his life, and talents, open every door
to him . . . he is a great man all over the East, in literary circles in
London, and in great parties where you and I would be part of the
crowd, he would be remarkable as a star. . . .

Isabel accompanied Richard to Brazil and Arabia, sharing all his hard-ships & pleasures. (See her letters on marriage and widowhood pp. 101 and 238).

CZARINA ALEXANDRA's letter to Czar Nicholas II expresses not only her love for him but an iron will.

Tsarskoje Selo, 4 December 1916

My Very Precious One,
Good-bye, sweet Lovy!

Its great pain to let you go – worse than ever after the hard times we have been living & fighting through. But God who is all love & mercy has let the things take a change for the better, – just a little more patience & deepest faith in the prayers & help of our Friend – then all will go well. I am fully convinced that great & beautiful times are coming for yr. reign & Russia. Only keep up your spirits, let no talks or letters pull you down – let them pass by as something unclean & quickly to be forgotten.

Show to all, that you are the Master & your will shall be obeyed – the time of great indulgence & gentleness is over – now comes your reign of will & power, & they shall be made to bow down before you & listen your orders & to work how & with whom you wish – obedience they must be taught, they do not know the meaning of that word, you have spoilt them by yr. kindness & all forgivingness.

Why do people hate me? Because they know I have a strong will & when am convinced of a thing being right (when besides blessed by *Gregory*), do not change my mind & that they can't bear. But its the bad ones.

Remember Mr. Philipps words when he gave me the image with the bell. As you were so kind, trusting & gentle, I was to be yr. bell, those that came with wrong intentions wld. not be able to approach me & I wld. warn you. Those who are afraid of me, don't look me in the eyes or are up to some wrong, never like me. – Look at the black ones – then Orlov & Drenteln – Witte – *Kokovtzev* – *Trepov*, I feel it too – *Makarov* – *Kaufmann* – *Sofia Ivanovna* – *Mary* – *Sandra* Obolensky, etc., but those who are good & devoted to you honestly & purely – love me, – look at the simple people & military. The good & bad clergy its all so clear & therefore no more hurts me as when I was younger.

Only when one allows oneself to write you or me nasty impertinent letters – you must punish.

Wartime love is of a special kind. MARION MERRIMAN, an American, was the only woman working fulltime in the International Brigade in the Spanish Civil War. She took the job in order to be with her adored young husband, Bob, who was first Commander of the Lincolns. Here she recounts incidents during the siege of Madrid.

Madrid was under bombardment every day. Bob said Did I want to go with him? I said I was in the war with Bob, for keeps. But I was scared – and I was curious about Hemingway. We went to the Hotel Florida, and directly up the stairs to Hemingway's room. 'Hello, I'm Merriman,' said Bob. 'I know,' said Hemingway, who then greeted me warmly. They got along. Each talked for a moment, then listened to the other. How different they were! Bob at twenty-eight. Hemingway at least a good ten years older, seemed complex. Big and bluff and macho. He didn't appear to be a braggart, but he got across the message through an air of self-assurance, that he could handle what he took on. . . .

The soldiers felt this was a democratic army, so they had the right to complain. I never heard any expression of resentment that Merriman had his wife around. Sometimes I was accepted a little too much. Occasionally the men made advances, I put them off quickly, whenever I could with kindness. The ones who really exasperated me were those with political arguments, about sharing. I told one enterprising young man that if I slept with him, I'd have to sleep with the other two thousand to be fair and that I wasn't up to it.

At eight o'clock next morning, May 30, I left for Murcia, on work, with two pleasant Slav officers. We had dinner on a terrace, overlooking a sleepy village, in moonlight. The pure beauty of where we were seemed to give one of my companions romantic ideas. In a woman-less war, I'd seen the look before and dismissed it.

That night I fell quickly asleep, but was suddenly wide awake. The man whose 'look' I'd noted was holding me down, one hand clamped over my mouth. I fought him, clawing, kicking. I couldn't scream. He raped me. I kicked him away. He fled the room.

I was stunned. I sobbed and sobbed, terrified. I climbed out of bed searched for water, and scrubbed for hours, but still felt filthy. Should

I tell Bob? I asked myself over and over. Finally I concluded I must not hurt Bob with this. This must be my secret burden. This war filled Bob's mind, so I finished my assignment, and joined him at Belchite.

As he explained the battle to me, the shadows lengthened across the empty fields. There one of our best machine gunners fell, beside that wall Burt was killed. Here Sidney fell, a sniper's bullet between his eyes. Our losses were low, but included some of our best and most loved men.

As Bob talked, I held his arm. I felt I had to support him. He seldom showed his needs to others, but since our college days, I'd always know when he needed me, and he needed me more than ever. As we hurried away I was filled with a weariness and heartsickness that only the warmth of the living could relieve.

Suddenly we heard piano music. There, across a street, in half a house, the front walls blown away, the inside looking like a stage, sat a Spanish soldier, at a grand piano, playing Beethoven. We stood there in the moonlight, and listened. But Bob had asked me to Belchite because there was work to do. I was to gather a first hand report for the ministry of war, of all the wounded and killed.

LOVE AFFAIRS

This section opens with two letters from the first epistolary novel in English, *Love Letters between a Nobleman and his Sister* by Aphra Behn (1683?). It was based on a real scandal at the time, and the language used influenced the discourse of many real letters subsequently, such as those written by Lady Mary Wortley Montagu, just before eloping. This is compared to George Sand, famous in the nineteenth century for her moral novels. After a disastrous marriage, she went to work in Paris. There she met leading intellectuals, such as Liszt, Flaubert, Lamartine – and Chopin, with whom she lived for ten years, nursing him through his final illness. She also fell in love with the outstanding Romantic poet, Alfred de Musset. He was younger than she and exceedingly demanding, which led her to ending their relationship.

Her tumultuous affair is followed by the relatively calm correspondence of Mrs Patrick Campbell to George Bernard Shaw. Their opening letters contrast dramatically with the final ones. Only G.B.S. is uninvolved enough to be kind and arrange for the selling of his love letters in order to provide for the actress in her impoverished old age. The twentieth-century letters are less passionate, more aware of the rapid passing of erotic desire.

APHRA BEHN (b. 1640), the first woman professional writer in England, was in love with a rake for some years. Her *Love-Letters Between a Nobleman and His Sister* is based on the abduction of Lady Henrietta Berkeley by her brother-in-law, Lord Grey of Werke. The heroine here is called 'Sylvia', her lover 'Philander', an obviously symbolic name, evoking the suffering of Lady Henrietta and Aphra Behn herself. Here is one of the first passionate outpourings of Sylvia to Philander.

Where a second time I open'd your letter, and read it again with a thousand changes of countenance, my whole mass of blood was in

that moment so discompos'd, that I chang'd from an ague to a fever
several times in a minute: oh what will all this bring me to? And where
will the raging fit end? I die with that thought, my guilty pen slackens
in my trembling hand, and I languish and fall over the un-employ'd
paper; – oh help me, some divinity, – or if you did, – I fear I should
be angry: oh *Philander*! a thousand passions and distracted thoughts
crowd to get out, and make their soft complaints to thee; but oh they
lose themselves with mixing; they are blended in a confusion together,
and love nor art can divide them, to deal them out in order; sometimes
I would tell you of my joy at your arrival, and my unspeaking transports
at the thought of seeing you so soon, that I shall hear your charming
voice, and find you at my feet making soft vows anew, with all the passion
of an impatient lover, with all the eloquence that sighs and cries, and
tears from those lovely eyes can express; and sure that is enough to
conquer any where, and to which coarse vulgar words are dull. The
rhetoric of love is half-breath'd, interrupted words, languishing eyes,
flattering speeches, broken sighs, pressing the hand, and falling tears:
ah how do they not persuade, how do they not charm and conquer;
'twas thus, with these soft easy arts, that *Sylvia* first was won; for sure
no arts of speaking could have talked my heart away, though you can
speak like any god: oh whither am I driven? [   ] my soul will sound
to nothing but to love: talk what you will, begin what discourse you
please, I end it all in love, because my soul is ever fix'd on *Philander*,
and insensibly its biass leads to that subject; no, I did not when I began
to write, think of speaking one word of my own weakness; but to have
told you with what resolv'd courage, honour and virtue, I expect your
coming.

Later Sylvia is abandoned.

Yes, perjured villain, at last all thy perfidy is arrived to my knowledge;
and thou hadst better have been damned, or have fallen, like an
ungrateful traitor, as thou art, under the public shame of dying by the
common executioner, than have fallen under the grasp of my revenge;
insatiate as thy lust, false as thy treasons to thy prince, fatal as thy
destiny, loud as thy infamy, and bloody as thy party. Villain, villain,
where got you the courage to use me thus, knowing my injuries and
my spirit?

GEORGE SAND (1804–76) enjoyed a turbulent winter with Alfred de Musset, which he celebrated in his poetry. They went to Venice together, a visit she expounds on here in her letter to him.

Paris (Winter 1834–1835)

I was quite sure that these reproaches would come the very day after happiness had been dreamt of and decided upon, and that you would make a crime of something that you had accepted as absolutely my own business. Oh! My God! Have we arrived at that already! All right! Do not let us go any further! Let me go away! I wanted to yesterday. There was an eternal adieu in my soul. Remember your despair and all that you poured out to me about being unable to live without me! And I was silly enough to try and save you again! But you are more impossible than ever to help because no sooner are you satisfied that you turn your anger and despair against poor me! My God! What can *I* do? Oh! my God, sometimes one wishes one were dead! What *do* you want me to do now? I wish I knew. And already you are fulminating with questions, suspicions and recriminations! And why do you ask me about Pagello when I forbade you ever to mention him? What right have you to question me about Venice either? Was I yours in Venice? The very first day I fell ill there, you flew into a bad temper and said that there was nothing so depressing as an ailing woman! And was not that the first day of our rupture? My dear boy! I do not wish to indulge in recriminations but I really must jog your memory, it is so very bad with regard to *facts*. I do not want to recount your shortcomings but, I must just point out that I never once complained of being torn from my children, my friends, my work and my affections and my duties and carried off three hundred miles from home and there abandoned with such offensive and wounding words, only because, *only* because I had a feverish attack and was out of looks and sadly out of spirits owing to your callousness.

I never complained, I kept back my tears while you were there, and then one evening that I shall never forget in the Danieli Casino, you said these awful words:

'George, I was mistaken, I must ask you to forgive me, but really I do *not* love you!' If I had not been so ill that a doctor was coming to bleed me the next day, I should have gone away at once; but then I reflected that you had no money, I did not know whether you would actually accept money from me, and I would not, could not desert you and leave you alone in a strange country without a farthing. Then we locked the door between our rooms and we tried to regain our former

good comradeship like our first days together here, but it was
impossible. We were both dispirited.

Pagello was the Venetian doctor who fell in love with her.

I did not care for Pagello at first, and as I was no longer yours I was
not obliged to consider you. . . . Did I not foresee that you would suffer
from that past which inspired you like a great poem as long as I refused
myself, and which, now that you have recaptured me appears to you
as a nightmare?

Let me go away! If I am the light woman you *imagine* me to be, why
are you frantic to regain possession? You are in torment because I
have been sincere . . . Oh! my God! what remains of the great beauty
of our passion?

Later . . .

Paris, 1834

Oh God! Oh God! Have I been reproaching you when you are suffering
so! Forgive me, my angel, my beloved, my poor boy, I am suffering
so much myself that I do not know which way to turn. I cry out to God
and entreat a miracle of Him. But He does not send one. What will
become of us? One or the other must find strength either to love enough
for *anything* or to forget; and do not deceive yourself, neither of us have
the strength for the one or the other! You think you will be able to
find that all-conquering love because you find hope every morning after
abandoning it every night. You are twenty-three, Alfred, and I am
thirty-one, with so many sorrows, sobs, and heart-breaks behind me!
What are you making for? What do you hope from the solitude and
exaltation of a grief which is already so piercing! Alas, I am as limp
and feeble as a crushed rope. I am stricken down, hanging over my
broken-hearted love as over a corpse, suffering too much to revive it
or to bury it. And you seem disposed to lash your own grief to further
furies. Have you not had enough of it, as it is? I do not think there
can be more desperate pain than the grief I feel now.

She elaborates on her feelings to the well-known critic Sainte-Beuve.

Nohant, end of 1834

My very dear friend,
I ought to have written to you sooner but you can well understand

that I needed a few days to come to myself again and to reach an understanding of the position this appalling nightmare has led me to. My awakening here has been fairly tolerable. I have met all my old comrades and found them as good to me as ever, but my worn out heart, alas! is very weary and very jaded! It will not recover easily.

Alfred has sent me a little letter, rather an affectionate one, repenting of his violence. Through it all he has such a kind heart! For all answer I sent him a little leaf from my garden, and he sent me a curl from his hair which I had often asked for before, that is a fortnight ago. And now it is all over.

George Bernard Shaw and MRS PATRICK CAMPBELL have a more sedate correspondence.

> 33 Kensington Square, W.
> [Postmark: 27th June 1912]

My dear Mr Shaw,

First of all my thanks for letting me hear the play, and for thinking I can be your pretty slut. I wonder if I could please you [as Eliza Doolittle in *Pygmalion*].

I want you to tell me what the business proposal is – when, where, and with whom.

Perhaps you will come and see me. We said so little yesterday. I mustn't lose time – my days are numbered surely.

It was a great pleasure to me to see you again.

Yours sincerely,

B. S. CAMPBELL.

> 20 July 1912

– My Stella used to sing a song which I told her was silly, and she declared was funny – your last letter reminds me more of it than your others –

> He's mad, mad, mad,
> He's clean gone off his nut
> He cleans his boots with strawberry jam
> He eats his hat whenever he can
> He's mad, mad, mad –

– I hope you too will have a lovely holiday and not need your 'cap and bells' all the time – and that bladder-whacking of yours, that makes my dear friend D.D. jump, and imagine its really a bump!

My address will be
    Hotel Mirabeau
        Aix-les-Bains
           Savoie
              France –

I start to-morrow after 8 days in bed – with two black eyes – and some screw-like pains in my shoulder.

Yours affectionately,

BEATRICE STELLA.

33, Kensington Square, W.
18th Nov. 1912

No more shams – a real love letter this time – then I can breathe freely, and perhaps who knows begin to sit up and get well –

I haven't said 'kiss me' because life is too short for the kiss my heart calls for. . . . All your words are as idle wind – Look into my eyes for two minutes without speaking if you dare! Where would be your 54 years? and my grandmothers heart? and how many hours would you be late for dinner?

– If you give me one kiss and you can only kiss me if I say 'kiss me' and I will never say 'kiss me' because I am a respectable widow and I wouldn't let any man kiss me unless I was sure of the wedding ring –

STELLA (LIZA, I MEAN)

Ayot St Lawrence, Welwyn.
18th Nov. 1912

. . . If I looked into your eyes without speaking for two minutes (Silent for two minutes with an audience even of one! Impossible, cried the fiend; but I don't care) I might see heaven. And then I should just trot off and do ten years hard work and think it only a moment, leaving you staring.

Do you know, I dont hate you one little bit. I am clearly in my second childhood (56, not 54); for you might be the Virgin Mary and I an Irish peasant, and my feeling for you could not be more innocent; and yet there is no relation into which we could enter which would not be entirely natural and happy for me. . . .

Goodnightest

GBS

1913

If you hadn't been so sleepy you would have noticed my 'goodbye'. They have given me permission to stay away until Monday. This heavenly place. I sat in the sea for an hour this morning – not two dozen houses, not a hundred people – The sea goes out miles and comes in up to the green in front of the house, and as far as you can see to right and to left just green and sand and glory – The peace is divine and soul-strengthening and soul-resting. I and my part – and Georgina to play with – the maid and the chauffeur at hand.

You with your eighteenth-century ribaldry habit. You lost me because you never found me. – I who have nothing but my little lamp and flame – you would blow it out with your bellows of self. You would snuff it with your egotistical snortings – you elegant charmer – you lady-killer – you precious treasure of friendship – for you do I keep my little lamp burning for fear you may lose your way in the dark. . . .

The drive to Rye and all about when the sun is low is lovely.
STELLA

Your two letters – considering – are very well.

Do you think it was nothing to me to hurt my friend –

Littlestone.
13 Aug. 1913

I am sure you have done splendid work and have had a divine rest.

You are trying to break my heart with your letters. You know I did *rightly*. What other thing was there for me to do? I had to behave like a man – and a gentleman hadn't I? I will see you Monday or Tuesday.
STELLA

10, Adelphi Terrace, W.C.
13th August 1913

Back from the land of broken promise.

I might ring you up and say this; but I am too proud.

Oh shallow hearted thing!

The world has changed horribly since Sunday afternoon.

What did you want? Oysters and champagne? Why did you go? How could you go? This morning Brabazon accosted me in the hotel. He has a house close by. He said the worst of the place is that he cannot sleep there. My heart snatched at the excuse for you. But no, not like that. At the Great Judgment they will say to you 'all your other sins are forgiven; but why did you do this?' There where I imagined heaven there is nothing. Oh mirage in the desert, I shall die of thirst after all, in spite of you.

I finished my play in time for lunch today, punctually at half past one. It is an old precept of mine: Do your work; and your sweetheart will never have too much of you. How I have thrust work between us lest I should plague you and tire you out! And now I am no better off than if I had thrown everything to the winds but temptation. Fool! Dupe! Dotard! Crybaby! Useless, these letters; the wound will not heal.
G.B.S.

> Littlestone-on-Sea.
> 15th Aug. 1913

I looked about thinking I might see you to-day I missed a letter from you tonight.

Perhaps you are gone to Scotland – or to Ayot – or you are busy reading your play to your friends and my enemies.

When the man brought the ginger beer he said 'You've paid your bill and ginger beer one shilling' I thought you would have guessed then but you were too sleepy – I owe you a shilling –

Your dear letters are not true – but they are wonders! – when I see you I can tell you what will make all clear – don't be hurt Joey dear – please PLEASE PLEASE
STELLA

The following letter is typewritten, but the words 'and that never did I think your lovemaking other than it was, sympathy, kindness, and the wit and folly of genius' have been inserted afterwards in pencil (possibly at a later date?)

> Ashfields, Lathom, Lancs.
> 21 December 1921

There is no mistake about it you are an extraordinary man.

Miss Morris is making a copy of the letters that I propose publishing if you agreed and consented.

I will send them to you to-morrow.

It is quite easy for me to come down from the clouds and realise there are other points of view than my own.

I did indeed hate speaking of George to you.

What I wanted was your clever opinion how to get just enough truth on the written page.

I thought you knew he left me two years ago.

You know you always thought me a fool, and that you never even pretended unfaithfulness to Charlotte and that never did I think your love making other than what it was – sympathy, kindness, and the wit and folly of genius.

What you sometimes think ignorance in me is often deliberate – Perhaps I see what I choose to see – I look at what I want to look at – a joy and a tragedy that –

Don't mix up your genius and your clay, which is what you will do if your lovely letters are tampered with now –

I am glad you both felt as I did over *Will Shakespeare* [a play].

There was nothing wrong excepting the bridge of Shakespeare's nose – he may have altered it since I saw the play.

I could have played Mary Fitton with more subtle danger –

Clemence Dane is a most dear woman and superlatively clever – Please send me your letter to her, it would interest me tremendously.

My love to you. If you had a good memory you would recollect that I always wanted to send my love to Charlotte. *You* led her to see me all askew.

I alone kept my head and saw you both as you are without any help from anyone – If you dare to pretend it is otherwise, you will assuredly boil in hell.

STELLA THE PEASANT
(Italian)

4, Whitehall Court, S.W.1.
18th March 1938

My dear Stella,

Now that you put me to it, I find this business of the letters much more complicated than I thought. I can do no more than confirm to you the gift of the pieces of paper on which your letters to me are written. The pieces of paper on which my letters to you are written are your property without question.

I can also declare, and do hereby declare, that my executors will be acting according to my wishes if, after my wife's death and mine, they consent to the publication of the letters for your benefit, or, if you also are no more, for the benefit of your daughter Stella. Failing her, the interest in the letters becomes an unencumbered part of my estate . . .

I strongly advise you to have two copies of the correspondence typed in sections of three or four letters at different offices so as to prevent the possibility of surreptitious copies. Send one copy to Stella and tell her to take special care of it. This will act as a fire insurance. You keep the originals yourself. The third copy will do for the printer; and if it also is kept in a separate place it will be an additional insurance against loss by theft, fire, accident, carelessness or the like. I have no copies myself, nor have I ever shewn your letters to anyone.

I think this is all I have to say, except that as you are nine years younger than we are your chances of surviving both of us are fairly good.
always
G.B.S.

> Hotel Sevilla, New York
> 5th April 1938

Dearest Joey,
I have your letter of March 18th. Your letter makes it quite clear that I possess nothing that enables me to continue my attitude towards the publication of the letters.

You have often urged me to sell the letters this I will now do. I will not sell them collectively but singly.

Circumstances may make it necessary for me to publish my letters to you, with notes to make them comprehensive [sic].

Sometime ago I wrote telling you that two photostated copies of all your letters to me were in the Chase National Bank. You had so often begged me to have copies made, and photostated copies seemed the safest.

Should the time come when the ban is lifted from your letters there will be these photostated copies in the possession of my family.
My love to you
STELLA

> Hotel Sirmione, Lago di Garda
> 3rd Sept. 1938

Dear Joey. It is miserable to read of your illness in the newspapers I wouldn't dare bother you with a letter were I not sure you would not read it if you are bidden not to tire yourself unnecessarily.

My beloved Italy has done wonders for me – I was carried on to the boat when I left the States, and off the boat when I arrived at Boulogne – a rheumatic knee – four months of agony, and the American Doctor

had said '18 months and crutches'. When the Italian Doctor saw it, he
smiled and said: 'I will have you dancing in a fortnight'
My love and prayers,
STELLA

REBECCA WEST (1892–1983) had various intense affairs after her relationship with H. G. Wells. Here she writes to her confidante, American
novelist Fannie Hurst. The man (Max) was Lord Beaverbrook, but she
was too considerate and discreet to allow any public knowledge of this
brief affair:

                                                    New York 1923
M[ax] called up and said he thought we wouldn't go tomorrow because
we ought both to reconcile ourselves to the fact that life together in
London is impossible and that it was torturing for him to see me. I
have no hope left and wish he had never come. I am obsessed by
him, though this is what had happened:
    We were alone. That was a queer thing, for nearly always he had a
crowd around him. We had lunch, and we walked round the garden for
a time. He then talked quite lightly of our past infatuation as if it were
a tremendous joke. He laughed about it. I suddenly realised that he
was physically quite indifferent to me. Fannie, I'm not telling you the
truth. I'm leaving out the point. He casually implied in a phrase that
when he had made love to me in London first he was drunk, and that
it had been very awkward for him when he found I took it seriously.
New York he didn't explain at all. Then he went back to town in the
car, and he dropped me on his way. Later that afternoon I heard he
is making ardent love to Gwen Ffrangcon-Davies, the young actress
who is playing Juliet very successfully. . . .
    Why had he set his secretaries to find out where I was in New York?
or was that only because he wanted to see me as a friend, and never
told me he was making enquiries in case he revived the hopes he had
raised in me when he was drunk? I loved Max for years. It's over but
I'm over too. . . . I thought at Christmas I'd got something to give Max
– that there was something worth while to be got out of it. But why
was he so stricken when I told him that I couldn't have a child? I shall
go mad wondering. The New York business was I suppose a

panic-stricken response to what he realised was my clinging to the idea
he loved me.
REBECCA

In her distress when Beaverbrook left New York – after sending her the
statutory load of roses – Rebecca became ill and the rest of her lecture
tour had to be delayed. On her recovery she went West, mildly consoled
by the attentions of other men. One New York admirer wrote to her of
his bitterness that 'what was so little a game to me was so much a game
for you', and supposed that by now 'you will have vamped half California,
and the other half of California will have tried (unsuccessfully) to rape
you. . . . Do be careful how you handle Charlie Chaplin – they say he
has quite a way with you intellectual women!'

LESBIAN LOVE

After the First World War there was more education for women, more women were being published, and expressing themselves eloquently in letters. Here the rich American patron, BRYHER, writes to Amy Lowell, whose *Tendencies in Modern American Poetry* had mentioned H.D. (Hilda Doolittle), a writer she longed to meet.

12 Aug 1918

At once I began to meditate an attack on her. Mr Shorter with some difficulty got me her address. Curiously enough she was staying in the very next village to the place we had chosen instead of Scilly this year. I sent her a copy of the pamphlet and wrote beseeching I might go and see her. Encouragement to a young enthusiasm seems to be a root of The Imagist nature for I had a letter back almost at once asking me to walk across. . . . I found the house without much difficulty – a solitary one by the cliff edge and seeing books scattered everywhere, I knocked. Mrs Aldington opened the door herself.

I am afraid my first impression was how magnificently you had expressed her and made her live in those few pages of 'Tendencies' and my next was that I was a whirlwind disturbing a calm Sicilian day. . . . I tried hard to keep from asking innumerable questions about you – but sometimes they would break out. . . . Mrs Aldington has promised to come and see me in London. . . . She was of exceeding interest to me and I owe the meeting, the knowledge of her and her poems to you through 'Tendencies'.

After this meeting between Bryher and H.D., the two women began to correspond. Soon they helped each other to begin new lives. H.D. searched for a flat in London for Bryher.

... there is no trouble with heating as there are gas-fires in all rooms, and I can get our breakfast & simple luncheons, and dinners even if you want to try a month with me.... I can arrange minor matters –

H.D. then poured out her own problems to Bryher:

19 Dec 1918

You must take pity on me and let me be with you part of the time. We could put aside certain afternoons of the week, and arrange to have people in then to tea, and we could go out together, you with me (as Mr Shorter says 'a good married woman') to chaperone.... At present, I am a little tied. Three years ago, I had a sad illness & lost my little child. I am expecting to have another towards the end of March....

KATHERINE MANSFIELD (1888–1923) loved both men and women. It is not clear whether this account is fact or fiction. It was found among her papers after her death, and offers a touching insight into an erotic relationship between two women.

1911

I had asked her to dine with me, and then go to the Opera. My room was opposite hers. She said she would come but – could I lace up her evening bodice, it was hooks at the back. Very well.

It was still daylight when I knocked at the door and entered. In her petticoat bodice and a full silk petticoat she was washing, sponging her face and neck. She said she was finished, and I might sit on the bed and wait for her. So I looked round at the dreary room. The one filthy window faced the street. She could see the choked, dust-grimed window of a wash-house opposite. For furniture, the room contained a low bed, draped with revolting, yellow, vine-patterned curtains, a chair, a wardrobe with a piece of cracked mirror attached, a washstand. But the wallpaper hurt me physically. It hung in tattered strips from the wall. In its less discoloured and faded patches I could trace the pattern of roses – buds and flowers – and the frieze was a conventional design of birds, of what genus the good God alone knows.

And this was where she lived. I watched her curiously. She was pulling on long, thin stockings, and saying 'damn' when she could not find her suspenders. And I felt within me a certainty that nothing beautiful could ever happen in that room, and for her I felt contempt, a little tolerance, a very little pity.

A dull, grey light hovered over everything; it seemed to accentuate the thin tawdriness of her clothes, the squalor of her life, she, too, looked dull and grey and tired. And I sat on the bed, and thought: 'Come, this Old Age. I have forgotten passion, I have been left behind in the beautiful golden procession of Youth. Now I am seeing life in the dressing-room of the theatre.'

So we dined somewhere and went to the Opera. It was late, when we came out into the crowded night street, late and cold. She gathered up her long skirts. Silently we walked back to the Thistle Hotel, down the white pathway fringed with beautiful golden lilies, up the amethyst shadowed staircase.

Was Youth dead? . . . *Was* Youth dead?

She told me as we walked along the corridor to her room that she was glad the night had come. I did not ask why. I was glad, too. It seemed a secret between us. So I went with her into her room to undo those troublesome hooks. She lit a little candle on an enamel bracket. The light filled the room with darkness. Like a sleepy child she slipped out of her frock and then, suddenly, turned to me and flung her arms round my neck.

(Signed)

KATHERINE MANSFIELD

The American writer DJUNA BARNES (1892–1982) came to Europe in the 1920s, like Hemingway and Scott Fitzgerald and so many others. She met a sculptress of nineteen, Thelma Wood, and they fell deeply in love. The early years of their relationship were idyllic. Djuna called herself Momma, while Thelma here uses the two names, Simon and Papa.

23 March 1922(?)

Dear little angel

This is where I have finally gotten to . . . I have a nice room – great big – and great big bed – for $5 a week. . . .

Old Papa begins to feel like a new papa – don't *forget me* – *because*
I'm really sort of a nice kid.

I dreamed last night you ran away with Bob Chandler – and I nearly
died. . . .

I love you sweetheart – I want you here. I would like to ride with
you.

I kiss your precious sweet face

SIMON

In 1927 they had their first major break. THELMA WOOD sailed back to
the United States, and wrote from the boat:

Dearest one – You said something just as I was leaving that makes
things seem a little less terrible . . . that we could meet in New York
and maybe Simon would be different.

But you see how silly Simon must clutch on anything to make him
stronger – you see I can't think of anything ahead that doesn't mean
you.

I keep saying – Simon, you've got to be a man and take your medicine
– but then always in my head goes – There is no Simon and no Irine
[Djuna] and I can't bear it and go crazy. . . .

I feel so shy at saying any thing for fear it sounds like excusing which
God knows I don't – but I've thought over it all and I think if I didn't
drink maybe things wouldn't have happened – as that is usely [sic] when
I get involved –

Now Simon will not touch one drop till you come to America and
I'll have my exhibition done. . . . Perhaps we could try it a new way
– . . . if you will I will never again as long as you love me take one
small drop of anything stronger than tea.

If this sounds like bunk to you precious – drop me a little note and
say no use. But if there is any slight chance for Simon if he bucks up
let him know that too – I tell you angel darling the only reason your
Simon doesn't drop off that boat is because I've made you sufficiently
unhappy as it is –

A few weeks later she wrote again:

at times Djuna things get very terrible – something will happen and I
go to pieces – for instance I dream of you every night – and sometimes
Djuna I dream we are lovers and I wake up the next day and nearly

die of shame – taking advantage in my sleep of something I know so intimately – and something you do not wish –

But Thelma had fallen in love with another woman. . . .

PART THREE

Marriage – Motherhood – The ordeals of childbirth – Baby-rearing
– Running a household – The joys and problems of growing
children

MARRIAGE

The first printed reference we have to marriage from a woman is a wedding invitation, dating from the third century AD, from the Oxyrhynchus papyrus: 'Herais requests your company at dinner in celebration of the marriage of her children at her house tomorrow, the fifth, at nine o'clock'.

Marriage presents contradictions. Women were expected to devote their lives to husbands, while coping with children, households and frequently work outside, to support the family. Christian marriage vows echo romantic love, in evoking an image of devotion and sharing, yet proved disastrous to many a woman who lost her few legal and economic rights.

The two opening letters suggest devoted medieval relationships, while the third describes a wretched Tudor marriage, recently republished thanks to Muriel St Clare Byrne. These Lisle Letters give invaluable information of the daily life and problems of an aristocratic Tudor family.

Then follows Madame de Sévigné's witty announcement of her daughter's forthcoming marriage. She is an extraordinarily varied writer, neglected today, yet writers like Jane Austen and Fanny Burney read her eagerly.

Two salacious letters from Lady Mary Wortley Montagu (1708–62), remarkable correspondent and early feminist, comment on contemporaries.

The nineteenth- and twentieth-century passages provide widely differing inside views on marriage.

ISABEL married against the wishes of her brother, King Henry of Castile. Isabel realized that to become Queen of Castile, and reunite most of the regions into modern Spain, she needed a strong husband to aid her. She decided on her cousin Ferdinand of Aragon, probably a model for *The Prince* of Machiavelli. However her brother King Henry was her legal guardian, and he wanted Ferdinand to marry his daughter, Juana. She therefore had to justify her marriage to the King, to the Royal Council, and the powerful at Court. She explains their marriage by stating that they hoped to serve Henry 'in the dignity of his estate' to bring 'concord and peace' to Castile and 'with all our might to favour justice, which because of recent disturbances is in a weak position'.

Her skilled arguments make the defence of her marriage into a political justification. First she acknowledges that it would have been 'very difficult' to gain consent; then she agrees that the marriage was a source of 'scandal', admitting their weakness, which was a fear among Castilians that Ferdinand, of neighbouring Aragon, would favour his countrymen. She ends by proclaiming a pragmatic policy which was in fact successful in bringing union, peace and prosperity.

We are joined in matrimony as the Holy Mother Church of Rome commands and should have waited till seeing your Grace's consent and the vows and counsels of all the prelates and great men ... but ... so clear and manifest was it ... that were it necessary to wait for everyone's accord and consent this would be very difficult to obtain or else so much time would have passed that in these realms great peril would arise because of the absence of children to continue the succession ... therefore ... we decided to contract our aforesaid marriage as much without scandal as we could ... and without favouring any foreigners.
(trans. O. Kenyon)

Isabel was eighteen when she chose her most suitable cousin as husband and co-ruler, and composed this skilful letter, adding that her capacity to produce an heir was decisive.

We sometimes imagine that a young widow with property would have been among the few fortunate women in the Middle Ages. Not so, according to this account in the recently published Lisle Letters. Here a nun, ANTOINETTE DE SAVEUSE, describes the wretched life of a young widow when she remarries.

10 September 1537

To Lady Lisle,
  Madame, my Lady Deputy, I recommend me most affectuously to your good favour. You have written to me to declare the secrets of these poor people.

After the death of the aforesaid Monsieur du Pont de Remy, Madame de Bours very slily tried to persuade the good widow to take in marriage her brother de Riou. She, being young, and well-disposed to have her pleasure, took him, to the displeasure of all her own relations, because she might have matched with two gentlemen of considerable standing, one of whom could spend 20,000 livres of income, and the other 30,000. Madame, I cannot express to you the distress that I have endured for the three weeks which I spent with her; for she told me so much of her grief that I could not listen without freely shedding tears with her. And it is great marvel to me how she hath had of this second marriage as many as twelve children, having suffered such distress as she hath told me. So much so, that she has even proved to me that one day Monsieur broke open a great coffer that had belonged to Monsieur de Saveuse, Madame's father, which was full of fine vessels, the which he placed on a table and staked at dice to the value of 14,000 livres in one afternoon; not to mention all his other follies and the great gifts which he hath made to his own near relations, as if he wished totally to destroy likewise his own children, of whom he makes as little account as if they were nothing to him.

The good lady doth consider the great charge of her six little children, of whom the eldest is not more than ten years old, and that all that they can have cometh from her, and that daily she sees thus pitifully wasted the goodly estate that the late gentleman her father left her – so much so, Madame, that she made her moan to me that during these twelve years that she had been married to him, he has diminished her inheritance by the value of more than 50,000 livres, for in her youth one could hardly have found a gentlewoman of her sort in all the realm of France; and as for wishing to return to any of her own relations, she can find in them neither loyalty nor the aid of good counsel in this cause. Beseeching you most humbly that of your kindness it may please you by means of your most discreet counsel to help in the necessity in which this good lady at this present finds herself, for she laments to me that she doth not know to whom to turn; but since the last letter received from you I have determined to apply to you in confidence, to know, Madame, whether one cannot prevent the said gentleman so that he may no longer give rein to such prodigality with her possessions and those of his children; because if he continues these expenses much longer, without brooking any hindrance, however much she resists, the good lady will, I fear, be obliged in the future to sell her lands.

I beseech you, Madame, that the report of this affair may not be
further divulged . . . thus praying God to grant you the
accomplishment of your virtuous, noble desires.
Your humble servant and friend,
ANTHOENETTE (SEUR)

Advice on an unwise marriage, from QUEEN ELIZABETH I to Mary Queen
of Scots, when the Scots rebelled soon after her precipitate marriage to
the ambitious Bothwell.

23 June 1567

Madam,
It has been always held for a special principal in friendship that
prosperity provideth but adversity proveth friends, whereof at this time
finding occasion to verify the same in our actions, we have thought well
both for our profession and your comfort in these few words to testify
our friendship not only by . . . you of the . . . but to comfort you for
the best.

We have understood by your trusty servant, Robert Melville, such
things as you gave him in charge to declare on your behalf concerning
your estate and specially of as much as could be said for and allowed
of your marriage. Madam, to be plain with you, our grief hath not been
small that in this your marriage no slender consideration has been had
that, as we perceive manifestly no good friend you have in the whole
world can like thereof, and, if we should otherwise write or say, we
should abuse you. For how could a worse choice be made for your
honour than in such haste to marry such a subject who, besides other
notorious lacks, public fame has charged with the murder of your late
husband, besides the touching of yourself in some part, though we trust
in that behalf falsely. And with what peril have you married him, that
hath another lawful wife alive, whereby neither by God's law nor man's
yourself can be his lawful wife nor any children betwixt you legitimate?
Thus you see plainly what we think of the marriage; we are heartily
sorry that we can conceive no better, what colourable reasons soever
we have heard of your servant to induce us therein. Whereof we wish
upon the death of your husband that first care had been to have
searched out and punished the murderers of our near cousin, your
husband, which having been done effectually, as easily it might have
been in a matter so notorious, there might have been many more things

tolerated better in your marriage than now can be suffered to be spoken of, and surely we cannot but for friendship to yourself besides the natural instinction that we have of blood to your late husband, profess ourselves earnestly bent to do anything in our power to prevent the due punishment of that murder against any subject you have, how dear soever you should hold him, and next thereto, to be careful how your son, the Prince, may be preserved to the comfort of you and your Realm. Which two things we have from the beginning always taken to heart, and therein do mean to continue, and would be very sorry but you should allow us therein, what dangerous persuasions soever be made to you for the contrary. Now for your comfort in such adversity as we hear you should be whereof we know (?) not well what to think to be ... having a great part of your nobility, as we hear, separated from you, we assure you that whatsoever we can imagine meet for your honour and surety that shall lie in our power, we will perform the same that it shall and will appear you have a good neighbour, a dear sister and a faithful friend, and so shall you undoubtedly always find and prove us to be indeed ... you for which purpose we are determined to send with all speed one of our own trusty servants, not only to understand your state but also thereupon so to deal with your nobility and people as they shall find you not to lack our friendship and power for the preservation of your honour in quietness. And upon knowledge had what shall be further right to be done for your comfort and for the tranquillity of your Realm we will omit no time to further the same as you shall and will see, and so we recommend ourselves to you good sister in as effectual a manner as heretofore we were accustomed.

LUCY HUTCHINSON married a colonel in Cromwell's army. She admired his Puritan ideals and devotion. After his death she wrote a book justifying his life. Here she explains his qualities to her children. Although she was born in 1620, this letter was not published until 1806.

Never man had a greater passion for a woman, nor a more honourable esteem of a wife; yet he was not uxorious, nor remitted he that just rule which it was her honour to obey, but managed the reins of government with such prudence and affection that she who would not delight in such an honourable and advantageable subjection, must have

wanted a reasonable soul. He governed by persuasion, which he never
employed but to things honourable and profitable for herself; he loved
her soul and her honour more than her outside, and yet he had even
for her person a constant indulgence, exceeding the common temporary
passions of the most uxorious fools. If he esteemed her at a higher rate
than she in herself could have deserved, he was the author of that
virtue he doated on, while she only reflected his own glories upon him;
all that she was, was *him*, while he was here, and all that she is now at
best is but his pale shade. So liberal was he to her, and of so generous
a temper, that he hated the mention of severed purses; his estate being
so much at her disposal, that he never would receive an account of
anything she expended; so constant was he in his love, that when she
ceased to be young and lovely, he began to show most fondness; he
loved her at such a kind and generous rate as words cannot express;
yet even this, which was the highest love he or any man could have,
was yet bounded by a superior, he loved her in the Lord as his
fellow-creature, not his idol, but in such a manner as showed that an
affection, bounded in the just rules of duty, far exceeds every way all
the irregular passions in the world. He loved God above her, and all the
other dear pledges of his heart, and at his command and for his glory
cheerfully resigned them. He was as kind a father, as dear a brother, as
good a master, and as faithful a friend as the world had, yet in all these
relations, the greatest indulgence he could have in the world never
prevailed on him to indulge vice in the dearest person; but the more
dear any were to him, the more was he offended at anything that might
take off the lustre of their glory. As he had great severity against errors
and follies pertinaciously pursued, so had he the most merciful, gentle,
and compassionate frame of spirit that can be imagined to those who
became sensible of their errors and frailties, although they had been
ever so injurious to himself.

MADAME DE SÉVIGNÉ adored her daughter, but began to feel a little
worried about her prospects after four years of unsuitable suitors. Mme
de Sévigné was married at seventeen; now her daughter was already
twenty-two.

The matter was settled at last. Mlle de Sévigné was to marry a man
who was neither handsome nor young (he was then about forty) and who
had had two wives already. But François Adhémar, Count of Grignan,

had other qualifications. He belonged to one of the oldest and best families in France.

Here Mme de Sévigné writes to her cousin for his consent.

Paris, 4 December 1668

I must tell you some news I am sure you will be delighted to hear. 'The prettiest girl in France' is to be married, not to the handsomest young fellow, but to one of the most worthy men in the kingdom – to M. de Grignan, whom you have known for a long time. All his wives have died to give place to your cousin; and, with extraordinary kindness, his father and son have died too, so that he is richer than he has ever been before. And since by his birth, his establishments and his own good qualities he is all that we could wish, we have not bargained with him in the usual way, but have relied on the two families that have preceded us. He seems very pleased at the thought of being allied with us; and as we expect to hear from his uncle, the Archbishop of Arles (his other uncle, the Bishop of Uzès, is here), the affair will no doubt be concluded before the end of this year.

As I like to do what is usual on all occasions I now ask for your advice and approval. People outside our family seem to be satisfied, which is a good thing, for we are foolish enough to be influenced by other people's opinions.

QUEEN MARY II to King William III: a queen in love and in danger.

1690
Whitehall, September.

. . . I never do anything now without thinking, it may be, you are in the greatest dangers, and yet I must see company upon my set days. I must play twice a-week – nay, I must laugh and talk, though never so much against my will. I believe I dissemble very ill to those who know me, – at least, 'tis a good constraint to myself, yet I must endure it. All my motions are so watched, and all I do so observed, that if I eat less, or speak less, or look more grave, all is lost in the opinion of the world. So that I have this misery added to that of your absence and my fears for your dear person, that I must grin when my heart is ready to break, and talk when it is so oppressed I can scarce breathe.

I don't know what I should do, were it not for the Grace of God,

which supports me. I am sure I have great reason to praise the Lord
while I live, for His great mercy that I don't sink under this affliction, nay,
that I keep my health, for I can neither sleep nor eat. I go to Kensington
as often as I can for air, but then I can never be quite alone; neither can
I complain, – that would be some ease; but I have nobody whose humour
and circumstances agree with mine enough to speak my mind freely.
Besides, I must hear of business, which, being a thing I am so new in,
and so unfit for, does not break my brains the more, and not ease my
heart. I see I have insensibly made my letter too long upon my own self,
but I am confident you love enough to bear it for once. I don't remember
I have been guilty of the like fault before, since you went, and that is
now three months; for which time of almost perpetual fear and trouble
this is but a short account, and so I hope may pass.

'Tis some ease to me to write my pain, and 'tis some satisfaction to
believe you will pity me. It will be yet more when I hear it from
yourself in a letter, as I am sure you must, if it be but out of common
good-nature; how much more, then, out of kindness, if you love me as
well as you make me believe, and as I endeavour to deserve a little by
that sincere and lasting kindness I have for you. But, by making
excuses, I do but take up more of your time, and therefore I must tell
you that this morning Lord Marlborough went away. As little reason
as I have to care for his wife, yet I must pity her condition, having
lain-in but eight days; and I have great compassion for wives, when their
husbands go to fight.

I have almost forgot to tell you, that in the *Utrecht Courant* they have
printed a letter of yours to the States of Holland, in which you promise to
be soon with them. I can't tell you how many ill hours I have had about
that, in the midst of my joy when I thought you were coming home, for it
troubled me to think you would go over and fight again there.

LADY MARY WORTLEY MONTAGU attempts to alleviate her sister's melan-
cholia with these disillusioned reflections on marriage.

                                                        Aug 1725
Dear Sister,
I am in hopes your King of France [Louis XV] behaves better than our
Duke of Bedford, who by the care of a pious mother certainly preserved
his virginity to his marriage bed, where he was so much disappointed

in his fair bride (who through his own inclination could not bestow on
him those expressless raptures he had figured to himself) that he
already pukes at the thought of her, and determines to let his estate
go to his brother, rather than go through the filthy drudgery of getting
an heir. This is true history and I think the most extraordinary has
happened in this last age. This comes of living till the age of sixteen
without competent knowledge of either practical or speculative anatomy,
and literally thinking fine ladies composed of lilies and roses. A propos
of red and white, Lady Hervey is more delightful than ever, and such a
politician that if people were not blind to merit, she would govern the
nation. . . . Adieu, dear sister, I take a sincere part in all that relates to
you, and am ever yours.

Lady Lechmere had gambling debts, which her husband refused to pay.
She took laudanum to kill herself, but vomited and recovered.

Twickenham, 3 February 1726
It is very true, dear sister, that if I writ to you a full account of all that
passes, my letters would be both frequent and voluminous. This sinful
town is very populous, and my own affairs very much in a hurry, but
the same things that afford me much matter give me very little time,
and I am hardly at leisure to make observations, much less to write
them down. But the melancholy catastrophe of poor Lady Lechmere
is too extraordinary not to attract the attention of everybody. After
having played away her reputation and fortune, she has poisoned herself
– this is the effect of prudence! All indiscreet people live and flourish.
Mrs Murray has retrieved his Grace, and being reconciled to the
temporal, has renounced the spiritual. Her friend Lady Hervey by
aiming too high has fallen very low, and is reduced to trying to persuade
folks she has an intrigue, and gets nobody to believe her, the man in
question taking a great deal of pains to clear himself of the scandal. Her
Chelsea Grace of Rutland is married to an attorney; there's prudence
for you! 'Tis a strange thing that women can't converse with a lawyer,
a parson, nor a man midwife without putting them all to the same use,
as if one could not sign a deed, say one's prayers, or take physic without
doing you know what after it. This instinct is so odd, I am sometimes
apt to think we were made to no other end. If that's true, Lord ha' mercy
upon me; to be sure, I shall broil in the next world for living in the
neglect of a known duty in this.

LADY MARY WORTLEY MONTAGU eloped with her future husband. Unfortunately she soon found him dull and cold. She turned her drive and
liveliness into mordant books on education and letters to her sister:

[1723]

To speak plainly. I am very sorry for the forlorn state of matrimony,
which is as much ridiculed by our young ladies as it used to be by young
fellows: in short, both sexes have found the inconvenience of it, and
appellation of rake is as genteel in a woman as a man of quality; it is no
scandal to say Miss – the maid of honour, looks very well now she is
up again, and poor Biddy Noel has never been quite well since her last
confinement. You may imagine we married women look very silly; we
have nothing to excuse ourselves but that it was done a while ago and
we were very young when we did it. This is the general state of
affairs.

Fortunately, some men agreed with women's rights. Here, in an extract
from *Roxana*, the novelist DANIEL DEFOE puts his ideas into the mouth
of his heroine:

[1724]

I told him, I had, perhaps, differing notions of matrimony from what
the received custom had given us of it; that I thought a woman was
a free agent, as well as a man, and was born free, and could she manage
herself suitably, might enjoy that liberty to as much purpose as the men
do; that the laws of matrimony were indeed otherwise, and mankind
at this time acted quite upon other principles; and those such that a
woman gave herself entirely away from herself, in marriage, and
capitulated only to be, at best, but an upper servant, and from the
time she took the man, she was no better or worse than the servant
among the Israelites, who had his ears bored, that is, nailed to the
door-post, who by that act gave himself up to be a servant during life.

    That the very nature of the marriage contract was, in short, nothing
but giving up liberty, estate, authority, and everything to the man, and
the woman was indeed a mere woman ever after, that is to say, a slave.

Marriage Egyptian-style is described here by FLORENCE NIGHTINGALE who travelled up the Nile in 1849. Her letters to her family are still interesting: her descriptions are sensitive and authoritative; she offers an amusing, valuable record of nineteenth-century travel, to compare with the lively Lucie Duff Gordon. And Nightingale's letters record sites in Nubia which were later destroyed.

On the boat from Alexandria to Cairo she saw a group of women, dressed for a Moslem wedding:

27 November

She was the prettiest woman I ever saw, more like a sylph than a Juno, except on that occasion, and sat in her close jacket and trousers, with a sash round her waist, when with us. The women who *stood* the onset, were a bride from the island of Lemnos, a fat ugly woman, who had been married at eleven, and was being brought up by two duennas, rather nice old hags in turbans, to Cairo to her husband. The bride was magnificently dressed, and would have been handsome if she had not looked such an animal and so old. Her duennas always sat on either side of her, like tame elephants, and let her speak to none. She was covered with diamonds and pearls, had one jacket on of blue velvet trimmed with fur over another of yellow silk, &c. Most of the women crouched on the floor all night, and talked the whole time. They were amazingly puzzled by us, and I was asked some fifty times if I were married. This redoubled the difficulty; I could not conceive why one said to me so often, 'But you *did* go to the opera at Alexandria,' and would believe no denial. What we could be going to do in Upper Egypt was another difficulty; and that we should not travel by a caravan. At last we heard them settling in Greek that we were the singing people of the opera at Alexandria; but what could we be going to sing at Dongola for? Another woman was explaining her views on marriage. English, she said, married late, and fifteen *was* late. She never would marry her daughter later than ten or twelve; and when you *began* to think of it, the man ought not to be more than seven. (By the by, we saw a marriage at Alexandria; one horse bore the wedded couple, of six and seven, the lady riding behind her bridegroom, and preceded by men playing single stick.)

FANNY BURNEY married a French general when she was forty. They had only one son, Alexander, who chose to study at Cambridge when her husband returned to France. They both considered their son lazy. To counteract this, Gen. d'Arblay wrote to say he'd found a well-born fiancée for the young man! Here his mother reflects on the state of marriage.

Bath, 20 Oct. 1816

A mistress and a bride would see him her devoted slave: but in the year following year, when ardent novelty is passed away, a mother loved as I am may form much judgment what will be the lot of the wife, always allowing for the attractions of reconciliation which belong exclusively to the marriage state, where it is happy.

Nevertheless, I am completely of your opinion, that a good and lovely wife will ultimately soften his asperity, and give him a new taste for existence, by opening to him new sources of felicity, and exciting, as you justly suggest, new emulation to improvement, when he is wise enough to know how to appreciate, to treat, and to preserve such a treasure. But will four months fit him for beginning such a trial? Think of her, *mon ami*, as well as of him. The "responsibility" in this case would be yours for both, and exquisite would be your agony should either of them be unhappy. A darling daughter – an only child, nursed in the lap of soft prosperity – sole object of tenderness and of happiness to both her parents; rich, well-born, stranger to all care, and unused to any control; beautiful as a little angel, and (be very sure) not unconscious she is born to be adored.

But could any permanent amendment ensue, from working upon his errors only through his passions? Is it not to be feared that as they, the passions, subside, the errors would all peep up again? And she, who so prudently has already rejected a nearly accepted *prétendant* for his want of order!!! (poor Alexander!) how will she be content to be a monitress, where she will find everything in useful life to teach, and nothing in return to learn? And even if he endure the perpetual tutoring, will not she sicken of her victories ere he wearies of his defeats?

The Victorian novelist MRS OLIPHANT (1828–97) cautions us to not rush into judgments about marriage. She herself supported her own *and* her brother's children through writing. Yet her public views on a wife's role do not support working wives.

1858

To Blackwood's Magazine
False delicacies there may be in ordinary education, but nothing can
well be more utterly false than that artificial courage which tempts many
women, to rush into subjects of which they can have little practical
knowledge and no personal experience – to discuss the delicate laws of
marriage, the subtle and intricate mutual rights and wrongs of the two
great portions of humanity, and to make arbitrary and sweeping
condemnations of those who may, in the real course and practice of
life, have neither leisure nor inclination to defend themselves.
MRS OLIPHANT, NOVELIST

Compare her to the harsh views of many:

12 November 1859

To Saturday Review
Married life is a woman's profession, and to this life her training – that
of dependence – is modelled. Of course by not getting a husband, or
by losing him, she may find that she is without resources. All that can
be said of her is she has failed in business, and no social reform can
prevent such failures.
ANONYMOUS

The letters of American women are a little franker than many European
counterparts. This extract is from MARY ELLEN CASTLE (1837–92). She
had the unusual privilege of parents allowing her to attend college. There
she fell in love with her professor, James Rankin. At first her family
opposed the marriage, as he was eighteen years older. This letter, written
after two years of marriage, while she was expecting their first child,
reveals intense love for her absent husband.

Wednesday, 16 May 1860
Two days have passed away since I last felt your *good-bye kiss* and I am
beginning to long earnestly for the sight of your dear face – and loving
embraces; Yet my darling I am better content than I thought I could
ever be away from you – and I will try not to be *unhappy* at all – I
know it is much better for me to be *here* for several reasons. I can have
some *exercise*, and that is what I *ought* to have, as hard as it is for me

to *endure* it now – I have had so little to do all winter that I find I must begin very *gradually* now, but I *shall* be cautious darling and you must not fear that I shall do myself any injury – I shall be more *quiet* here too than I could be in Seymour [Indiana] – shall not see so many people. . . .

I wonder where you are tonight my own darling, and if you miss your *absent wife*. – Does your little room look desolate, or are you so very busy that you do not think of it? – I hope to get a letter from you by *tomorrow* night at farthest – write to me often dearest as I shall get the *blues* sometimes terribly – I *did* have such a *heart-ache* the last night I slept in your arms, I could not talk to you at all – but you must forgive my foolishness dearest – as you have often done before – and will have cause to do many times again – I am too tired to write more tonight – my heart is *full* of love to you *all* the time darling, I am still *your own* Ellen.

QUEEN VICTORIA writes on the institution of marriage to her favourite granddaughter Princess Alice.

Through my experience, I am becoming more and more convinced that the only true happiness is to be found in the domestic circle. . . . I must emphasise that give and take are essential. It is very necessary to look on marriage in a serious light. So many girls think to marry is to be independent and amuse oneself, whereas it is the reverse of independence: two wills have to be made to act together. It is only by mutual agreement and mutual yielding to one another that a happy marriage can be arrived at.

Queen Victoria spent a great deal of time attempting to matchmake for her many relatives, especially for the heir to the throne her son Edward.

To Alice:
I must observe that excessive gentleness, unless coupled with great cleverness and firmness would not do in his particular case. Superiority of mind and a certain determination are very necessary else invariably advantage is taken, and rudeness and an amount of tyrannising people takes place. You will understand me – those who never knuckle under but hold their own are always those most admired and who get

on best with this individual. Touch your brain dear, try to find someone
for him.

To which the Princess Royal replied: 'Unfortunately Princesses do not
spring up like mushrooms from the earth – or grow upon trees. . . .
However you may go far before you find another Princess like Princess
Alex [of Denmark, whom Edward eventually married in 1863].' Queen
Victoria finally answered:

You are, I know, a little inclined to be carried away if you are pleased
with a person, but Fritz is not. And as he coincides with what you
have to say, I feel sure she must be charming, in every sense of the
word: a pearl not to be lost. But, dearest, we only look on one side of
the question – have you at all thought if *she* will have him?

ISABEL BURTON adored her demanding, outwardly unresponsive husband
all her life. She accompanied him on tiring expeditions throughout the
Middle East, and even hired a doctor to live in, when he became ill in 1887.

I always think that a man is one character to his wife, another to his
family, another to *her* family, a fourth to a mistress or an *amourette* . . .
if he have one – and so on, *ad infinitum*; but I think the wife, if they
are happy and love each other, gets the pearl out of all the oyster
shells. . . . My husband, whose character naturally expanded with me
in the privacy of our domestic life, became quite another man the moment
anyone else entered the room. I have often, in the early days of my
married life, watched with great interest and astonishment things that
in after life I became quite used to. . . . He was the best of husbands
and the easiest man to live with. He was a man with whom it was possible
to combine, to keep up, all the little refinements of the honeymoon,
which tends to preserve affection and respect. . . .

OUÏDA, the novelist, was a loyal friend to both Burtons – husband and
wife. She wrote:

To women, Burton had one unpardonable fault: he loved his wife. He
would have been a happier and a greater man if he had had no wife
– but his love for her was extreme: it was a source of weakness as most

warm emotions are in the lives of strong men. Their marriage was romantic and clandestine; a love-marriage in the most absolute sense of the words, not wise on either side, but on each impassioned. . . . Throughout the chief part of their lives he was implicitly obeyed by her, but during the close of his, ill-health made him more helpless, and compelled him to rely on her in all things, and then the religious ogre raised its head and claimed its prey.

JANE CARLYLE proved a supportive lively wife, though the marriage may not have been consummated. Her husband, Thomas, was revered in his time for his writing on history. She subordinated her life to comfort him, as seen in this letter to him.

Craigenvilla, Edinburgh: Monday, 24 August, 1857
Oh, my dear! What a magnificent book this is going to be! The best of all your books. I say so, who never flatter, as you are too well aware; and who am 'the only person I know that is always in the right!' So far as it is here before me, I find it forcible and vivid, and sparkling as 'The French Revolution,' with the geniality and composure and finish of 'Cromwell' – a wonderful combination of merits! And how you have contrived to fit together all those different sorts of pictures, belonging to different sorts of times, as compactly and smoothly as a bit of the finest mosaic! Really one may say, of these two first books at least, what Helen said of the letters of her sister who died – you remember? – 'So splendidly put together one would have thought that hand couldn't have written them!'

It was the sheets that hindered me from writing yesterday; though I doubt if a letter posted at Morningside (the Scotch *Campo Santo*) yesterday (Sunday) would have reached you sooner than if posted to-day. Certainly it is a devil of a place for keeping the Sunday, this! Such preaching and fasting, and 'touting and praying,' as I was never before concerned in! But one never knows whence deliverance is to come any more than misfortune. I was cut out of all, or nearly all, my difficulties yesterday by the simple providential means of – a bowel complaint! It was reason enough for staying away from church; excuse enough for declining to be read to; and the loss of my dinner was entirely made up for by the loss of my appetite! Nothing could have happened more opportunely!

Fecklessness with money, more often than not, is a cause of friction in marriage. JEAN RHYS (1894–1970) left her native Dominica in her early twenties. She lived in London, then Paris, earning pitifully little as a typist. Her unhappy love affairs often became the themes of her brief novels, romances with tragic endings. Throughout her life she corresponded with supportive women friends about her financial and emotional problems. Max was her third husband, Leslie her first lover. This letter to Peggy Kircaldy shows her narrative gifts, her wry humour in analysing predicaments.

Monday [1950]
Stanhope Gardens

Peggy my dear,

Max's case comes on tomorrow, he's with his lawyer now, and as I'm too weary to tramp about the stony streets I'll talk to you instead and risk boring you. My dear if I'm confusing about what has happened – well I'm pretty confused too. But I'll tell you all I know and make it as short as possible – thank you for listening.

You remember don't you that when you came to see me at Beckenham I was full of plans for fixing up the poor old house. That was the start (at any rate so far as I know). A very plausible man who called himself a 'builder' had agreed to repair the water pipes, make the basement habitable and all the rest. I was very enthusiastic about this, I was simply delighted when I thought of settling in that house and just flopping for the rest of my life. I'm awfully tired, tired to my soul, and I am not brave at all now but an almighty coward. I hadn't the slightest reason to distrust Max. He was Leslie's cousin, he knew I had no money when he asked me to marry him, none better, for he was the trustee [of Leslie's will]. He'd been very kind to me. Also I am perfectly certain even now that Max is not a bad hat. He's potty. I *look* potty, he *is* potty. There's no other explanation. Listen. This builder (so called) got a hundred quid from me and *three* hundred from Max (to start off with). He sent some workmen along and they made a hell of a row for a week.

MOTHERHOOD

Motherhood has been central to the existence of most women. Our culture states that women should be fulfilled by childbearing. Yet most of these letters express more pain than joy in childbirth. Some, including Queen Victoria, admit to feeling 'like a dog'. They unveil with honesty the real suffering caused by much childbearing – before contraception and painkillers. There exist few letters which describe mothering during early childhood, probably because of exhaustion and illiteracy; so the letters from an ordinary middle-class American mother (who died when her eldest child was only nine) are valuable primary evidence.

In a culture which judges women by their ability to produce children, sterility causes misery. We read about Mary I longing to give Philip II of Spain an heir, and an unknown Frenchwoman unable to bring her pregnancies to fruition because of her husband's syphilis – a suffering that must have ruined many homes before the discovery of antibiotics. This section ends with a letter from Fay Weldon attempting to make a young woman today understand the many difficulties connected with pregnancy in the past.

Longing for motherhood is expressed in this letter by HILDEGARD OF BINGEN (1098–1179) who writes to sympathize with Bertha, Queen of Greece and Empress of Byzantium, in her longing for a son. Note the joy and certainty conveyed by her images of sprouting branches and 'bubbling waters'.

1153

God's Spirit breathes and speaks: in wintertime, God takes care of the branch that is love. In summer, God causes that same branch to be green and to sprout with blossoms. God removes diseased outgrowths that could do harm to the branch.

It is through the little brook springing from stones in the east that other bubbling waters are washed clean, for it flows more swiftly. Besides, it is more useful than the other waters because there is no dirt in it.

These lessons also apply to every human being to whom God grants one day of the happiness and the glowing sunrise of glory. Such a person will not be oppressed by the strong north wind with its hateful foes of discord.

So look to the One who has moved you and who desires from your heart a burnt offering, the gift of keeping all of God's commandments. Sigh for the Divine. And may God grant you what you desire and what you pray for in your need, the joy of a son. The living eye of God looks on you: it wants to have you and you will live for eternity.

Queen Mary I was forty when she married the handsome young King Philip II of Spain. She longed for a child to unite their two countries under Catholicism – and to please Philip, with whom she had fallen in love. Mary's stomach grew in size for nine months, so that she and most onlookers believed she was pregnant – but it was a false pregnancy. ONE OF QUEEN MARY'S LADIES-IN-WAITING wrote the following.

21 May 1555

Mrs Clarentius and divers others, as parasites about her, assured her to be with child, insomuch as the Queen was fully so persuaded herself, being desirous thereof, if God had been so pleased, that it might have been a comfort to all Catholic posterity, as she declared by her oration in the Guild Hall at London, at the rising of Wyatt, which was so worthy a speech, made by her there, touching the cause of her marriage and why, that it made them that were there, though of contrary religion, to relent into tears, and hardly could she suffer any that would not say as she said, touching her being with child. Mrs Frideswide Strelly, a good honourable woman of hers would not yield to her desire, and never told her an untruth. . . .

When the rockers and cradle and all such things were provided for the Queen's delivery, that her time should be nigh, as it was supposed, and those parasites had had all the spoil of such things amongst them, and no such matter in the end . . . then when the uttermost time was come, and the Queen thus deluded, she sent for Strelly her woman again, to whom she said, 'Ah, Strelly, Strelly, I see they be all flatterers

and none true to me but thou,' and then was she more in favour than she ever was before.
[Sloane MS 1583]

MARY TUDOR was unable to have a child, perhaps because of her father's syphilis. A prayer can be construed as a letter to God (as in *The Color Purple* by Alice Walker), so I include this prayer by Mary:

Most benign Lord Jesu! Behold me wretched beggar, and most vile sinner, prostrate here before the feet of thy mercy. Behold the wounds, sores, griefs and vices of my soul, (which alas! I have brought into the same by sin) that they may be healed. Most Merciful Lord Jesu! Have pity upon mine infirmities, captivity and infelicity: by means whereof my miserable soul is pressed down to earthly things, and divided into sundry desires.

THE ORDEALS OF CHILDBIRTH

Mothers were not asked if their many babies symbolized beauty and innocence. In fact they were seldom asked their views on any aspect of childbirth, so their letters on this topic are particularly revealing. Labour could cause intense physical suffering before the use of chloroform popularized by Queen Victoria. Many women died in childbirth, or soon after, as in some Third World countries today. Lengthy labour and child-rearing left most women too exhausted to find time to write.

SUZANNE NECKER, wife of the powerful French minister, had received a good education for the time, but nothing she had been told had prepared her for the ordeal of childbirth. The first and only daughter, Germaine de Staël, was born on 22 April 1766. Soon afterwards, she reported the pain and terror she had gone through.

1766

I confess that my terrified imagination fell far short of the truth. For three days and nights I suffered the tortures of the damned, and Death was at my bedside, accompanied by his satellites in the shape of a species of men who are still more terrible than the Furies, and who have been invented for the sole purpose of horrifying modesty and scandalizing nature. The word *accoucheur** still makes me shudder. . . . The revolting details of childbirth had been hidden from me with such care that I was as surprised as I was horrified, and I cannot help thinking that the vows most women are made to take are very foolhardy. I doubt whether they would willingly go to the altar to swear that they will allow themselves to be broken on the wheel every nine months.

**accoucheur* = someone who delivers a baby.

23 May 1877

I am glad baby is a boy for he will suffer in a different (less hopeless, perhaps, since it is fate) way than women suffer. Certain things come as an inheritance to women. A man can escape pain – a woman is prone to it as the sparks fly upward.

MARY H. FOOTE
(1847–1938)
To her friend Helena de Kay Gilder

Many mothers died of puerperal fever, which could have been prevented if more were understood about hygiene. This letter to Mr C. White describes the problem.

21 November 1774

We had a puerperal fever in the infirmary last winter. It began about the end of February, when almost every woman, as soon as she was delivered, or perhaps about twenty-four hours after, was seized with it; and all of them died, though every method was tried to cure the disorder. What was singular, the women were in good health before they were brought to bed, though some of them had been long in the hospital before delivery. One woman had been dismissed the ward before she was brought to bed; came into it some days after with her labour upon her; was easily delivered, and remained perfectly well for twenty-four hours, when she was seized with a shivering and the other symptoms of the fever. I caused her to be removed to another ward; yet notwithstanding all the care that was taken of her she died in the same manner as the others.

DR YOUNG
Edinburgh.
[C. White, *Treatise on the Management of Pregnant and Lying-In Women*]

This American mother had lost her first child, a daughter. Here she describes the difficulties, and subsequent relief at the birth of her second baby.

I was confined 13th April, 1847, Tuesday, before 2 o'clock in the morn'g, after having been sick 20 hours – very sick but a short time.

Sent for my friends Mrs. N. Marble & Mrs. G. K. Shaw & the
physician, Doct. Brown about eight o'clock Monday eve'g. Upon the
whole, they called it a pretty *comfortable time*. I was not much
disappointed in a daughter, tho' I wished for a son. I felt all the time
that I wo'd rather have another daughter than never have any other child.
The Nurse Miss H. Chesley came early the same day & is yet with me.
She is one of the most skilful & experienced in the State – Aged about
43 – healthy & smart & has nursed 200 women – is proud of her calling
& has a genuine love for infants that amounts to passion. I sho'd have had
a good getting up had I not been attacked with canker in the mouth &
throat of the most violent & obstinate character. It affected the nerves of
the face so that they pained me like ague, & the cheeks swelled much –
blood flow'd to the head & the inflamation became high – then it seized
upon the brain – I suffered several days the most distracting nervous
headache & my physician feared brain fever. For many days I co'd not
open my mouth – nor co'd I quite shut it – & for ten days I took no
nourishment except simple drinks & that with the greatest difficulty, & I
am still much afflicted with sore mouth.

   The babe appears smart & healthy. She has a little round solid head
& snug body, looked very small to my nurse, but upon weighing her
found her just six pounds to the surprise of all. She has a very pretty
forehead – high like her fathers – blue eyes light eyebrows lashes etc. –
thus we think she will be complected like him. She does not look much
as Charlotte did – has not near as much hair – nor is it as dark. All
agree in calling her an uncommon handsome child of her age – & I
really think they must be sincere – tho' I know this is no indication that
she will be pretty a few months hence. The first day I proposed to call
her Elizabeth for hus-' Mother, he was rather desirous to have her
named for me & proposed Persis Elizabeth, & tho' this is not the *kind*
of name I fancy most – I did not object & unless we change our minds
this will be her name. . . .

   It has been a matter of surprise with me that so much interest has
been manifested by the ladies – *every* married lady in the village having
called since I was confined – all classes – ten or twelve who never
called before. Something owing to custom of the place perhaps, but I
wo'd fain believe the longer we live here the more friends we have.
PERSIS SIBLEY ANDREWS

There was sadness at *not* producing children. SUZANNE VOILQUIN married, in 1825, a construction worker with venereal disease. Here she writes with unusual directness of the effects of his disease.

As for me, in the first five years of my marriage I had to abandon the hope of becoming a mother because of it. Three times I felt a dear tiny being moving about in my womb only to die there before having seen the light of day. How many tears I shed in the silence of the nights as I saw my hopes disappointed again and again. Oh, to have felt near my heart this young life that I bore with so much love perish without my having heard that so-long-desired first cry. Believe me, you would have had to experience these sorrows to appreciate all their bitterness. Words are powerless to express to you the lassitude and disgust for life that each of these crises left deep in my heart. I even came to doubt divine justice. 'Must I accept the ruin of my health,' I asked myself, 'the even more terrible loss of my child as expiations for a sin against society's laws and not against divine indulgence? If God is just, why these new sufferings? Wasn't I recently wronged in a cowardly way? Did I not cry and pray enough? If I was at fault, haven't I redeemed myself by work, courage, and devotion? Oh, sacred maternity, my beloved ideal! Why have you always eluded me? What can I cling to? This marriage to which I have given so much of my life, and from which I have received so little happiness in return, is it not to be blessed?' During such moments of discouragement or during the nights I was unable to sleep, I began to regret the loss of my Catholic faith. I told myself that if I still had the strong faith that had sustained my mother in her laborious and painful life, then perhaps I, like her, would be more resigned. But now that was no longer possible, and there was nothing left in me to control the internal flame that was destroying me.

However she did not give way to despair, but trained as a midwife and joined the movement for social reform of Saint-Simon.

QUEEN VICTORIA became the symbol of a devoted mother, with nine children. Her letters to her eldest daughter reveal the pain and discomfort she went through.

24 March 1858

Now to reply to your observation that a married woman has much more
liberty than an unmarried one; in one sense of the word she has, – but
what I meant was – in a physical point of view – and if you have
hereafter (as I had constantly for the first 2 years of my marriage) –
aches – and sufferings and miseries and plagues – which you must
struggle against – and enjoyments etc. to give up – constant precautions
to take, you will feel the yoke of a married woman! Without that –
certainly it is unbounded happiness – if one has a husband one worships!
It is a foretaste of heaven. And you have a husband who adores you,
and is, I perceive, ready to meet every wish and desire of your's. I
had 9 times for 8 months to bear with those above-named enemies
and real misery (besides many duties) and I own it tried me sorely;
one feels so pinned down – one's wings clipped – in fact, at the best
(and few were or are better than I was), only half oneself – particularly
the first and second time. This I call the "shadow side" as much as
being torn away from one's loved home, parents and brothers and sisters.
And therefore – I think our sex a most unenviable one.

21 April 1858

I can not tell you how happy I am that you are not in an unenviable
position. I never can rejoice by hearing that a poor young thing is
pulled down by this trial.

  Though I quite admit the comfort and blessing good and amiable
children are – though they are also an awful plague and anxiety for
which they show one so little gratitude very often! What made me so
miserable was – to have the two first years of my married life utterly
spoilt by this occupation! I could enjoy nothing – not travel about or
go about with dear Papa and if I had waited a year, as I hope you
will, it would have been very different.

15 June 1858

What you say of the pride of giving life to an immortal soul is very fine,
dear, but I own I cannot enter into that; I think much more of our
being like a cow or a dog at such moments; when our poor nature
becomes so very animal and unecstatic – but for you, dear, if you are
sensible and reasonable not in ecstasy nor spending your day with
nurses and wet nurses, which is the ruin of many a refined and
intellectual young lady, without adding to her real maternal duties, a
child will be a great resource. Above all, dear, do remember never to

lose the modesty of a young girl towards others (without being prude); though you are married don't become a matron at once to whom everything can be said, and who minds saying nothing herself – I remained particular to a degree (indeed feel so now) and often feel shocked at the confidences of other married ladies. I fear abroad they are very indelicate about these things. Think of me who at that first time, very unreasonable, and perfectly furious as I was to be caught, having to have drawing rooms and levées and made to sit down – and be stared at and take every sort of precaution.

30 June 1858

I delight in the idea of being a grandmama; to be that at 39 (D.V.) and to look and feel young is great fun, only I wish I could go through it for you, dear, and save you all the annoyance. But that can't be helped. I think of my next birthday being spent with my children and a grandchild. It will be a treat!

MARY WOLLSTONECRAFT (1759–97), author of *Vindication of the Rights of Women*, was shoddily treated by her womanizing husband, American businessman Gilbert Imlay. She attempted suicide when he left her. However, moments of depression did not cloud her ability to argue for the rights of mothers to keep their own children, as is shown in this letter to her husband.

1 January 1794

Considering the care and anxiety a woman must have about a child before it comes into the world, it seems to me, by a *natural right*, to belong to her. When men get immersed in the world, they seem to lose all sensations, excepting those necessary to continue or produce life! – Are these the privileges of reason? Amongst the feathered race, whilst the hen keeps the young warm, her mate stays by to cheer her; but it is sufficient for man to condescend to get a child, in order to claim it. – A man is a tyrant!

FAY WELDON writes a letter to her niece, Alice, describing the real
dangers of pregnancy at the time of Jane Austen, and her creation Mrs
Bennet, mother of Elizabeth in *Pride and Prejudice*.

November 1983

My dear Alice,

Just imagine yourself living at the time of Jane Austen.

Now, Alice, there you are, a typical young woman of the 1799s.
We're supposing you're working on the land, and of peasant stock.
You've scraped your dowry together and you've found your young (or
old, often quite old!) man, and got yourself married. Your prime duty is
to have children. The clergyman has told you so at the wedding
ceremony. 'Marriage is designed by God for the procreation of
children. . . .' Everyone believes it. (If you turned out to be barren,
that was a terrible disaster, not just personally but socially. It made you
a non-woman. No infertility clinics then. Just the image of the barren
fig tree, blasted by Jesus for what it couldn't help.) But such disasters
apart, you're likely to be pregnant within a year of marriage and carry
one child successfully to term every two years until the menopause. This
seems to be the rate which nature, uninterfered with, decrees for human
reproduction. Fifty per cent of all the babies would die before they were
two: from disease due to malnutrition, ignorance, or infection. Every
death would be the same misery it is today. Your many pregnancies
would be plentifully interrupted by miscarriages, and one baby in every
four would be still-born. Midwives, mercifully, did not customarily allow
imperfect babies to live, nor were they expected to. Child delivery was
primitive and there were no analgesics. Child care was not considered
a full-time job. Babies were swaddled and hung on pegs out of the way
while mothers went on keeping the wolf from the door. If the mother's
milk failed, the babies would be fed on gruel, soaked into sacking and
sucked out by the baby.

Your own chances of dying in childbirth were not negligible and
increased with every pregnancy. After fifteen pregnancies (which meant
something like six babies brought to term and safely delivered) your
chances of dying were (Marie Stopes later claimed) one in two. Mrs
Bennet, giving birth to Mary, must have been worried indeed. Her
nerves were bad: she was considered ridiculous, poor thing, for saying
so. (I take a very tender view of Mrs Bennet, more tender than her
creator does. But I am looking at a society from the outside in, not the
inside out.)

Jane Austen herself was the sixth child of a family of seven. Or eight, really. Her mother's second child was epileptic, sent away from home – or presumably, simply not collected from the wet-nurse – and never mentioned again. An older brother, Edward, was reared in a family not his own, where there was more money and more time. Children, coming in large numbers to comparatively few households – as in Ireland today, where contraception is still disallowed – were quite frequently reared in homes better able to accommodate them than their own. Emma, in *The Watsons*, is brought up outside the family, and meets her sisters for the first time when she is a young woman.

BABY-REARING

This letter written in Italy in the second century BC, contains advice from a mother, MYIA, to a young woman, Phyllis, who has just had a baby.

The wet-nurse should not be temperamental or talkative or uncontrolled in her appetite for food, but orderly and temperate. It is best if the baby is put down to sleep when it is well filled with milk. Such rest is sweet for little ones and such feeding most effective. If other food is given, it should be as simple as possible. One should stay away from wine completely because it has such a powerful effect, or mix it sparingly with its evening meal of milk. She should not give him continual baths; it is better to have occasional temperate ones. Along the same lines, the atmosphere around the baby should have an even balance of hot and cold, and his housing should be neither too airy nor too close. Moreover, his water should not be hard nor too soft, nor his bed too rough – rather, it should fall comfortably on his skin. In each of these areas Nature desires what is rightfully hers, not luxuries.

This much then I think it is useful to write at present – my hopes based on Nursing according to Plan. With the gods' help, I shall in the future provide the possible and appropriate reminders about the child's upbringing.

Many parents, even those who could afford expert help, experienced difficulties in baby-rearing. This is from LORD AMBERLEY, who felt very close to his wife, Kate Stanley (1842–74). Their son was Bertrand Russell.

22 August 1865

Papa & Mama came today. Mama admired the baby and thought him very fine. I thought he looked pale, & am afraid we must get him a wet-nurse if he is to thrive. However, all who saw him seemed to be pleased with him. Dear Kate struggled hard against the wet nurse, but in the evening declared her readiness to give up breast-feeding if the child's health would be better with another woman. A terrible disappointment to her, for we both care very much about ladies nursing, but I doubt not her strong sense of duty will overcome the reluctance to relinquish this harassing attempt to feed her baby when nature does not provide the means of doing so.

KATE AMBERLEY could afford good nursing, but experienced many problems with the care of her first baby over breast-feeding and nurses.

5 Sept 1865

Powell (the wetnurse) came – baby fought a good deal with her about sucking but took it in the evg. . . . A [Lord Amberley] has been too dear & tender all the time of my confinement; full of care gentleness & thought for me, very low several times which made me sad when I did not feel strong enough to cheer him up. He is very dear too about his boy very fond of him & admires him as much as I do – My nurse Mrs. Cotton thinks baby has A's eyes but otherwise like me. He frowns too much but he has been so bothered since his birth – This is the 5th woman he has had poor darling – He weighed 9 lbs when born 10 lbs at a fortnight old & he was 23 inches tall altogether very large & very strong.

To Georgiana Peel, Amberley's half-sister:

24 Oct 1865

I have been deceived over the new nurse, Davies. I am too furious. When he cried she used to shake him – when she washed him she used to stuff the sponge in his little mouth – push her finger (beast!) in his dear little throat – say she hated the child, wished he were dead – used to let him lie on the floor screaming while she sat quietly by & said screams did not annoy her it was good for his lungs, besides she liked me to hear him scream as she thought otherwise I should think she had nothing to do & as soon as I came into the room she would take him into her arms & cant over him as if she loved him dearly. She hated being at Alderley because Mama & Mde [Kate's sister] used always to be coming into the room & to Mama she used to lie & when asked if Baby had been out say yes, when she had never stirred fr. the room – She thought she could manage me as she liked & that I would never find her out or find fault with her, & no more I think I should as I trusted her so implicitly. She would not let the wetnurse suckle him before he came to me, that he might scream & that I might know what a trouble he was – she sat in her room most of the day I find reading novels & never nursed the baby or spoke to it.

MRS GASKELL writes to her sister-in-law, Anne Robson, about her fears as a mother.

23 December 1840
Wednesday evening 9 o'clock

My dearest Nancy,
I am sitting all alone, and not feeling over and above well, and it would be such a comfort to have you here to open my mind to – but that not being among the possibilities, I am going to write you a long private letter. MA [Marianne] is better; she has jelly and strengthening eggs twice a day and seems much less languid. . . . Mr Partington [the doctor] was encouraging this morning but one can't help having 'Mother's fears' and William [her husband] I dare say kindly, won't allow me ever to talk to him about anxieties, while it would be SUCH A RELIEF often.

I have of course had MA with me more during this delicacy of hers, and I am more and more anxious about her – not exactly her health, but I see hers is a peculiar character – *very* dependent of those around her – almost as much as Meta is independent and in this point I look to Meta to strengthen her. But I am convinced that love and sympathy are *very* much required by MA. The want of them would make her an unhappy character, probably sullen and deceitful – while sunshine and tenderness would do everything for her. She is very conscientious and tender-hearted.

Now Anne, will you remember this? It is difficult to have the right trust in God almost, when thinking about one's children – and you know I have no sister or near relation whom I could entreat to watch over any peculiarity in their disposition. Dear William feels kindly towards his children, is yet most reserved in *expressions* of either affection or sympathy – & in the case of my death, we all know the probability of widowers marrying again – would you promise dearest

Anne, to remember MA's PECULIARITY OF CHARACTER, & as much as circumstances permit, watch over and cherish her. Meta is remarkably independent, and will help MA *if she is spared*. Now don't go and fancy that I am low-spirited – I do often pray to God with regard to what becomes of my children . . .

Looking after four small daughters when a baby son is born, MRS GASKELL describes her full day, not unlike a modern mother's, to Eliza Holland.

Summer 1845
Sunday morning
Willie asleep everyone else out. . . . I am so busy & so happy. My laddie is grunting so I must make haste. . . . I have Florence & Willie in my room which is also nursery, call Hearn at six, ½ p 6 she is dressed, comes in, dresses Flora, gives her breakfast the first; ½ p. 7 I get up, 8 Flora goes down to her sisters & Daddy, & Hearn to her breakfast. While I in my dressing gown dress Willie. ½ p. 8 I go to breakfast with parlour people, Florence being with us & Willie (ought to be) in his cot; Hearn makes beds etc in nursery only. 9 she takes F. & I read chapter & have prayers first with household & then with children, ½ p. 9 Florence & Willie come in drawing room for an hour while bedroom & nursery windows are open; ½ p. 10 go in kitchen, cellars & order dinner. Write letters; ¼ p. 11 put on things; ½ p. 11 take Florence out. I come in, nurse W. & get ready for dinner; ½ p. 1 dinner; ½ p. 2 children, two little ones, come down during servants' dinner half hour open windows upstairs; 3 p.m. go up again & I have two hours to kick my heels in (to be elegant & explicit). 5 Marianne & Meta from lessons & Florence from upstairs & Papa when he can comes in drawing room to 'Lilly a hornpipe', i.e. dance while Mama plays, & make all the noise they can. Daddy reads, writes or does what he likes in dining room. ½ p. 5 Margaret (nursemaid) brings Florence's supper, which Marianne gives her, being answerable for slops, dirty pinafores & untidy misbehaviours while Meta goes up stairs to get ready & fold up Willie's basket of clothes while he is undressed (this by way of feminine & family duties). Meta is so neat & so knowing, only, handles wet napkins very gingerly. 6 I carry Florence upstairs, nurse Willie; while she is tubbed & put to bed. ½ past 6 I come down dressed leaving (hitherto) both asleep & Will & Meta dressed (between 6 and ½ p.) & Miss F. with tea quite ready. After tea read to M. A. & Meta till

bedtime while they sew, knit or worsted work. From 8 till 10 gape. We are so desperately punctual that now you know what we do every hour.

RUNNING A HOUSEHOLD

The labour of women in the home has been undervalued, culturally and financially. Women have worked long hours, running households, rearing children, cleaning, cooking, yet have never been paid wages. Society decreed the home to be 'women's sphere'. Yet in the Middle Ages both sexes shared labour, inside the home and on the land. Powerful men, when away on business, or fighting, often entrusted the management of their estates to their wives, whose expertise deserved to be considered 'professional'. From Anglo-Saxon to Tudor times, propertied women were allowed to keep their titles to property on marriage, which lent them more prestige in patriarchal eyes. By the seventeenth century life appeared more settled and prosperous. The eighteenth century saw family life increase in importance. Fanny Burney and Jane Austen wrote fascinating accounts of the way their households spent their time. They transform the ordinary into a valuable female way of viewing daily life.

Nineteenth-century books on good household management stated that domesticity should satisfy women, though writers like Mrs Beeton declared it a demanding profession. It did satisfy Elizabeth Browning when she experienced it for the first time, in Italy, with servants to do most of the work. But the books of advice seldom dealt with the problems of overload, which occurred whenever women had children and needed to continue with other work. Mrs Gaskell and Louisa May Alcott counsel ways of coping with household and writing. By the twentieth century women are explicitly underlining the competing demands on their time which interfere with intellectual concentration; the writer Katherine Mansfield is compared to a black single parent of the 1980s. Both are overworked, yet find time to turn housework into homemaking, the creating of a caring place – for men.

The Pastons, living in the fifteenth century, suffered from attacks on their property and tenants. When Sir John was away, MARGARET PASTON

(*c.* 1420–84) took over as 'captainess' of their estate. In 1448 the Duke
of Suffolk's soldiers with battle-axes ransacked her church and kitchens.
This letter shows Margaret's exact knowledge of the weapons needed
to protect their estate against plundering.

1448

Right worshipful husband, I commend myself to you and ask you to get
some crossbows, and windlasses to wind them with, and crossbow
bolts, for your houses here are so low that no one can shoot out of
them with a longbow, however much we needed to. I expect you can
get such things from Sir John Fastolf if you were to send to him. And
I would also like you to get two or three short pole-axes to keep indoors,
and as many leather jackets, if you can.

Partridge [Moleyns' bailiff] and his companions are very much afraid
that you will try to reclaim possession from them, and have made
great defences within the house, so I am told. They have made bars
to bar the doors crosswise, and loopholes at every corner of the house
out of which to shoot, both with bows and hand-guns; and the holes
that have been made for hand-guns are barely knee high from the floor,
and five such holes have been made. No one could shoot out from
them with hand bows.

Purry made friends with William Hasard at Querles' house and told
him that he would come and drink with Partridge and him; and he said
he would be welcome. That afternoon he went there to see what they
did and what company they had with them. When he came there the
doors were bolted fast and there was no one with them but Margaret
and Capron and his wife and Querles' wife, and another man in black,
who walked with a limp; I think from what he said that it was Norfolk
of Gimingham. And Purry saw all this, and Marriott and his company
boasted greatly; but I will tell you about that when you come home.
Yours,
MARGARET PASTON

Managing a medieval household was similar to running a business today.
It represented the largest grouping of people together under one roof at
that time. There might be a hundred servants, and many relatives and
workmen to deal with. MARGARET PASTON's lawyer husband was often
in London on business, and her letters to him show how professional

the lady of the manor was. Margaret, a careful housewife, recommended her husband to look not only for good quality, but reasonable prices when he ordered food in London which could not be produced on their estate:

I pray you that ye will buy for me 1 lb of almonds and 1 lb of sugar, some freize [material] to maken of your childer's [children's] gowns. Ye shall have best cheap and best choice of Hay's wife, as it is told me. And that ye would buy a yarn of broadcloth of black for an hood for me, of 44d or 4s a yard.

Part of a housewife's job in those days was to get ready stores of food to be salted for the winter months when there was no fresh food. In this note Margaret Paston's bailiff advised her to stock up with herrings for the winter while they were cheap:

Mistress, it were good to remember your stuff of herring now this fishing time. I have got me a friend in Lowestoft to help buy me seven or eight barrels and they shall not cost more than 6s 8d a barrel. You shall do more [better] now [autumn] with 40s [£2] than you shall do at Christmas with 5 marks [worth over £3].

During the reign of Henry VIII, the Lisle family prospered until the King needed money. They moved to Calais in 1533 and dispersed some of their English household. Lady Lisle left her step-daughter, JANE BASSET in charge. Jane had obviously agreed to oversee her stepmother's property, including the accounts, bedding, and fishing. Her main worry is caused by an elderly local priest, Sir John Bonde, about whom she complains for stealing and treating the house like a brothel.

Thanks to Muriel St Clare Byrne, we can now read transcriptions of the letters of the Lisle family from 1533–40. Jane used Roman numerals.

[1535]

Madame, as for your feather beds and your testers of silks, they were not put out this iij quarters of a year until the vj day of June last was, and that was by the sight of a letter that was come upon him. Whether the said letter came from you or no, I cannot tell, but I had neither letter, neither word of the ij letters that I sent your ladyship afore these.

Also, madame, it is your will and pleasure that I shall have a chamber here at your place; but now I am taken up with Sir John Bonde, and

also with Bremelcum, that I cannot tell what to do, for they had liefer
that any brothel in this parts were here than I, and so the said woman
that I wrote unto you is here daily, and so she said unto me herself
and defined also: And this, good madame, doth grieve me very sore.

Also, madame, as for your fishing, what accompt they make upon
you I cannot tell, but I can prove that when he goeth to market with
your fish and receiveth xx^s a day, they put nothing in the book of
accompt but iiij^s; that is one week with another, and he goes to market
lightly, one week with another, iij times a week, beside that he doth
sell otherwise. Also, good madame, I heartily desire you to send word
that all this may be amended and specially that this foresaid woman
come not to your place, for all the country speak of it; and so Jesu
have you in his protection and keeping. Amen.

Also, as I hear say, Sir John Bonde will be with you shortly for to
excuse him and Bremelcum and give you a pig of your own sow.
By [your] daughter Jane Bassett
in all thing to her small power

Daily life under Henry VIII: the move to Calais of one branch of the
Lisle family produced an interchange of letters that tell us a great deal
about the Lisle family's interests and activities. Here MADAME DE BOURS,
who had been hostess to Lady Lisle, keeps in touch, sends her a present
and gives news about her son, Montmorency.

13 October 1538

Madame. The commencement of this present letter shall be to beseech
you to pardon me that I have not been able for such a long time to make
my recommendations to you. I am waiting to send you the two goshawks
for which you wrote me. I have been able to procure but one, the which
hath still an injury to its leg. I understand that there is a certain
gentleman who hath made promise to Monsieur de Riou to send a couple
to my Lord. It is now six weeks since Montmorency went to the Court.
I have required him to take pains to procure them if he could, for me
to send you. For the most part of this time I have been continuously
away from home, for love of one of my brothers who hath been ill, and
whom it hath pleased God to take to himself some fifteen days ago.
Ever since my return hither I have been acrased, and do not yet find
myself strong enough to be able to write you a longer letter. I beseech

you to be so good as to make me partaker at large of your news. By your last letters you tell me that Mademoiselle my good daughter hath been sore sick for a long time and yet is. I am greatly desirous to know how she doth at this present. Madame, after being most humbly recommended to the good grace of my Lord and you, I pray Our Lord to grant you good life and long.

From Bours, this xiij day of October.

Ever most ready to do you service,

Signed ANNE ROUAUD

Madame, there is a great personage of this realm who hath prayed me to obtain for him a large English greyhound. I beseech you to do me this favour to procure for me one that will be very good. This is the desire of your very good friend.

The interchange across the Channel of food of all kinds from Calais is constant, usually in the form of birds (as well as those for sport), and from England usually of venison. Thus in a business letter from London to her husband, on 28 November, LADY LISLE writes:

... most heartily thanking you for your partridges and the baked hare, which I this day received from you, with your two letters. ... I do send you by Vernam, packed in a barrel, ij does.

Managing a household during a king's visit is here described in one of MADAME DE SÉVIGNÉ's frequent witty detailed letters to her beloved daughter. Here she recounts the suicide of a cook, who thought he could not provide a good enough feast for Louis XIV. Probably copies of this letter would have been handed round to friends, in the place of newspapers.

Paris, Sunday 26 April 1671

I wrote to you on Friday, telling you Vatel had stabbed himself. Here is the story in detail: The King arrived on Thursday evening, when all went well – the hunting, the lanterns, the moonlight, the walks in the garden, the supper in a place decorated with jonquils. But there was no roast served at some of the tables, because of the great number of unexpected guests. This upset Vatel very much. He went about saying, 'I have lost my honour – I can't endure this.' And he told Gourville that he had been so much worried by the preparations that he had not slept for the last twelve nights. Gourville did all he could to comfort him; but he could not get the failure of the roast (though there was plenty at the King's table) out of his head.

Gourville spoke to the Prince, who went to Vatel's room and said to him, 'Vatel, everything is going well. Nothing could have been better than the King's supper.' He replied, 'Your Highness's kindness completes my distress. I know there was no roast for two tables.' 'Not at all,' said the Prince, 'don't distress yourself, for everything is going well.'

Midnight comes – the fireworks are a failure. They can hardly be seen, the sky is so cloudy. They had cost 16,000 francs. At four o'clock in the morning Vatel gets up and wanders about. The whole household is asleep. He comes across one of the purveyors who has just arrived. He finds that he has brought only two loads of fish. 'Is this all?' he asks. 'Yes, Monsieur,' says the man, not knowing that orders had been given to others. Vatel waits for some time; but as no more carts arrive, he thinks there is no more fish to be had. He goes to Gourville and says, 'Sir, I shall not be able to bear this disgrace. I shall not survive the loss of my honour and reputation.' Gourville makes light of the matter; whereupon Vatel mounts to his chamber, puts his sword against the door and runs himself through. Twice he merely wounds himself, but at the third stroke he falls down dead.

Loads of fish arrive from all quarters. Vatel is not to be found. People go to his chamber; they knock; they force the door; they find him lying in his blood. The Prince is greatly distressed. His son weeps, for all the arrangements for his journey to Burgundy depended on Vatel.

The Prince having related the whole affair to the King, it was regarded as the result of too nice a sense of honour. Some praised him for his courage, others thought he was too rash. The King said he had put off his visit to Chantilly for five years, because he was aware of the trouble it would give.

LADY MARY WORTLEY MONTAGU had an eventful life. She eloped with a husband whom she discovered to be boring and cold. Nevertheless she bore him a son and daughter, of whom she was very fond. She accompanied him to Turkey for two years when he became ambassador. She went to Italy for her remaining years where she made a pleasant quiet life for herself which she describes to her son:

10 Jy 1753

I believe my description gives you but an imperfect idea of my garden. Perhaps I shall succeed better in describing my manner of life, which is as regular as that of any monastery. I generally rise at six, and as soon as I have breakfasted, put myself at the head of my needle-women and work with them till nine. I then inspect my dairy, and take a turn among my poultry, which is a very large enquiry. I have, at present, two hundred chickens, besides turkeys, geese, ducks, and peacocks. All things have hitherto prospered under my care; my bees and silk-worms are doubled, and I am told that, without accidents, my capital will be so in two years' time. At eleven o'clock I retire to my books, I dare not indulge myself in that pleasure above an hour. At twelve I constantly dine, and sleep after dinner till about three. I then send for some of my old priests, and either play at piquet or whist, till 'tis cool enough to go out. One evening I walk in my wood, where I often sup, take the air on horse-back the next, and go on the water the third. The fishery of this part of the river belongs to me; and my fisherman's little boat (to which I have a green lutestring awning) serves me for a barge. He and his son are my rowers without any expense, he being very well paid by the profit of the fish, which I give him on condition of having every day one dish for my table. Here is plenty of every sort of fresh water fish (excepting salmon); but we have a large trout so like it, that I who have almost forgot the taste, do not distinguish it.

We are both placed properly in regard to our different times of life; you amidst the fair, the gallant, and the gay; I, in a retreat, where I enjoy every amusement that solitude can afford. I confess I sometimes wish for a little conversation; but I reflect that the commerce of the world gives more uneasiness than pleasure.
Your most affectionate mother,
M. WORTLEY.

JANE AUSTEN writes to her beloved sister Cassandra.

Sunday 25 Jan 1801

I shall want the two new coloured gowns for the summer, for my pink one will not do more than clear me from Steventon. I shall not trouble

you, however, to get more than one of them, and that is to be a plain
brown cambric muslin, for morning wear; the other, which is to be a
very pretty yellow and white cloud, I mean to buy in Bath. Buy two
brown ones, if you please, and both of a length, but one longer than the
other – it is for a tall woman. Seven yards for my mother, seven and
a half for me a dark brown, but the kind of brown is left to your own
choice, and I had rather they were different, as it will always be
something to say, to dispute about which is the prettiest. They must be
cambric muslin.

How do you like this cold weather? I hope you have all been earnestly
praying for it as a salutary relief from the dreadfully mild and
unhealthy season preceeding it, fancying yourself half putrified from
the want of it, and that now you will all draw into the fire, complain that
you never felt such bitterness of cold before, that you are half starved,
quite froze, and wish the mild weather back again with all your hearts.

Your unfortunate sister was betrayed last Thursday into a situation
of the utmost cruelty. I arrived at Ashe Park before the Party from
Deane, and was shut up in the drawing-room with Mr Holder alone
for ten minutes. I had some thoughts of insisting on the housekeeper
being sent for, and nothing could prevail on me to move two steps
from the door, on the lock of which I kept one hand constantly fixed.
We met nobody but ourselves, and were very cross.
Yours ever, J A

MRS BEETON (1836–65) died young, leaving a lasting memorial of her
dedication to domestic work in the famous book *Household Management*.
I include this passage to show the time-consuming demands such writing
laid on middle-class women.

1859

Early rising is one of the most essential qualities which enter into good
Household Management, as it is not only the parent of health, but of
innumerable other advantages. Indeed, when a mistress is an early
riser, it is almost certain that her house will be orderly and
well-managed. On the contrary, if she remain in bed till a late hour,
then the domestics, who, as we have observed, invariably partake
somewhat of their mistress's character, will surely become
sluggards. . . .

Cleanliness is indispensable to health, and must be studied both in
regard to the person and the house, and all that it contains. Cold or
tepid baths should be employed every morning, unless, on account of
illness or other circumstances, they should be deemed
objectionable. . . .

Frugality and economy are home virtues, without which no household
can prosper. . . . The necessity of practising economy should be
evident to every one, whether in the possession of an income no more
than sufficient for a family's requirements, or of a large fortune which
puts financial adversity out of the question. . . .

In marketing, that the best articles are the cheapest, may be laid
down as a rule; and it is desirable, unless an experienced and
confidential housekeeper be kept, that the mistress should herself
purchase all provisions and stores needed for the house. If the mistress
be a young wife, and not accustomed to order 'things for the house,'
a little practice and experience will soon teach her who are the best
tradespeople to deal with, and what are the best provisions to buy.
Under each particular head of Fish, Meat, Poultry, Game, &c., will
be described the proper means of ascertaining the quality of these
comestibles.

A housekeeping account-book should invariably be kept, and kept
punctually and precisely. The plan for keeping household accounts,
which we should recommend, would be to enter, that is, write down
in a daily diary every amount paid on each particular day, be it ever
so small; then, at the end of a week or month, let these various payments
be ranged under their specific heads of Butcher, Baker, &c.: and thus
will be seen the proportions paid to each tradesman, and any week's
or month's expenses may be contrasted with another. The
housekeeping accounts should be balanced not less than once a month
– once a week is better; and it should be seen that the money in hand
tallies with the account. Judge Haliburton never wrote truer words than
when he said – 'No man is rich whose expenditure exceeds his means,
and no one is poor whose incomings exceed his outgoings.' Once a
month it is advisable that the mistress overlook her store of glass
and china, marking any breakages on the inventory of these
articles.

When, in a large establishment, a housekeeper is kept, it will be
advisable to examine her accounts regularly. Then, any increase of
expenditure which may be apparent can easily be explained, and
the housekeeper will have the satisfaction of knowing whether her

efforts to manage her department well and economically have been successful.

How to combine looking after a family with writing and running the house? MRS GASKELL answers an unknown correspondent:

25th Sept 1862

My dear Madam

My first piece of advice to you would be *Get strong* – I am almost sure you are out of bodily health and that, if I were you, I would make it my first object to attain. Did you ever try a tea-cup full of *hop-tea* the first thing in the morning? It is a very simple tonic, and could do no harm. Then again try *hard* to arrange your work well. That is a regular piece of headwork and taxes a woman's powers of organization; but the reward is immediate and great. I have known well what it is to be both wanting money, & feeling weak in body and entirely disheartened. I do not think I ever cared for literary fame; nor do I think it *is* a thing that ought to be cared for. It comes and it goes. The exercise of a talent or power *is* always a great pleasure; but one should weigh well whether this pleasure may not be obtained by the sacrifice of some duty. When I had *little* children I do not think I could have written stories, because I should have become too much absorbed in my *fictitious* people to attend to my *real* ones. I think you would be sorry if you began to feel that your desire to earn money, even for so laudable an object as to help your husband, made you unable to give your tender sympathy to your little ones in their small joys & sorrows; and yet, don't you know how you, – how every one, who tries to write stories *must* become absorbed in them, (fictitious though they be,) if they are to interest their readers in them. Besides viewing the subject from a solely artistic point of view a good writer of fiction must have *lived* an active & sympathetic life if she wishes her books to have strength & vitality in them. When you are forty, and if you have a gift for being an authoress you will write ten times as good a novel as you could do now, just because you will have gone through so much more of the interests of a wife and a mother.

All this does not help you over present difficulties, does it? Well then let us try what will – How much have you in your own power? How much must you submit to because it is God's appointment? You have it in your own power to arrange your day's work to the very best of your ability, making the various household arts into real studies (& there is plenty of poetry and association about them – remember how the Greek princesses in Homer washed the clothes &c &c &c &c.) You would perhaps find a little book called The Finchley Manual of Needlework of real use to you in sewing; it gives patterns and directions &c. Your want of strength may be remedied *possibly* by care & attention; if not, you must submit to what is God's ordinance; only remember that the very hardest day's bodily work I have ever done has never produced anything like the intense exhaustion I have felt after writing the "best" parts of my books.

Have you no sister or relation who could come & help you a little while till you get stronger, – no older friend at hand who would help you to plan your work so that it should oppress you as little as possible? If this letter has been of *any* use to you, do not scruple to write to me again, if I can give you help. I may not always be able to answer you as soon as I do now, for at home my life is very very much occupied, but I will always *try* & do so. And do my dear, always remember to ask God for light and help – for with Him all things are possible – and it almost astonishes one sometimes to find how He sends down answers to one's prayers in new bright thoughts, or in even more bright & lovely peace.

Your sincere though unknown friend,

E. C. GASKELL

LUCIE DUFF GORDON became head of an Egyptian household, with slaves, after she had been ill with tuberculosis, and was advised to go to Egypt, for her health. She fell in love with the country, and stayed there for eight years.

Cairo, 18 April 1863

My dear Tom

By no need of my own have I become a slave-owner. The American Consul-General turned over to me a black girl of eight or nine, and in consequence of her reports the poor little black boy who is the slave and marmiton of the cook here has been entreating Omar to beg me to buy him and take him with me. It is touching to see the two poor little black things recounting their woes and comparing notes. I went yesterday to deposit my cooking things and boat furniture at my washerwoman's

house. Seeing me arrive on my donkey, followed by a cargo of
household goods, about eight or ten Arab women thronged round
delighted at the idea that I was coming to live in their quarter, and
offering me neighbourly services. Of course all rushed upstairs, and my
old washerwoman was put to great expense in pipes and coffee. I think,
as you, that I must have the 'black drop,' and that the Arabs see it,
for I am always told that I am like them, with praises of my former
good looks. 'You were beautiful Hareem once.' Nothing is more
striking to me than the way in which one is constantly reminded of
Herodotus. The Christianity and the Islam of this country are full of
the ancient worship, and the sacred animals have all taken service with
Muslim saints. At Minieh one reigns over crocodiles; higher up I saw
the hole of Æsculapius' serpent at Gebel Sheykh Hereedee, and I fed
the birds – as did Herodotus – who used to tear the cordage of boats
which refused to feed them, and who are now the servants of Sheykh
Naooneh, and still come on board by scores for the bread which no Reis
dares refuse them. Bubastis' cats are still fed in the Cadi's court at
public expense in Cairo, and behave with singular decorum when 'the
servant of the cats' serves them their dinner. Among gods, Amun Ra,
the sun-god and serpent-killer, calls himself Mar Girgis (St. George),
and is worshipped by Christians and Muslims in the same churches,
and Osiris holds his festivals as riotously as ever at Tanta in the Delta,
under the name of Seyd el Bedawee. The *fellah* women offer sacrifices
to the Nile, and walk round ancient statues in order to have children.
The ceremonies at births and burials are not Muslim, but ancient
Egyptian.

Male writers usually have a wife to 'service' them. Since Lady Mary
Wortley Montagu, women have been pointing out the problems involved
in being expected to perform two jobs at once. Here KATHERINE MANS-
FIELD writes to her lover, John Middleton Murry.

[1913]

. . . the house seems to take up so much time if it isn't looked after
with some sort of method. I mean . . . when I have to clear up twice
over or wash up extra unnecessary things I get frightfully impatient and
want to be working. So often this week, I've heard you and Gordon
talking while I washed dishes. Well, someone's got to wash dishes and

get food, otherwise – 'There's nothing in the house but eggs to eat'.
Yes, I hate hate *hate* doing these things that you accept just as all men
accept of their women. I can only play the servant with a very bad
grace indeed. It's all very well for females who have nothing else to do
. . . and then you say I am a tyrant, and wonder because I get tired
at night! The trouble with women like me is – they can't keep their
nerves out of the job in hand – and Monday after you and Gordon
and Lesley have gone I walk about with a mind full of ghosts of
saucepans and primus stoves and 'Will there be enough to go round?'
. . . and you calling (whatever I am doing) 'Tig, isn't there going to be
tea? It's five o'clock' as though I were a dilatory housemaid.

I loathe myself today. I detest this woman who 'superintends' you
and rushes about, slamming doors and slopping water – all untidy with
her blouse out and her nails grimed. I am disgusted and repelled by
the creature who shouts at you. 'You might at least empty the pail
and wash out the tea leaves!' Yes, no wonder you 'come over silent'.

Housekeeping is chiefly homemaking, a creative activity, devoted to the
people women live with. Here KATHERINE MANSFIELD writes to her sister
Chaddie about life in Paris with Middleton Murry, in the flat she found
for them in the Rue de Tournon, near the Luxembourg Gardens.

Paris, 22 Dec 1913

Dear Chaddie,
The weather is icy, but Paris looks beautiful. Everything is white &
every morning the sun shines & shines all day until finally it disappears
in a pink sky. The fountains are just a bubble in their basins of ice –
and now the little green Xmas booths are lining the streets – I am going
to enjoy life in Paris, I know.

Unfortunately, Murry did not enjoy life there, and left. Two years later
she wrote to him.

29 Dec. 1915

Dearest only, only one
. . . I have found a tiny villa for us . . . It stands alone in a small garden
with terraces. It faces the 'midi' & gets the sun all day long. It has a
stone verandah & little round table where we can sit & eat or work. A

charming little tiny kitchen with pots and pans and big coffee pot. Electric light, water downstairs and upstairs too. A most refined 'water-closet' *with* water in the house . . . The salle à manger is small and square with the light low over the table. It leads on to the verandah and overlooks the sea. So does the chambre à coucher. It is very private and stands high on the top of a hill. It's called the Villa Pauline.

On the last day of that year, she awaited his telegram to say he was coming.

I've ordered the little stoves and the wine and the wood. All the windows are open – all the doors – the linen is airing. I went to the flower market and stood among the buyers and bought, wholesale you know, at the auction in a state of lively terrified joy 3 dozen rose buds and 6 bunches of violets.

How a single parent copes is reflected in this letter from a young black mother whom I taught and who became a friend of mine. When she began studying at a polytechnic, she wrote me this letter about coping with a son of three, study, and housework. Her degree course opened a whole new world for her, yet her son seems even more important.

17 April 1989

Dear Olga,

Today has been another hectic and exhausting day. Firstly the trains were late at East Dulwich, so I missed my connection. Luckily David enjoyed the train journey and chattered away as usual. I had to race to get him to his new Nursery School on time.

College was very interesting, as the literature lecture was absorbing. Sometimes the course is too political for me, but today we studied Alice Walker's *The Color Purple* which is about a young Black girl trying to find a sense of identity. Rather like me!

After the classes I raced to fetch David and he told me all about his new friends. When we get back to my little flat, I start to prepare supper at about five o'clock. We eat at about six and immediately afterwards it's bathtime for David. He loves splashing and playing with the bubbles. He chooses three stories (because he's only three years old). Story time is important for us – to be together. I treasure it and so does he. Finally at 7.30 he is fast asleep, peace at last!

No housework after this, it's my time for reading and studying. And writing to friends like you, because writing letters is my LIFELINE to the outside world.

Take care. Best wishes,

ERNETT AND LITTLE DAVID

THE JOYS AND PROBLEMS OF GROWING CHILDREN

The earliest of these letters deal with political problems, and demand physical support from sons in war-troubled times. By the seventeenth century mothers such as Madame (King Louis XIV's sister-in-law) and Madame de Sévigné express greater preoccupation with emotional reactions and lifestyles.

Women in power often used their influence privately and are seldom given due credit for what they achieved. Here the Austrian Empress Maria Theresa forcefully persuades her headstrong daughter, Marie-Antoinette, to be less impetuous and tactless, in order to avoid war. She was successful for a brief time, as she had been with her own husband.

We see remarkably clear-sighted mothers judging their offspring. Fanny Burney and Mrs Gaskell are certainly not prejudiced in favour of the children they very much loved, proof that maternal love is not blind. Until 'Women's Lib' the mother-daughter relationship, like most relationships between women, had been either trivialized or ignored. And as many women had to repeat the behaviour patterns of their mothers, the intrinsic interest was not always perceived, except by the few who rebelled against a culture dictating a 'women's place is in the home'. The twentieth century has seen outstanding women poets such as Sylvia Plath and Anne Sexton analyse the complex loves and resentments binding them to their parents and their children.

This section ends with two little-known letters, emphasizing the enjoyment the suffragette Mrs Pankhurst experienced with her daughter, and the maternal love that persuaded her to become a stepmother, while never ceasing work to help women get the vote.

This letter demanding help from her sons purports to be from QUEEN EMMA, widow of both Ethelred the Unready and Canute. Her sons were in Normandy. The letter was probably written in St Omer, about 1041.

Her sons obeyed, and sailed from Boulogne. This suggests that the tone of the letter was that expected by well-born young men from a powerful mother.

Emma, queen in name only, imparts motherly salutation to her sons, Edward and Alfred. Since we severally lament the death of our lord, the king, most dear sons, and since daily you are deprived more and more of the kingdom, your inheritance, I wonder what plan you are adopting, since you are aware that the delay arising from your procrastination is becoming from day to day a support to the usurper of your rule. For he goes round hamlets and cities ceaselessly, and makes the chief men his friends by gifts, threats and prayers. But they would prefer that one of you should rule over them, than that they should be held in the power of him who now commands them. I entreat, therefore, that one of you come to me speedily and privately, to receive from me wholesome counsel, and to know in what manner this matter, which I desire, must be brought to pass. Send back word what you are going to do about these matters by the present messenger, whoever he may be. Farewell, beloved ones of my heart.
[*Encomium Emmae Regina*]

A mother asks her son for help during the Crusades. LADY HAVISIA DE NEVILLE's first husband died in 1246. Her son Hugh went to fight in the Holy Land, leaving his mother overseeing all his property. During the Crusades it was often difficult to obtain funds, and here she writes of her serious need for money. This letter was written in French, in 1258.

Havisia de Neville to her very dear son, Hugh de Neville, wishes health and the blessing of God and her own.
    Know, dear son, that I am well and hearty, thanks to God, and am much rejoiced at the news that William Fitz Simon brought me of your health. God be thanked for it! Know, dear son, that our necessities of receiving the returns from your lands can avail nothing, on account of the great rule your adversary has in the king's court, unless you yourself were present. Wherefore your father-in-law and I, and all your other friends, agree that you should come to England, and we pray and entreat you, by the faith and love that you owe us, that you will not by

any means fail in this; since you ought once again to return. For we know well that it would be a very great dishonour and we consider it a great sin, to suffer us and ours to be disinherited by your indolence. Therefore I anxiously pray you, dear son, that you will travel with all possible haste, and also, according to the counsel of all your friends, that you go to the court of Rome, and procure if you can the letter of the pope, express and stringent, to the king of England, that he should restore your lands, and have them restored. And that you may make a proper understanding at the court of all our needs, without omitting or concealing anything; that is, how you are placed with the king, and that you are compelled by a writing to hold the (obligation), without contradiction and without ever making an acquisition to the contrary. For wise persons have said the acquisition would be worth nothing, unless it made express mention of this, that it was through no fault of yours that you made this the aforesaid obligation when in war, and through fear of prison.

Dear son, I pray you not to trust too much to the money of the crusade allowance, for they say that more great lords of England will take the cross; and they will take away as much as shall be raised for the crusade, as certain friends have given me to know. But do not ever cease, as you dearly love me, for no waiting for money, to borrow all the money that you can, and to go to the court of Rome to acquire for our necessities, and to hasten to come to England to accomplish our needs. For I hope, by the help of God, if you could well accomplish what you have to do about the acquisition of our lands, that you will see such change in England, that never in our time could you have better accomplished your wish, or more to your honour. Wherefore cease not to solicit again about your coming, since you can here best serve God. I commend you to the true body of God, who give you life and health. Sir Walter de la Hide, Joanna your sister, and all our household, salute you. And know, dear son, that my counsel is that you obtain the letters of request of the legate of that country, and the letters of the master of the Temple and of the Hospital, to the legate of England and to other rich men, for your needs, and in testimony of your deeds in that country on the occasion of your coming. And ever take care of your house that you have there, if God give you courage to return.

MADAME DE SÉVIGNÉ is here writing to her beloved married daughter about
her son Charles, for whom she had bought a commission in Louis XIV's
army. Their relationship was frank and intimate. Charles joined the
numerous admirers (including his father) of Ninon, a celebrated beauty at
Court. In this letter she shows how determined yet amusing she could be
when her son's honour – and another woman's – were at risk:

Paris, 22nd April, 1671

A word about your brother, my dear. . . . I give him a little preaching,
now and then, and he agrees with everything I say; but it doesn't
make the slightest change in his ways. He has left his actress, after
having followed her up and down. When he was with her or writing to
her he was all in earnest; but the next moment he would be making a
jest of her. Ninon has quite given him up. He was anything but happy
while she loved him; and now that she does not, he is very much hurt
by the way she talks about him. She said the other day, 'His mind is
like porridge, his body is like wet paper, and his heart is like a pumpkin
fried in snow.'

She was jealous of the actress, and asked him for the letters he had
from her. He was foolish enough to give them. She wanted to hand them
over to some lover of that princess! When I heard this I pointed out
to him that it was a shameful thing to injure a poor girl who had loved
him; that she had not parted with his letters, but had given them back
to him; that his behaviour was mean and unworthy of a man of quality;
that honour must be observed even in things that are not honourable.
He saw how right I was in this, ran off to Ninon, and partly by skill and
partly by force got hold of the poor devil's letters. I made him burn
them at once.

My son has told all his follies to M. de la Rochefoucauld, who loves
original characters. He agrees with what I said the other day – that my
son is not foolish in the head, but in the heart; that his feelings are all
true and all false, all cold and all hot, all deceitful and all sincere; that,
in short, he has a foolish heart. We laughed at this a good deal, and
my son joined in; for he is very good company, and says 'agreed' to
everything people say. We get on very well together. I am his confidant;
and I have to listen to most disagreeable things, so as to be able to
give my opinion on everything. He believes me as much as he can, and
begs me to put matters right, which I do in a friendly way.

He wants to come with me to Brittany for five or six weeks, and if
there is not to be a camp in Lorraine, I shall take him.

What a letter full of follies! But, as you have an interest in your brother, I hope it won't bore you.

The difficulties of bringing up a family at Versailles were increased by the paternal interest of Louis XIV. Here his sister-in-law, 'MADAME', describes her problems with her granddaughter, whom she calls by her title, the Duchesse de Berry. Her letter is to the Duchess of Hanover.

14 January 1712, Versailles

Heavens, what a tribulation stubborn children are! Last Monday I spent the entire morning scolding the Duchesse de Berri and telling her that she ought to beg the King's forgiveness. At the end of it she said to me, 'My memory will be very bad, Madame, if I do not remember what you have said to me.' My son, contrary to his usual custom, also exhorted her as fervently as he was able, so that we hoped that all would go off well and that the King would be satisfied with her. Her mother had already begged the King on Monday graciously to permit her to see him, he having forbidden her, through me, to enter his presence again until further orders. My son also interceded for her, but the King told him that he would do nothing further in the matter without consulting me first. That evening, as I was following the King into his cabinet, I saw that he looked quite embarrassed, and I said laughingly, 'Your Majesty need not be annoyed at seeing me in this cabinet against your wishes, because I shall leave it as soon as I have had the honour of speaking to you, and what I have to say will not take long. I beg you, therefore, sir, not to be annoyed with me, for I never intentionally do anything which will displease you. The reason I have followed you into your cabinet without having been commanded by Your Majesty to do so is that my son and Madame d'Orléans have told me that you will only allow the Duchesse de Berri to appear before you and beg Your Majesty's pardon when I have added my entreaties to theirs, and that is all I have come here for.' ... The King made no reply to the first part of my speech, but referring to the latter part he exclaimed, 'What, Madame, do you advise me to receive Madame de Berri again so soon?' I replied with a laugh, 'As for advice, it would ill become me ever to offer advice to Your Majesty, but I do beseech you to grant this consolation to the Duchesse de Berri, as I assure you she feels very much humiliated.' The King replied very politely, 'You have such good sense that your advice is always good, and I will receive Madame de Berri again to-morrow evening. You may tell her so yourself or send her a message.' I made a deep reverence, put my hand on the door handle, and said, 'I will not reply to Your Majesty in the manner it behoves me to, lest I keep you longer from the company which awaits you,' and I retired forthwith.

On Tuesday evening the Duchesse de Berri went to visit Madame de Maintenon, but did not say a single word to her, although I had expressly bidden my granddaughter to begin by saying that she would like to meet the King in her room because she hoped that Madame de Maintenon would be kind enough to help her to conciliate the King. Instead of speaking thus she never opened her mouth to speak either to her or to the King, and never stopped weeping from beginning to end, so that the King was constrained to say to her, 'It is evident that I must be the one to break the ice.' According to the account which the King very kindly gave me afterwards, everything passed off very frigidly, at which you will not be surprised.

MADAME showed more caring than most courtiers towards the misery of impoverished parents, as is revealed in this letter to the Raugravine Louisa.

2 March 1709

Never in my life have I seen such miserable times. The common people are dying like flies. The mills have stopped working and many people have therefore died of hunger. Yesterday I was told a sad story about a woman who had stolen a loaf from a baker's shop in Paris. The baker wanted to have her arrested. She wept and said, 'If you only knew my misery you would not take the bread away from me. I have three small children without any clothes, and they are crying for food. I couldn't endure it any longer, and that is why I stole this loaf.' The magistrate before whom the woman was brought told her to take him to her home. He went thither with her and found three little children bundled up in rags sitting in a corner shivering with cold as if they had a fever. He asked the eldest, 'Where is your father?' and the child replied, 'He is behind the door.' The magistrate went to see what the man was doing behind the door and fell back horror-stricken. The poor wretch

had hanged himself in a fit of despair. Such things are happening every
day.

MARIA-THERESA was married at sixteen to the Emperor of Austria, by
whom she had sixteen children. The youngest was Marie-Antoinette,
who became Queen of France, and whose young husband showed a
preference for Madame Du Barry, whom she publicly snubbed. Louis
XV, furious at this contempt of his mistress, threatened to break off
Franco-Austrian relations. Maria-Theresa was the only person in
Europe with any influence over Marie-Antoinette. Here she deploys that
influence in order to make her daughter condone publicly an adulterous
liaison which would never have been tolerated in Vienna.

1771

The dread and embarrassment you show about speaking to the King,
the best of fathers, about speaking to persons you are advised to speak
to! What a pother about saying 'Good day' to someone, a kindly word
concerning a dress or some trumpery. Mere whimsy, or something
worse. You have allowed yourself to become enslaved to such an extent
that reason and duty can no longer persuade you. I cannot keep silent
about this matter any longer. After your conversation with Mercy and
after all he told you about the King's wishes and your duty, you actually
dared to fail him. What reason can you give for such conduct? None
at all. It does not become you to regard the Dubarry in any other light
than that of a lady who has the right of entry to the court and is admitted
to the society of the King. You are His Majesty's first subject, and you
owe him obedience and submission. It behoves you to set a good
example, to show the courtiers and the ladies at Versailles that you are
ready to do your master's will. If any baseness, any intimacy, were
asked of you, neither I nor any other would advise you to consent;
but all that is expected is that you should say an indifferent word,
should look at her beseemingly – not for the lady's own sake, but for
the sake of your grandfather, your master, your benefactor!

Marie Antoinette capitulated at last. On New Years Day 1772 the
alliance between Austria and France was saved.

MADAME DE SÉVIGNÉ idolized her only daughter. When she got married she and her husband lived with her mother for some time. But a year later Monsieur de Grignan was appointed to work in Provence. This is Mme de Sévigné's first letter after her daughter's departure.

Paris, Friday 6 February 1671

To Madame de Grignan

My affliction would be very ordinary if I could describe it to you, so I won't undertake it. I look in vain for my dear daughter, but can no longer find her, and her every step takes her further from me. So I went off to Sainte-Marie, still weeping, still lifeless. It seemed as if my heart and soul were being torn out of me, and truly, what a brutal separation! I asked to be free to be alone. I was taken into Mme du Housset's room, where they lit a fire for me. Agnes looked at me but didn't speak; such was our understanding. I stayed there until five and never stopped sobbing; all my thoughts were killing me. I wrote to M. de Grignan, in what tone you can well imagine. I went on to Mme de La Fayette's, and she intensified my grief by the sympathy she showed. She was alone and ill, and depressed about the death of one of her sisters who was a nun – in fact she was just as I would have wished her. M. de La Rochefoucauld came. We talked of nothing but you, of the justification I had for being upset . . . I came home eventually from Mme de La Fayette's at eight, but coming in here, oh God! Can you imagine what I felt as I came up the stairs? That room where I always used to go – alas, I found the doors open but everything empty and in a muddle, and your poor little girl to remind me of my own. Can you understand all I went through? Black awakenings during the night, and in the morning I was not a step nearer finding rest for my soul. The time after dinner I spent with Mme de La Troche at the Arsenal. In the evening I had your letter, which threw me back into my first grief, and tonight I shall finish this at Mme de Coulanges's, where I shall hear some news. For my part this is all I know about, together with the regrets of all those you have left here. If I felt like it the whole of my letter could be full of people's good wishes.

The French novelist GEORGE SAND sends some advice to her godson, the younger Alexandre Dumas:

Nohant, 7 November 1861

My dear son,
The mere fact of my dedication giving you pleasure is enough thanks
for me without your saying a single word. You gave me a hearty kiss
at Nohant and all your thanks were in that. People want to make me
out a personage, but I only want to be your 'mother'. The fact that you
are fond of me shows that you have a heart and that is all I want. I
have never been conscious of *superiority* in any direction, because I have
never been able to accomplish all that I have dreamed and conceived,
except in a way utterly inferior to my ideal. Therefore no one will ever
make me believe that I know better than other people. Having remained
a child myself in so many ways what I admire most in characters of your
strong individuality, is their kind-heartedness and their doubt of their
own powers. In the sense I mean, those are the principles of their
vitality; for whosoever crowns himself with his own hands has said his
last word. If he is not done for altogether one may at least say that
he has come to an end of himself and may keep his end up, but will
not be able to go any further.

Then try to keep your soul young and quivering, right up to old age,
and to imagine right up to the brink of death that life is only beginning.
I think that is the only way to keep adding to one's talent, to one's
affections and one's inner happiness.

This feeling that the *All* is greater, finer, stronger and more beautiful
than oneself, keeps one always within the lovely dream which is called
the illusion of youth, and which I call the Ideal, that is to say the vision
and sense of what is true raised above the heights of heaven. *In spite
of all that has combined to rend me, I am an optimist.* That is perhaps my
only good quality. You will see that you will acquire it too.
Your devoted godmother

MRS GASKELL assesses her first son-in-law. Her daughter Florence had
fallen in love when she was only nineteen. She became engaged to
Crompton, Fellow of Trinity College, already thirty years old. The letter
is to Charles Eliot Norton.

13 July 1863

I suppose he has those solid intellectual qualities which tell in action,
though not in conversation. But his goodness is what gives me the

thankfullest feeling of confidence in him. They will have to live in London, and will have to begin economically. One of his nice feelings is his thorough approval of his father's plan of dividing his property among his 7 children equally. Florence is very economical and managing. We tell her she will starve her husband, she is so full of economical plans.

Mr Crompton is not exactly a Unitarian, nor exactly broad Church, but perhaps rather more of the latter than the former. He is so good-principled he may be called a religious man; for I am sure the root of his life is in religion. But he has not imagination enough to be what one calls *spiritual*. It is just the same want that makes him not care for music or painting, nor much for poetry. In these tastes Florence is his superior, although she is not 'artistic'. Then he cares for science, in which she is at present ignorant. His strong, good, *un*sensitive character is just what will, I trust, prove very grateful to her anxious, conscientious little heart. They are to be married *here* and by Mr Gaskell. No one but the two families are to be at the wedding. They go into Scotland; return here to pay us a little visit before settling into the Northern Circuit, and bring her here to stay as often as he can.

MRS GASKELL frequently expressed concern over the health and personality of the third of her four daughters, Meta. When Meta's engagement was broken off by her rich fiancé, she underwent a religious crisis, which she attempted to appease by intense work in a Lancashire cotton factory during the famines of the early 1860s. She suffered from headaches, fainting fits and unnecessary stress. The letter is to Anne Robson.

2 January 1865

She is bodily strong excepting for the violent pain in two places in her spine, which the least worry still brings on; and it is almost impossible to keep her from worry. For instance the other day, when I was unable to be with her; three people came in unexpectedly to lunch; we have a new cook and Meta did(n't) think we had enough meat for lunch etc. *so* her pain in her back came on and then, unless she exercises very great self-control crying that is almost hysterical succeeds. She does not like to have all this spoken about, so don't allude to it, as she has a horror of being thought hysterical but I think these fits of crying are of that nature, though accompanied with this pain in the spine. Mr Erichsen is still prescribing for her – a great deal of open air, 6 hours a day – but no fatigue early hours, a *great deal of meat* to eat, bitter beer, a little society, but not large assemblies, as much change as possible and tonics. He has already greatly improved her health; which had never been strong since the sewing days.

MILLICENT FAWCETT had good relationships with her husband and daughter, both of whom shared her ideals, and fought with her, through persuasion, for women's rights. She represents an English approach to social change. She wrote to her friend Lady Frances Balfour:

5 March 1910

I never believe in the possibility of a sex war. Nature has seen after that; as long as mothers have sons and fathers daughters there can never be a sex war. What draws men and women together is stronger than the brutality and tyranny which drive them apart. I am for going on with all our work just as before. If we are mobbed or our meetings wrecked it won't harm our cause.

Difficulties in family life were given a little help when advice columns began. This letter was written in 1906 to 'Aunt Jennie', the agony aunt of *Progressive Farmer*. It is from a NELLIE TAYLOR, a farmer's wife, about her troubles with in-laws and a jealous stepmother.

1906

Well Aunt Jennie you trusted me with your troubles and I must trust you with mine. As every sweet have a drop of bitter. My husband is twenty one years older than myself. He is one of the best men in his family I ever saw. If he has ever felt worried with me in the eight years we have been married I have never known it. And he is so ready and willing to help me about the house. His mother died when he was a child. She left two boys and one girl. Soon after the war ended father married a second wife, she was a widow with one child. The children were all taken home together. In a few years there were three more, one boy and two girls. One of the girls died at six, and the other lived to get grown, and died. That left her one son, *and her daughter* who soon married. Willie their youngest left home before he was free, and the other two of the first wifes children married, so that left Mord *my husband* the only one left at home. He has staid right here all this *long long* time and worked for them. And hasent had a single thing only what he lived on. And for several years they have been dependent for they are both old and feeble. We do all in our power to make them comfortable. We are nothing but common poor farmers but we live comfortable and happy except one thing and that is *this and the secret* I am *trusting you with*. She cant be *suited* with any thing on earth. Father told me not long ago that he had been living with her now forty years. And he had never been able to do the first thing that was right. She will be seventy nine next month, and you know she cant do much. I do every thing I can for her. And has for eight years. And I have never done any thing to please her yet. Since she has not been able to take the responsibility of the house and its surroundings, I am just compelled to take charge myself. Father has given up every thing to us to manage as we see best, and has told *me to go* ahead and pay no attention to what she says. But you know that is hard to do, still I do my best. And the poor old creature cant even appreciate my hard endevers to work for and take care of her. And very often tells me how offensive it is for me to come in and take possession of her house. She is a constant reader of the Bible and professes to be a great christion and any one who does not know would think she is the best woman on earth. But oh, my they don't know. She does not love the first children and therefore she doesnt love me. I think where the big trouble lie is this. She is afraid her son will not get every thing and the older ones will get something she wants him to have. Aunt Jennie Please dont let any one see this or they may think I am *curious* as the children say for writing such to a stranger but you do not feel like a stranger to me, altho I have never seen you.

MRS EMMELINE PANKHURST, remembered as a leading suffragette, was very close to her eldest daughter Christabel. In between imprisonments in 1912 and 1913 she managed to cross the Channel to stay in Paris, where Christabel was working. Here she is just the mother enjoying a brief stay with her daughter. This was written to Dr Ethel Smyth, the composer, a close friend and fellow militant.

Paris, 1913

This is more like home than anything I have known for years. Paris suits me and Berthe [Christabel's maid in the flat on the Avenue de la Grande Armée] cooks food that agrees with me. I can potter about seeing things, get up and go to bed when I LIKE, SEE WHOM I LIKE. AND I LOVE TO BE WITH C IN THIS WAY AND TIDY HER UP ... I am at peace for a few weeks and I snatch the fearful joy and mean to make the most of it before the fight begins again.

Soon afterwards, she married a widower, Tam Walsh, partly out of compassion for his three motherless children. When she was in prison again in January 1918, Sarah, the youngest of her three step-daughters, wrote:

Dear Mother,
I will not see you on Saturday, so don't worry. You don't know what might happen, you might be out before you can say Jack Frost. I am reading Oliver Twist. I think you have read it and it's a very sad story, I almost cried when I read it. But it's nice in the end, how Mr Brownlow adopted Oliver for his son. I think I will close my little letter hoping you will like it, and I also send it with my fondest love,
Your loving child, Sally.

PART FOUR

Divorce and adultery – Work, duty and money – Writers comment
on their work – Travel

DIVORCE AND ADULTERY

Before the end of the nineteenth century divorce was almost impossible to obtain, except by a few rich and powerful men. Henry VIII set a precedent, as did the Prince Regent in 1796. For most, death performed the task of divorce.

The difficulties for women are enumerated here by the courageous activist Caroline Norton, in her famous letter to Queen Victoria. In 1848 a Mrs Dawson had been refused a divorce, although her adulterous husband frequently flogged her with a horse whip. Summing up the judge declared 'a husband may beat his wife, a husband may even imprison his wife'.

Some years after Norton's persistent campaigns, in 1857, Parliament passed the Matrimonial Causes Act, which set up civil courts to grant judicial separations and divorces. Yet even in 1870 Queen Victoria wrote to Sir T. Martin, 'The Queen is most anxious to enlist everyone to join in checking this mad, wicked folly of "Women's Rights".'

European attitudes and customs are compared to those in Moslem countries, recounted by Lady Mary Wortley Montagu and Lucie Duff Gordon. In many countries today it is virtually impossible for a woman to obtain a divorce. In some countries she can be rejected if she proves sterile – so undergoing a double rejection, by man and by nature. (The Pali Text Society has translated early poems by Buddhist women who had been sent home to fathers by unloving husbands, even when they were beautiful and had tried to please both husband and in-laws.) To counterbalance the unhappiness, I include George Sand; she made the most of the freedom given her by divorce – to live and to write.

LADY MARY WORTLEY MONTAGU writes from Turkey to Abbé Conti, Italian philosopher and poet; her letter describes divorce in a Moslem country.

Constantinople 29 May 1717

When I spoke of their religion I forgot to mention two particularities, one of which I had read of, but it seemed so odd to me I could not believe it. Yet 'tis certainly true that when a man has divorced his wife in the most solemn manner, he can take her again upon no other terms than permitting another man to pass a night with her, and there are some examples of those that have submitted to this law rather than not have back their beloved. The other point of doctrine is very extraordinary: any woman that dies unmarried is looked upon to die in a state of reprobation. To confirm this belief, they reason that the end of the creation of women is to increase and multiply, and she is only properly employed in the works of her calling when she is bringing children or taking care of 'em, which are all the virtues that God expects from her; and indeed their way of life, which shuts them out of all public commerce, does not permit them any other. Our vulgar notion that they do not own women to have any souls is a mistake. 'Tis true they say they are not of so elevated a kind and therefore must not hope to be admitted into the paradise appointed for the men, who are to be entertained by celestial beauties; but there is a place of happiness destined for souls of the inferior order, where all good women are to be in eternal bliss.
I am, Sir, etc

Although this was true, other travellers remarked that the husband usually chose a friend whose tactful continence he could rely on.

Divorce proved impossible in Italy. When LADY MARY WORTLEY MONTAGU followed her lover to that country and settled there, she wrote entertainingly to her daughter. Here she describes the discovery of her neighbour's unfaithfulness, during a husband's brief absence:

You please me extremely in saying my letters are of any entertainment to you. I would contribute to your happiness in every shape I can, but in my solitude there are so few subjects present themselves, it is not easy to find one that would amuse you, though as I believe you have some leisure hours at Kenwood, when anything new is welcome, I will venture to tell you a small history in which I had some share.

I have already informed you of the divisions and subdivisions of estates in this country, by which you will imagine there is a numerous gentry of great names and little fortunes. Six of those families inhabit this town. You may fancy this forms a sort of society, but far from it, as there is not one of them that does not think (for some reason or other) they are far superior to all the rest. There is such a settled aversion amongst them, they avoid one another with the utmost care, and hardly ever meet except by chance at the castle (as they call my house), where their regard for me obliges them to behave civilly, but it is with an affected coldness that is downright disagreeable, and hinders me from seeing any of them often.

I was quietly reading in my closet when I was interrupted by the chambermaid of the Signora Laura Bono, who flung herself at my feet, and in an agony of sobs and tears begged me for the love of the Holy Madonna to hasten to her master's house, where the two brothers would certainly murder one another if my presence did not stop their fury. I was very much surprised, having always heard them spoke of as a pattern of fraternal union. However, I made all possible speed thither, without staying for hoods or attendance. I was soon there (the house touching my garden wall) and was directed to the bedchamber by the noise of oaths and execrations, but on opening the door was astonished to a degree you may better guess than I describe, by seeing the Signora Laura prostrate on the ground, melting in tears, and her husband standing with a drawn stiletto in his hand, swearing she should never see tomorrow's sun. I was soon let into the secret.

The good man, having business of consequence at Brescia, went thither early in the morning, but as he expected his chief tenant to pay his rent that day, he left orders with his wife that if the farmer came, to make him very welcome. She obeyed him with great punctuality. The money coming in the hand of a handsome lad of eighteen she did not only admit him to her own table and produced the best wine in the cellar, but resolved to give him *chère entière*. While she was exercising this generous hospitality, the husband met midway the gentleman he intended to visit, who was posting to another side of the country. They agreed on another appointment, and he returned to his own house, where, giving his horse to be led round to the stable by the servant that accompanied him, he opened his door with the *passe-partout* key, and proceeded to his chamber without meeting anybody, where he found his beloved spouse asleep on the bed with her gallant. The opening of the door waked them. The young fellow immediately leaped out of the window, which looked into the garden and was open (it being summer), and escaped over the fields, leaving his breeches on a chair by the bed.

I can not be persuaded that any woman who had lived virtuous till forty (for such was her age) could suddenly be endowed with such consummate impudence to solicit a youth at first sight, there being no probability, his age and station considered, that he would have made any attempt of that kind. I must confess I was wicked enough to think the unblemished reputation she had hitherto maintained, and did not fail to put us in mind of, was owing to a series of such frolics; and to say truth, they are the only *amours* that can reasonably hope to remain undiscovered. Ladies that can resolve to make love thus *ex tempore* may pass unobserved, especially if they can content themselves with low life, where fear may oblige their favourites to secrecy. There wants only a very lewd constitution, a very bad heart, and a moderate understanding to make this conduct easy, and I do not doubt it has been practised by many prudes beside her I am now speaking of.

You may be sure I did not communicate these reflections. The first word I spoke was to desire Signor Carlo to sheathe his poniard, not being pleased with its glittering. He did so very readily, begging my pardon for not having done it on my first appearance, saying he did not know what he did; and indeed he had the countenance and gesture of a man distracted. I did not endeavour a defence that seemed to me impossible, but represented to him as well as I could the crime of a murder which, if he could justify before men, was still a crying sin before God, the disgrace he would bring on himself and posterity, and irreparable injury he would do his eldest daughter (a pretty girl of fifteen, that I knew he was extreme fond of). I added that if he thought it proper to part from his lady he might easily find a pretext for it some months hence, and that it was as much his interest as hers to conceal this affair from the knowledge of the world. I could not presently make him taste these reasons, and was forced to stay there near five hours (almost from five to ten at night) before I durst leave them together, which I could not do till he had sworn in the most serious manner he would make no future attempt on her life. I was content with his oath, knowing him to be very devout, and found I was not mistaken.

How the matter was made up between them afterwards I know not, but 'tis now two year since it happened, and all appearances remaining as if it had never been. The secret is in very few hands; his brother, being at that time at Brescia, I believe knows nothing of it to this day. The chambermaid and myself have preserved the strictest silence; and the lady retains the satisfaction of insulting all her acquaintance on the foundation of a spotless character that only she can boast in the parish, where she is most heartily hated, from these airs of impertinent virtue, and another very essential reason, being the best dressed woman amongst them, though one of the plainest in her figure.

The discretion of the chambermaid in fetching me, which possibly saved her mistress's life, and her taciturnity since, I fancy appears very remarkable to you, and is what would certainly never happen in England. The first part of her behaviour deserves great praise, coming of her own accord and inventing so decent an excuse for her admittance; but her silence may be attributed to her knowing very well that any servant that presumes to talk of his master will most certainly be incapable of talking at all in a short time, their lives being entirely in the power of their superiors. I do not mean by law but by custom, which has full as much force. If one of them was killed it would either never be inquired into at all or very slightly passed over; yet it seldom happens and I know no instance of it, which I think is owing to the great submission of domestics, who are sensible of their dependence, and the national temper not being hasty and never enflamed by wine.

The PRINCE REGENT took an immediate dislike to his highly sexed Queen Caroline. They lived apart till the birth of Princess Charlotte, after which he demanded an official separation. Lady Cholmondeley had been deputed to inform the princess, who requested a written statement.

Windsor Castle, 30 April 1796

Madam,
As Lord Cholmondeley informs me that you wish I would define, in writing, the terms upon which we are to live, I shall endeavour to explain myself upon that head, with as much clearness, and with as much propriety, as the nature of the subject will admit. Our inclinations are not in our power, nor should either of us be held answerable to the other, because nature has not made us suitable to each other. Tranquil and comfortable society is, however, in our power; let our intercourse therefore be restricted to that, and I will distinctly subscribe to the condition which you required, through Lady Cholmondeley, that even in the event of any accident happening to my daughter, which I trust providence in its mercy will avert, I shall not infringe the terms of the restriction by proposing, at any period, a connection of a more particular nature. I shall now finally close this

disagreeable correspondence, trusting that as we have completely
explained ourselves to each other, the rest of our lives will be passed
in uninterrupted tranquility.
I am, Madam,
With great truth,
Very sincerely, yours,
(Signed) GEORGE P.

To this letter QUEEN CAROLINE sent the following answer, written originally in French, but here translated:

6 May 1796

The avowal of your conversation with Lord Cholmondeley, neither
surprises, nor offends me. It merely confirms what you have tacitly
insinuated for this twelvemonth. But after this, it would be a want of
delicacy, or rather an unworthy meanness in me, were I to complain
of those conditions which you impose upon yourself.

I should have returned no answer to your letter, if it had not been
conceived in terms to make it doubtful, whether this arrangement
proceeds from you or from me, and you are aware that the credit of it
belongs to you alone.

The letter which you announce to me as the last, obliges me to
communicate to the king, as to my sovereign and my father, both your
avowal and my answer. You will find enclosed the copy of my letter to
the king. I apprize you of it, that I may not incur the slightest reproach
of duplicity from you. As I have at this moment no protector but his
Majesty, I refer myself solely to him upon this subject, and if my conduct
meets his approbation, I shall be in some degree at least consoled. I
retain every sentiment of gratitude for the situation in which I find myself,
as Princess of Wales, enabled by your means, to indulge in the free
exercise of a virtue dear to my heart, I mean charity.

It will be my duty likewise to act upon another motive, that of giving
an example of patience and resignation under every trial.

Do me the justice to believe that I shall never cease to pray for your
happiness, and to be,
Your much devoted
CAROLINE

GEORGE SAND explains to her mother why she needs to free herself from an unsatisfactory marriage. In fact her husband was a profligate womanizer, and no partner for her intellectually. She married young and left him when she was twenty-five. Her words sound contemporary, especially when compared with the letter she wrote to her daughter Solange, when *she* wanted a divorce, twenty-five years later.

Nohant, 31 May 1831

Dear Maman,
Are you not a little hasty in condemnation? For me, my dear, liberty of thought and action is the first of blessings. If one could combine with that the little cares of bringing up a family it would be much sweeter, but is that at all possible? The one is always a nuisance to the other, liberty to one's home-circle, and one's home-circle to liberty! You are the only judge in the question of which you would prefer to sacrifice! I know that my own greatest fault lies in the fact that I *cannot* submit to the least shadow of constraint. Everything that is imposed on me as a duty becomes odious at once; whatever I do of my own free will is done with all my heart. It is often a great misfortune to be made like that and all my failings towards other people when they do occur, originate there.

But can one change one's own nature? If people are very indulgent to this fault of mine I find that it corrects itself in the most wonderful way. But when I am perpetually reproached about it, it gets much worse, and really that is not out of a spirit of contradiction; it is just involuntary, irresistible! I really must venture to tell you, dear Maman, that you have very little idea what I am really like. It is a long time now since we lived together and you often forget that I am now twenty-seven years old and that my character was bound to undergo many changes since I was quite a girl.

You seem to impute a love of pleasure and a need of frivolous amusement to me that I am far from possessing. It is not society, and noise, and theatres and new dresses that I want; you are the only person to make that mistake, it is liberty that I long for. I want to be able to walk out quite alone and say to myself: 'I will dine at four, or at seven, just as I like. I will go to the Tuileries through the Luxembourg instead of the Champs Elysées if the whim seizes me.' That would please me far better than the ordinariness of ordinary people and the stiffness of drawing-rooms. . . . Write soon dear Maman. Kisses with all my soul.

When GEORGE SAND's daughter, Solange, insisted on a divorce, her mother wrote in quite distinct discourse:

Nohant, 25 April 1852

I see you are down in the dumps, my poor thing! That will soon be over, like everything else which happens to you. As you have had an unexpected victory and will recover your little daughter in a few days' time, you can bring her here to stay, if you like, till the news of the law-suit is over. You need not be in despair for a few days spent in your dismal room; for I see that is weighing on you most. But it is not a mortal grief! I have lived and worked alone between four dingy walls during the best years of my youth, and it's not what I regret having experienced.

The isolation that you complain of is another matter. It is inevitable for the moment, a natural sequence of the attitude you have adopted. Your husband, whose character is intolerable, I daresay, is not worth so much hatred. The separation might have been carried out with greater dignity and prudence. However you willed it and cannot reasonably complain of the immediate results of a resolution you arrived at alone, without consulting family, friends or the child whose absence you are now feeling. The existence of the child should have given you patience, while relations were immensely anxious that the moment should be better chosen, the motives better substantiated, and your manner gentler and more generous.

Solange, you always try to swallow iron bars, and are always astonished to find that you cannot digest them. You are lucky not to have worse indigestion than you do! The friends you were bent on making by living far away from me have been no more faithful than the friends you have through me. So really your greatest misfortune consists in being my daughter, which I'm powerless to change, so face it once and for all.

The novelist Balzac received many letters from women admirers. Here an anonymous reader tells him of her adulterous affair and begs him to turn it into fiction – as she is beginning to do.

1835

A woman endowed with soul, heart, imagination, and the love of virtue, but also passionate, quixotic, and full of energy, was married to a man who did not love her. For fifteen years she suffered all the *frightful consequences* that a big city can impose on the unfortunate wife of a husband whose passions are excessively intense and all too physical.

(This woman owes it to the truth to state here that she alone in all the world suffered from her husband's life. He was considered delightful by everyone but her – but the passions!)

She remained pure, even in her thoughts, despite the efforts of several men, all of whom wanted to be something in her life. This woman is not at all pretty, she can circulate in a *salon* without being noticed; yet from the time she was thirteen years old, the men admitted to her circle of acquaintances loved her; she was never able to figure out why, but nothing could be more true. Until that time, she had only understood of love what she had read about it, and her severe glance always stopped the improper speeches that were addressed to her. Then a mysterious suffering took hold of her, she cried constantly, everything became dull and cold to her, an illness of the nerves and blood seized her, ennui and disgust with life came to weigh heavily on her heart and stop its beating. They said it was aneurism, poor people!

A man was then received at her home, his position admitted him to her intimate circle; he said he was unhappy, she pitied him, he said he was suffering, she suffered with his suffering, he loved her, she also loved him! A hundred times she wanted to break it off, said so, tried, but circumstances and her heart were both opposed. This frightful battle lasted two years!

It was the third of November last year – my God! she gave herself to him, without wanting to, without second thoughts, carried away by the agitation of her heart, her senses, by unknown new, strong, unbelievable sensations, and especially by the fear of seeing him kill himself or leave for a journey that would compromise his future and his life (ten years before she had almost been responsible for a bloody drama, the effects of which had darkened her entire life); she was afraid, she trembled; finally she forgot everything except for the love she felt for this man! She dishonoured the respectable white hair of her father, she did not think of her thirteen-year-old daughter and her beautiful child of seven. In sum, she gave herself.

The hours that followed her error, ah! Monsieur, what pages to write! You understand so well – do I need to depict this desperate shame, mixed nonetheless with happiness, infinite happiness, for here it is my heart and my life that write, and they are expressing the utter truth.

For about six months my emotional life was tumultuous – despair, pleasures, tears, intoxication – but always accompanied by remorse that could not be vanquished! She was jealous, she hid her jealousy; impetuous and violent, she became sweet and fearful, and brought nothing to this liaison but the most absolute truth, without coquetry.

Knowing nothing of this passion she had never experienced, she was visited by too many good feelings, good intentions – even when the criminal feelings continued – to break with him; separate from him, no, for he wanted always to be something in her life, but finally this man was no longer the same; his character, which she had so admired, gave way to hard demands, sweet attentions to irritation, sweet endearments to words that were hard, offensive; finally, two months ago, after two hours of unbearable heartache, she became delirious for almost a day, she opened the gate of the garden in which she happened to live at the time . . . the Seine rolled by below . . . she restrained herself only when the mother in her revealed to her the stain she would place on the lives of her two poor children!

Ah! Please, Monsieur, write of the experience of a woman guilty of such an offence, clinging to the affection of her father who, knowing how difficult her experience as a wife has been, praises her, thanks her for living a life he believes to be pure, and to the respect of her family, which she merits so little; of her daughter's presence, a perpetual reproach; of the remorse that torments her like a cancer, all of which make her life horrible. I beg you, write of this dreadful situation. What does one do when one has reached this point?

CAROLINE NORTON (1808–77), a novelist, played a leading role in reforming the restrictive divorce law, which she analysed in this letter to Queen Victoria in 1855. Queen Victoria remained unconvinced.

An English wife has *no legal rights*; her being is absorbed into that of her husband. Years of separation or desertion cannot alter this position. Unless divorced by special enactment in the House of Lords, the legal fiction holds her to be 'one' with her husband, although she may never see or hear of him.

She has no possessions, unless by special settlement. *Her* property is *his*.

An English wife has no legal right even to her clothes or ornaments;

her husband may take them and sell them if he pleases, even though they be the gifts of relatives or friends, or bought before marriage.

An English wife cannot make a will. She may have children or kindred whom she may earnestly desire to benefit; – she may be separated from her husband, who may be living with a mistress; no matter: the law gives what she has to him, and no will she could make would be valid.

An English wife cannot legally claim her own earnings. Whether wages for manual labour, or payment for intellectual exertion, whether she weed potatoes, or keep a school, her salary is *the husband's*; and he could compel a second payment, and treat the first as void, if paid to the wife without his sanction.

She cannot claim support, as a matter of right, from her husband. The belief is that he is bound to maintain her. That is not the law . . . Separation from her husband, by consent, or his ill usage, does not alter their mutual relation. He retains the right to divorce her, though he himself be unfaithful. Her being, on the other hand, of spotless character, gives her no advantage in law. *As her husband* he has a right to all that is hers: *as his wife*, she has no right to anything that is his. As her husband, he may divorce her: as his wife the utmost 'divorce' she could obtain is permission to reside alone, married to his name. Marriage is a civil bond for him, an indissoluble sacrament for her.

This account of divorce Egyptian-style is by LUCIE DUFF GORDON who spent eight years travelling in Egypt, to cure tuberculosis.

Thursday 3 December 1862

Dearest Mutter,

When I call my crew black, don't think of negroes. They are elegantly-shaped Arabs and all gentlemen in manners, and the black is transparent, with amber *reflets* under it in the sunshine; a negro looks *blue* beside them. I have learned a great deal that is curious from Omar's confidences, who tells me his family affairs and talks about the women of his family, which he would not to a man. He refused to speak to his brother, a very grand dragoman, who was with the Prince of Wales, and who came up to us in the hotel at Cairo and addressed Omar, who turned his back on him. I asked the reason, and Omar told me how his brother had a wife, 'An old wife, been with him long time, very good wife.' She had had three children – all dead. All at once the dragoman, who is much older than Omar, declared he would divorce her and marry a young woman. Omar said, 'No, don't do that; keep her in your house as head of your home, and take one of your two black slave girls as your Hareem.' But the other insisted, and married a young Turkish wife; whereupon Omar took his poor old sister-in-law to live with him and his own young wife, and cut his grand brother dead. See how characteristic! – the urging his brother to take the young slave girl 'as his Hareem,' like a respectable man – that would have been all right; but what he did was 'not good.' I'll trouble you (as Mrs. Grote used to say) to settle these questions to everyone's satisfaction. I own Omar seemed to me to take a view against which I had nothing to say. His account of his other brother, a confectioner's household with two wives, was very curious. He and they, with his wife and sister-in-law, all live together, and one of the brother's wives has six children – three sleep with their own mother and three with their *other* mother – and all is quite harmonious.

WORK, DUTY AND MONEY

'Women's work' has a pejorative ring in our male-dominated culture. Yet women have always worked, continuously and continually, in every culture and country. These letters show women involved in a wide variety of tasks. Work was often a shared experience in field and household before the nineteenth century, for poor and for powerful. Here medieval Margaret Paston and Honor Lisle deal with financial and estate matters competently. Queen Elizabeth I shrewdly assesses the needs of a Protestant monarchy.

The death of a husband frequently precipitated a widow into his business, or job-hunting. After the deaths caused by the Great Plague in 1665, widows like the playwright Aphra Behn accepted any remunerative work. As she spoke Dutch, she agreed to spy for the English government, at war with Holland, dangerous work for which she was briefly imprisoned – but not paid! Though women were more vulnerable financially than men, they complain little about money. The Ladies of Llangollen, for example, though from wealthy aristocratic families, were given only £100 a year – because they refused to marry. But they turned their penury into a model of subsistence living, sharing work in kitchen and garden, and studying daily together.

More typical of the nineteenth century is the real misery of the Brontës exploited and undervalued as governesses. Many uneducated girls were unable to find remunerative work, except as prostitutes. I include an anxious plea to Dickens from Mrs Gaskell, working to help a prostitute. Social work became a lifelong mission for Harriet Martineau and Florence Nightingale. Their Victorian seriousness is echoed in what George Sand and George Eliot say about their work as writers, in the following section.

This part ends with a letter to me from a modern businesswoman. It is included because she represents an aspect of the 1980s: success in business while not losing sight of women's values. She comments on her attempts to instil the 'feminine' qualities of caring and respect for others into a work place which has achieved growth at a time of recession under her leadership.

HILDEGARD OF BINGEN was a nun and a mystic, Eberhard, to whom this letter is addressed, was consecrated bishop of Salzburg in 1149. Caught in the endless struggles between emperor and pope, Eberhard became one of the staunch supporters of Pope Alexander III. Eberhard and Hildegard met personally at least once, and her letter here is in response to Eberhard's request for prayer and advice – spiritual work.

O you, you who in your office represent the Son of the living God, I see now that your situation resembles two walls joined together through one cornerstone. The one appears like a shining cloud; the other is somewhat shaded. And yet their situation is such that the brightness of the one doesn't affect the shadows; nor does the shadiness of the other mix with the light. The walls stand for your concerns, and these concerns meet in your spirit [the cornerstone]. For, on the one hand, your desires and feelings sigh for the narrow path that leads to God. But, on the other hand, you have a whole realm of worries about the people entrusted to you. The former is in light; the latter in shadow. Your own desires are in the brightest light and you regard them as house guests, but this worldly concern lies in shadows and you look on it as an intruder. You don't allow yourself to see that they belong together and this is why you so frequently experience depression in your spirit. For you fail to see your striving for God and your concern for your people as a unity. And yet they both can be bound together as one gain – whether you are sighing for heavenly things with great yearning, or whether you concern yourself in a godly way for the people. After all, Christ too adhered to heavenly things and yet at the same time he drew close to the people. It stands written in Scripture: 'I say, "You are gods, sons of the Most High, all of you."' (Psalms 82:6) I interpret this text to mean that we are 'gods' in relation to the Divine and 'sons of the Most High' in our concern for the people.

MARGARET PASTON looked after major matters on the Norfolk estate and offered sensible advice to her distant husband, John Paston at Caister.

8 April 1465

... Please you to know that I am sending you a copy of the deed that
John Edmonds of Taverham sent to me through Dorlet. He told
Dorlet that he had a deed that would help in checking the title that
the Duke of Suffolk claims in Drayton. On the deed he sent me, the
seal of arms is like the copy I am sending you, and nothing like the
Duke of Suffolk's ancestors' arms. The said Edmonds says that if he
can find any other thing that may help you in that matter he will do
his part to help. . . .

Item, there are divers of your tenements at Mautby that have great
need of repair, but the tenants are so poor that they have no power
to repair them; wherefore, if it please you, I should like the marsh that
Brygge had to be kept in your own hand this year, so that the tenants
might have rushes to repair their houses with. And also there is windfall
wood at the manor that is of no great value, that might help them towards
their repairs, if you like to let those that are in most need have it. . . .

I understand by John Pamping that you will not let your son be taken
into your house nor be helped by you until a year after he was put out
of it, which will be about the feast of St. Thomas [probably 7 July but
possibly December]. For God's sake, Sir, have pity on him. Remember
that it has been a long time since he had anything from you to help
him, and he has obeyed you and will do at all times, and will do all
that he can or may to have your good fatherhood. And at the reverence
of God, be his good father and have a fatherly heart towards him; and
I hope that he shall always know himself the better hereafter and be
the more careful to avoid such things as should displease you. Pecock
shall tell you by mouth of more things than I have time to write to you
now. The Blessed Trinity have you in his keeping. . . .

QUEEN MARGARET OF ANJOU works to defend commoners in this letter
to Sir John Forrester, Knight.

[before 1482]

Trusty and well-beloved.
This is to tell you that today there have come before us a great number
of men and women, tenants of our lordship of Hertingfordbury,
complaining that you have been and still are daily setting about their
destruction and permanent undoing: specifically, that you have caused

many of them to be wrongfully indicted for felonies before the Coroner on the words of your own close employees and adherents, not having discovered the truth of the matter; and you have put many of them in prison, and the remainder of our tenants dare not remain in their houses for fear of death or other injuries, that you do them daily; and all on account of a farm of ours which you rent there, and that, it is said, for your own sole benefit, you wrongfully expand so that it consumes all the livelihood of our tenants; not only to the great disadvantage and undoing of our tenants, but also to the dishonour and prejudice of our lordship and ourself. We are greatly surprised by this, especially that you who are a judge should tolerate so complaisantly the destruction of our said tenants.

Therefore we wish, and expressly exhort and require, that you cease from such activities, and especially against ourselves and our said tenants, until such time that you have replied and explained yourself to us in this matter; and that meanwhile, you allow our tenants who are in prison to be released under reasonable bail; and the remainder of our tenants, who are guiltless and have fled for fear of being destroyed by yourself, may come home to our said lordship [i.e., manor]. And if any of our tenants have offended against the law, it is our intention that when the truth is known they shall be severely punished and chastised, as is justified by the circumstances. And you will advise us by the messenger that brings you this what reaction you intend to make to this, which we trust you will fulfil, if you intend in future to stand in our tender and favourable regard.
Given at Windsor etc.

Lord and Lady Lisle were requested to hand over their manor of Painswick to Thomas Cromwell, Lord Privy Seal. Here LADY LISLE recounts to her husband her skilful, but unsuccessful negotiation with Cromwell, on behalf of herself and her husband. The property of Painswick belonged to Lady Lisle, making her socially acceptable as negotiator.

16 November 1538

Mine own good lord, With whole heart and mind I commend me unto you, not a little desirous to hear from you, but wholly and entirely to be with you. And this shall be signifying you that I was this morning with

my Lord Privy Seal, to whom I declared how good and gracious the
King's Majesty was unto me, and that his pleasure was that I should
resort unto his lordship for the expedition of mine affairs, desiring
him to be good unto you for your annuity, which he said might be no
more than ij¢ll yearly: to whom I answered, that it lay in him to obtain
the iiij¢ll, and that was his first motion and promise: whereunto he
answered, that he thought you would not charge him with his promise.
Finally he said that he would do the best therein for you and all others
that lay in his power.

Then resumed I with him of the taking of possession of my son's
lands, how the good earls had handled me; and his lordship made me
answer that they should undo that was done, and that he would be in
hand with them for the same within ij hours after. And forasmuch as
he moved me not for Painswick, I opened the matter unto him myself;
saying that Mr. Pollard had moved me in his behalf for it, and how
that notwithstanding I had refused divers and sundry great offers for
mine interests therein, yet forasmuch as I found him always good lord
unto me, and specially now in my need, I could be content to depart
with it unto him, so that he would see me no loser, as I trusted of
his goodness he would not, and that this his request should not be for
Mr. Kingston nor none other, but for himself; to the which he
promised faithfully that it should be for no creature but himself; and
thus we departed, for he had no more leisure at that time. Howbeit,
I trust within a day or two I shall know further of his mind. Sir Anthony
Browne hath sent me a doe, whereof I send you half by this bearer; and
the other half I keep, because I think Mr. Richard Cromwell and Mr.
Pollard will sup with me tomorrow night: wherewith I trust you will
be content, for otherwise surely I would have sent you the whole
doe. . . .
ffrom London the xvjth day of Novembre
yours more then my nowne
HONOR LYSSLE

QUEEN ELIZABETH I was frequently asked by worried ministers to appoint
an heir to give stability to the kingdom. Early in her reign she understand-
ably refused. Here she uses her verbal skills to work her will in a letter
to the House of Commons.

1559

I will be Queen of England so long as I live; after my death let them succeed to whom in right it shall appertain if that be your Queen (as I know not who should be before her), I will not be against it . . . you assume . . . that, upon this declaration, the friendship would be more firm between us. I fear you are deceived; I fear it would be rather an origin of hatred between Mary (of Scots) and me.

Is it like that I shall be well pleased in regard of her, with a continual view of mine own hearse?

. . . I am well acquainted with the nature of this people; I know how easily they dislike the present state of affairs; I know what nimble eyes they bear to the next succession. . . . I have learned this from experience of mine own times. When my sister Mary was Queen, what prayers were made by many to see me placed in her seat. . . . Now then, if the affections of our people grow faint . . . what may we look for when evil-minded men shall have a foreign prince appointed the certain successor to the crown? In how great danger shall I be . . . when a prince so powerful, so near unto me, shall be declared my successor.. . . Assuredly, if my successor were known to the world, I would never esteem my state to be safe.

[Hayward, *Annals*.]

Similarly, MARY QUEEN OF SCOTS, in prison, to Babington, attempts to organize her return to power with clear and precise instructions.

17 July 1586

Everything being prepared, and the forces as well within as without . . . then you must set the six gentlemen to work and give order that, their design accomplished, I may be in some way got away from here and that all your forces shall be simultaneously in the field to receive me while we await foreign assistance. . . .

Now as no certain day can be appointed for the performance of the said gentlemen's enterprise, I desire them to have always near them, or at least at Court, four brave men well horsed to advertise speedily the success of their design, as soon as it is done, to those appointed to get me away from hence, so as to be able to get here before my keeper is informed of the said execution. . . .

FANNY BURNEY describes her work as lady-in-waiting to Queen Charlotte, to Mrs Burney.

Windsor, Dec. 17

My dearest Hetty,

I am sorry I could not more immediately write; but I really have not had a moment since your last.

Now I know what you next want is, to hear accounts of kings, queens, and such royal personages. O ho! do you so? Well.

Shall I tell you a few matters of fact? – or, had you rather a few matters of etiquette? Oh, matters of etiquette, you cry! for matters of fact are short and stupid, and anybody can tell, and everybody is tired with them.

Very well, take your own choice.

To begin, then, with the beginning.

You know I told you, in my last, my various difficulties, what sort of preferment to turn my thoughts to, and concluded with just starting a young budding notion of decision, by suggesting that a handsome pension for nothing at all would be as well as working night and day for a salary.

This blossom of an idea, the more I dwelt upon, the more I liked. Thinking served it for a hothouse, and it came out into full blow as I ruminated upon my pillow. Delighted that thus all my contradictory and wayward fancies were overcome, and my mind was peaceably settled what to wish and to demand, I gave over all further meditation upon choice of elevation, and had nothing more to do but to make my election known.

My next business, therefore, was to be presented. This could be no difficulty; my coming hither had been their own desire, and they had earnestly pressed its execution. I had only to prepare myself for the rencounter.

You would never believe – you, who, distant from Courts and courtiers, know nothing of their ways – the many things to be studied, for appearing with a proper propriety before crowned heads. Heads without crowns are quite other sort of rotundas.

Now, then, to the etiquette. I inquired into every particular, that no error might be committed. And as there is no saying what may happen in this mortal life, I shall give you those instructions I have received myself, that, should you find yourself in the royal presence, you may know how to comport yourself.

DIRECTIONS FOR COUGHING, SNEEZING, OR MOVING BEFORE THE KING AND QUEEN.

In the first place, you must not cough. If you find a cough tickling in your throat, you must arrest it from making any sound; if you find yourself choking with the forbearance, you must choke – but not cough.

In the second place, you must not sneeze. If you have a vehement cold, you must take no notice of it; if your nose-membranes feel a great irritation, you must hold your breath; if a sneeze still insists upon making its way, you must oppose it, by keeping your teeth grinding together; if the violence of the repulse breaks some blood-vessel, you must break the blood-vessel – but not sneeze.

In the third place, you must not, upon any account, stir either hand or foot. If, by chance, a black pin runs into your head, you must not take it out. If the pain is very great, you must be sure to bear it without wincing; if it brings the tears into your eyes, you must not wipe them off; if they give you a tingling by running down your cheeks, you must look as if nothing was the matter. If the blood should gush from your head by means of the black pin, you must let it gush; if you are uneasy to think of making such a blurred appearance, you must be uneasy, but you must say nothing about it. If, however, the agony is very great, you may, privately, bite the inside of your cheek, or of your lips, for a little relief; taking care, meanwhile, to do it so cautiously as to make no apparent dent outwardly. And, with that precaution, if you even gnaw a piece out, it will not be minded, only be sure either to swallow it, or commit it to a corner of the inside of your mouth till they are gone – for you must not spit.

I have many other directions, but no more paper; I will endeavour, however, to have them ready for you in time. Perhaps, meanwhile, you would be glad to know if I have myself had opportunity to put in practice these receipts?

HARRIETTE WILSON, a celebrated courtesan, was born in 1786 to an impoverished watchmaker. She was one of fifteen children, of whom nine survived. The Regency period could be crude and tough as her best-selling *Memoirs* reveal. She opens: 'I became mistress of the Earl of Craven at the age of fifteen.' Her witty revelations about the sexual behaviour of the powerful led to Wellington's well-known 'Publish and be damned'. Towards the end of her life she was short of money and wrote a brief note to beg help from Byron, who promptly complied.

Paris, 30 rue de la Paix

Ten thousand thanks, dear Lord Byron, for your prompt compliance with my request. You had better send the money to me here and I shall get it safe. I am very glad to learn that you are more tranquil. For my part, I never aspired to being your companion, and should be quite enough puffed up with pride, were I permitted to be your housekeeper, attend to your morning cup of chocolate, darn your nightcap, comb your dog, and see that your linen and beds are well aired, and, supposing all these things were duly and properly attended to, perhaps you might, one day or other in the course of a season, desire me to put on my clean bib and apron and seat myself by your side, while you condescended to read me in your beautiful voice your last new poem! . . .

It would serve me right, were you to refuse to send me what you promised after my presumption in writing you this sermon. However, I must be frank and take my chance, and, if you really wish to convince me you bear no malice nor hatred in your heart, tell me something about yourself; and do pray try and write a little better, for I never saw such a vile hand as yours has become. Was it never a little more decent? True, a great man is permitted to write worse than ordinary people; *mais votre écriture passe la permission.* Anyone, casting a hasty glance at one of your effusions, would mistake it for a washerwoman's laboured scrawl, or a long dirty ditty from some poor soul just married, who humbly begs the favour of a little mangling from the neighbouring nobility, gentry and others! Look to it, man! Are there no writing-masters at Ravenna? Cannot you write straight at least? Dean Swift would have taken you 'for a lady of England!'

God bless you, you beautiful little ill-tempered, delightful creature, and make you as happy as I wish you to be.

HARRIETTE

Can I forward you a bundle of pens, or anything?

Ravenna, May 15th

I enclose a bill for a thousand francs, a good deal short of fifty pounds; but I will remit the rest by the very first opportunity. Owing to the little correspondence between Langle, the Bologna banker, I have had more difficulty in arranging the remittance of this paltry sum, than if it had been as many hundreds to be paid on the spot. Excuse all this, also the badness of my handwriting, which you find fault with and which was once better; but, like everything else, it has suffered from the late hours and irregular habits.

The Italian pens, ink and paper are also two centuries behind the like articles in other countries.
Yours very truly and affectionately,
BYRON

NELLIE WEETON describes the work of a governess to her friend Mrs. Dodson. Weeton kept an insightful *Journal*.

Aug. 18, 1812

You don't know how much you are indebted for this scrawl; it has been almost the work of a week, my leisure moments are so very limited.

The children appear to have been allowed full liberty to a riotous degree; yet Mrs. A. seems to expect that I shall now, speedily, bring them into the exactest order ... the task is a most arduous one! The eldest, a girl, is of that strange kind of temper, that she will purposely do the very thing that she thinks will excite most displeasure. I often wish that I could exchange her for one of yours. Of this girl, I shall never reap any credit, I fear; but the 2d, a boy, not six yet, will evince to his friends whether or no I possess any talents in the education of children. He is a fine little fellow, and understands, with great quickness, every thing I attempt to teach him. I have begun to instruct him in writing, and the elements of grammar and arithmetic; and they all learn to dance. I have four under my care.

Mr. and Mrs. A. are pleasant and easy in their temper and manners, and make my situation as comfortable as such a one can be; for it is rather an awkward one for a female of any reflection or feeling. A *governess* is almost shut out of society; not choosing to associate with servants, and not being treated as an equal by the heads of the house or their visitors, she must possess some fortitude and strength of mind to render herself tranquil or happy; but indeed, the master or mistress of a house, if they have any goodness of heart, would take pains to prevent her feeling her inferiority. For my own part, I have no cause of just complaint; but I know some that are treated in a most mortifying manner.

CHARLOTTE BRONTË and her sisters had to earn their living, as their father's stipend was tiny. The three who worked as governesses had unpleasant experiences. These extracts are from letters to Charlotte's friend Ellen Nussey:

3 March 1841

... I am fairly established in my new place. It is in the family of Mr. White of Upperwood House, Rawdon. The house is not very large but exceedingly comfortable and well regulated; the grounds are fine and extensive. In taking the place I have made a large sacrifice in the way of salary, in the hope of securing comfort by which word I do not mean to express good eating and drinking, or warm fire, or soft bed, but the society of cheerful faces, and minds and hearts not dug out of a lead mine, or cut from a marble quarry. My salary is not really more than £16 p.a., though it is nominally £20, but the expense of washing will be deducted therefrom. My pupils are two in number, a girl of eight [Sarah Louisa] and a boy of six.

As to my employers, you will not expect me to say much respecting their characters when I tell you that I only arrived here yesterday. I have not the faculty of telling an individual's disposition at first sight. Before I venture to pronounce on a character I must see it first under various lights and from various points of view. All I can say, therefore, is, both Mr. & Mrs. White seem to me good sort of people. I have as yet had no cause to complain of want of consideration or civility. My pupils are wild and unbroken, but apparently well disposed. I wish I may be able to say as much next time I write to you. My earnest wish and endeavour will be to please them. ...

21 March 1841

... This place is far better than Stonegappe, but, God knows, I have enough to do to keep a good heart in the matter. ... Home-sickness afflicts me sorely. I like Mr. White extremely. Respecting Mrs. White I am for the present silent. I am trying hard to like her. The children are not such little devils incarnate as the Sidgwicks, but they are over-indulged, and at times hard to manage. *Do, do, do* come to see me; if it be a breach of etiquette, never mind. If you can only stop an hour, come. ...

4 May 1841

Well can I believe that Mrs. White has been an excise man's daughter, since she possesses a very coarse unlady-like temper, and I am convinced also that Mr. White's extraction is very low – Mrs. White when put out of her way is highly offensive – She must not give me any more of the same sort – or I shall ask for my wages and go. . . .

Charlotte left after six months.

London was infamous for the number of child prostitutes. MRS GASKELL attempted to rescue one from New Bayley Prison, as she describes in this letter to Charles Dickens.

Jan. 8, 1850

I am just now very much interested in a young girl, who is in our New Bayley prison. She is the daughter of an Irish clergyman who died when she was two years old; but even before that her mother had shown most complete indifference to her; and soon after the husband's death, she married again, keeping her child out at nurse. The girl's uncle had her placed at 6 years old in the Dublin school for orphan daughters of the clergy; and when she was about 14, she was apprenticed to an Irish dress-maker here, of very great reputation for fashion. Last September but one this dress-maker failed, and had to dismiss all her apprentices; she placed this girl with a woman who occasionally worked for her, and who has since succeeded to her business; this woman was very profligate and connived at the girl's seduction by a surgeon in the neighbourhood who was called in when the poor creature was ill. Then she was in despair, & wrote to her mother, (*who had never corresponded with her all the time she was at school and an apprentice;*) and while awaiting the answer went into the penitentiary; she wrote 3 times but no answer came, and in desperation she listened to a woman, who had obtained admittance to the penitentiary solely as it turned out to decoy girls into her mode of life, and left with her: & for four months she has led the most miserable life! in the hopes, as she tells me, of killing herself, for 'no one had ever cared for her in this world,' – she drank, 'wishing it might be poison,' pawned every article of clothing – and at last stole. I have been to see her in prison at Mr. Wright's request, and she looks quite a young child (she is but 16) with a wild wistful look in her eyes, as if searching for the kindness she has never known, – and she pines to redeem herself; her uncle (who won't see her, but confirms fully the account of her mother's cruel hardness,) says he has 30£ of her father's money in his hands; and she agrees to emigrate to Australia, for which her expenses would be paid.

MILLICENT FAWCETT and her husband worked together to help women gain greater rights. In 1870 an Act was passed allowing women possession of their earnings, but Fawcett wanted a much more comprehensive Bill. Here she mentions her somewhat unsuccessful electioneering.

Those present were mostly Suffolk farmers. I explained my petition, and asked for signatures, but obtained very few. One old farmer voiced the feelings of the majority. 'Am I to understand you, ma'am, that if this Bill becomes law, and my wife had a matter of a hundred pound left her, I should have to arst her for it?' Of course I was obliged to confess that he would have to suffer this humiliation, and then I got no more signatures.

During the Spanish Civil War, a group of Quakers and Republican sympathizers went to Bilbao, to bring orphaned children to Britain. Among them was one of my dons, Mrs Helen Grant. She told me of the correspondence of her colleague, EDITH PYE, a veteran Quaker relief worker, who received the Légion d'Honneur for her work in France with refugees, before and after the First World War.

Perpignan. 20 January 1939

Dear Hilda,
It is a terrible tragedy here – up till today the pass leading to Spain has been one solid block of refugees, of all ages, wounded soldiers etc. They spent the nights standing, as one stands in the tube in rush hour. They were prevented from coming into France by Senegalese soldiers. (They said 'Moors behind us and now Moors in front!' and the crowd simply got wedged tighter and tighter.) Some of our people set up a canteen on the French side giving a piece of bread and drink of hot milk to all the women and children and old people.
    Today things are a little better. They are letting a few thousand through and they have at last begun to issue rations. The French intend

to feed 150,000 on Spanish soil, but there is no sign and no possibility of their beginning this at present. These poor people have absolutely no shelter – it poured in buckets last night and you can imagine what it was like. Today we met the Gerona lot of workers at the frontier and brought them back. They were bombed out of Gerona and out of Figueras, had been three days on the way and slept two nights in the lorry.

Dr Audrey Russell Ellis had an awful time in a car on the road full of refugees that they were bombing and machine-gunning. She was alone and said the road was full of bodies of refugees.

I spent the morning at Le Perthuis watching the crowd. In the middle of it a poor woman went suddenly mad, stripped off every stitch of clothes and ran down the middle of the road screaming. She was very fat and pink, and it made the most awful contrast. The gendarmes were very nice about it, very decent. I offered to help and said I was a nurse, but they said they did not need help – the poor thing was out of her mind. After, I saw her in an ambulance.

We shall see tonight what more can be done – nothing in Spain itself, I fear, except on the border.

29 January 1939

No time to write – a tragedy so immense that one hardly sees how to tackle it. Margarita has a canteen for bread and milk at the frontier, but the French are only beginning today. Refugees have had five nights in the open – and last night pouring wet. All our workers out, safe. I shall probably not be here long.
Yours, Edith

The following letter from a Buddhist friend of mine which describes looking after handicapped young people in the 1990s reveals how well the female psyche can mould itself to this type of work and enhance it.

Bath, 5 Sept 1991

Dear Olga,
You wanted to hear more about my work, so here is the promised letter. My work is in a home for profoundly handicapped young people, our current age group is between 12–33 years. I am a registered nurse and had previously been working with the elderly in a NHS hospital but

the stress of all that made me rather ill, so I had to literally follow my heart and work in this place. I say literally follow my heart because every time I thought about the home my heart felt as if it were swelling and I knew sometime I had to be there in this capacity of Care person.

It is quite remarkable the wonderfully individual personalities which emerge from these beings who have no need for words and the things we would consider 'normal'. Communication for me is very much at heart level and I do say to people that it is a wonderful place to exercise using one's heart, though they often don't know what I mean. The humdrum chores of daily life there are fun because I now work with young people who have revived my zest for life somewhat; and also working for young people is just something completely different.

Feelings on soul levels come through at times and with no words to express needs, communication can vary between loud and incoherent and very subtle and sensitive. We use a lot of complementary medicine and wholefoods to try and keep a harmony and balance, both inside, in their own quiet place of being and in order to help them calm down any stormy behavioural disturbances. The residents get a varied life and do far more in the way of outings etc. than we ever do at home! Many staff enjoy getting out and about and creating lots of fun, going to the sea and around town or boating and concerts with them. I love these things too – and also very special and quiet moments.

A few nights ago when it was dusky and very balmy, I took a young man outside to look at how the evening sky had changed to an almost purple shade. It was misty over the valley and I talked to him about it and how nice I would find it to walk over the fields into that mist and smell it and feel it. I pulled up his hand to touch the sky and he giggled as he touched it. Then we went over the garden to where a fountain ripples and gurgles all day.

He cannot see well but I sat him on the cool stones and said, 'Will you look at the fountain. Can you hear where it is?' His head turned towards it and I put his hand down to where the water was, cold and still with leaves floating on top. He pulled back his hand in surprise, then in a moment slowly let it down and touched the cold wetness again, then again and again till he was laughing freely at his new pleasure. That to me was worth more than any trip out, to be in the dusk and the quiet, sharing something that was just ours and appreciating the feel and sounds of nature.

I feel very free having found this kind of work, somehow it helps me as much as I can help them and I feel great joy and love and gratitude that I had been pointed towards this place. Life is such an adventure and I try to remain very sensitive to the directions shown to me by the elements and the Universe; I think meditation helps a great deal here to keep my mind clear so that I don't miss signposts. This is a lesson which I learned the hard way.

Love,

NANDA

Business School,
Croydon College
11 Sept. 91

Dear Olga,

We talked of core values very briefly when we last spoke about how women could make management more caring and spiritual. Core values – heart values – valuing myself – valuing others – valued by others! These are not merely important core issues for me, but for many others in the world of work today.

My life is a search for value and meaning. Integral to that search is a personal path linked strongly to my working life and organizational change and growth. That is why I try to change management systems. I am very fortunate – my personal growth and transformation has been facilitated, even mirrored in the organizations I have worked in, from my time as classroom teacher to my present post.

Work for me has provided a primary means of developing a daily practice of skilful living and right livelihood. Too often I fall short of my intentions but my Buddhist framework and practice and personal therapy have helped me to learn, grow and most importantly – accept, to learn from my mistakes, and to celebrate success.

I found myself eighteen months ago at age 34 appointed as the Head of a Business School – over 100 staff, 2,500 students – a huge responsibility – lots of fear and doubt. Attendance at a conference entitled Spirituality in Organizations one week after my appointment helped to clear my way.

The key issue for me became how to raise the 'spirit' within the Business School. How to lead mindfully, facilitating empowerment and the full potential of all staff and students. Many people are afraid of the word and concept of 'spirit', so Core Values became the way – the focus.

We began as a Business School to develop and articulate Core Values as an integral part of our Strategic Plan and way of working – PEOPLE, QUALITY, CUSTOMERS, SUCCESS, DIVERSITY, INTEGRITY, EQUALITY, DEVELOPMENT, ACTION.

The culture and atmosphere have begun to change, many staff feel more motivated and valued. Trust and openness are growing. In these times of recession, and suffering caused by cutbacks, I feel grateful for the opportunities I receive daily.

Much love,

LYNNE

WRITERS COMMENT ON THEIR WORK

Since women writers are more likely than most to pen letters, we have many views on the joys, aims and difficulties inherent in their work. Jane Austen answers the Prince Regent's request for a romance, by saying: 'If it were indispensable for me to keep it up and never relax into laughing at myself or other people, I am sure I should be hung before I had finished the first chapter'. George Sand emphasizes the morality for which Proust and his mother admired her: 'A conscience which is pure and honest like mine finds a moral purpose to pursue, outside all party questions. I am and always have been an artist before all else.'

Mrs Oliphant, only a few years later, stresses inspiration, though she chose to write to support her own children and those of her brother: 'I went home to my little ones, and as soon as I got them to bed, I sat down and wrote . . . I sat up all night in a passion of composition, stirred to the very bottom of my mind.' Emily Dickinson, in isolation in New England, writes for help when rejected by this male critic, in prose which resembles her intense staccato poetry: 'I had a terror – I could tell no-one – and so I sing. . . . I would like to learn – Could you tell me how to grow?'

George Eliot explains some of her intentions to a fellow novelist. Deeply serious commitment is also noticeable in the words of Anaïs Nin to a critic. Some twentieth-century writers sound more light-hearted; Vita Sackville-West and Virginia Woolf took commitment to writing for granted, and had the support of writer husbands. Colette and Jean Rhys comment amusingly on financial difficulties which both endured till they achieved fame. My first letter is in the form of a poem, a form which became popular in Europe in the Renaissance; it is from the remarkable Sei Shonagon in tenth-century Japan.

SEI SHONAGON wrote her *Pillow Book* in the last decade of tenth-century Japan. She recounts daily happenings in the court of the sophisticated, affectionate, enlightened Empress. Their letters to each other were often in the form of poems, sometimes sent when they were together, to communicate intimate feelings. Here the letter becomes an art form.

When the Empress was staying in the Third Ward, a palanquin arrived full of irises for the Festival of the Fifth Day and Her Majesty was presented with herbal balls from the Palace. The Mistress of the Robes and a few of the younger ladies prepared special balls, which they attached to the clothing of the Princess Imperial and of the little Prince. Then other very pretty herbal balls arrived from other palaces. Someone also brought a green-wheat cake; I presented it to Her Majesty on the elegant lid of an inkstone on which I had first spread a sheet of thin green paper carrying the words, 'This has come from across the fence.' The Empress tore off a piece of the paper and wrote the following splendid poem:

> Even on this festive day,
> When all seeking butterflies and flowers,
> You and you alone can see
> What feelings hide within my heart.

JANE AUSTEN deploys the weapon of her wit to deal with problems from male correspondents. First to James Stanier Clarke:

Chawton, near Alton, 1 April 1816.

My dear Sir

I am honoured by the Prince's thanks and very much obliged to yourself for the kind manner in which you mention the work. I have also to acknowledge a former letter forwarded to me from Hans Place. I assure you I felt very grateful for the friendly tenor of it, and hope my silence will have been considered, as it was truly meant, to proceed only from an unwillingness to tax your time with idle thanks. Under every interesting circumstance which your own talents and literary labours have placed you in, or the favour of the Regent bestowed, you have my best wishes. Your recent appointments I hope are a step to something still better. In my opinion, the service of a court can hardly be too well paid, for immense must be the sacrifice of time and feeling required by it.

You are very very kind in your hints as to the sort of composition which might recommend me at present, and I am fully sensible that

an historical romance, founded on the House of Saxe Cobourg, might be much more to the purpose of profit or popularity than such pictures of domestic life in country villages as I deal in. But I could no more write a romance than an epic poem. I could not sit seriously down to write a serious romance under any other motive than to save my life; and if it were indispensable for me to keep it up and never relax into laughing at myself or other people, I am sure I should be hung before I had finished the first chapter. No, I must keep to my own style and go on in my own way; and though I may never succeed again in that, I am convinced that I should totally fail in any other.
I remain, my dear Sir,
Your very much obliged, and very sincere friend,
J. AUSTEN

To her publisher, John Murray.

(Monday) 1 April 1816
Dear Sir,
   I return you the Quarterly Review with many Thanks. The Authoress of *Emma* has no reason I think to complain of her treatment in it – except in the total omission of Mansfield Park. – I cannot but be sorry that so clever a Man as the Reviewer of *Emma* should consider it as unworthy of being noticed. – You will be pleased to hear that I have received the Prince's Thanks for the *handsome* Copy I sent him of *Emma*. Whatever he may think of *my* share of the Work, *Yours* seems to have been quite right.

Professor Elaine Showalter claims that women novelists care about their families' feelings more than some male writers. Here FANNY BURNEY shows similar respect for correspondents:

August 1823
What an interesting letter is this last, my truly dear Hetty; 'tis a real sister's letter, and such a one as I am at this time frequently looking over of old times! For the rest of my life I shall take charge and save my own executor the discretionary labours that with myself are almost endless; for I now regularly destroy all letters that either may eventually do mischief, however clever, or that contain nothing of instruction or entertainment, however innocent. This, which I announce to all my

correspondents who write confidentially, occasions my receiving letters that are real conversations. Were I younger I should consent to this condition with great reluctance – or perhaps resist it: but such innumerable papers, letters, documents, and memorandums have now passed through my hands, and, for reasons prudent, or kind, or conscientious, have been committed to the flames, that I should hold it wrong to make over to any other judgment than my own, the danger or the innoxiousness of any and every manuscript that has been cast into my power.

GEORGE SAND explains her work and its importance in a letter to Prince Jerome.

Nohant, 16 July 1854

My Dear Prince,
You told me to write to you but I do not like to, very often as you must have so little time for reading letters. This is only a line to let you know that my affection for you is unchanged and that I think of you more than you can have time to think of me. It is quite natural; you are in action, and we are spectators.

As for the allusions that you regret not having seen in certain works of mine, you cannot know much of what is going on in France if you think that they would be possible. And then perhaps you have not sufficiently considered that when there is a shortage of liberty, frank and courageous souls prefer silence to insinuation. Besides, were liberty to be re-established for us, it is by no means certain that I want to touch yet upon questions which humanity is not yet worthy of solving, which would have divided up the greatest and best minds of the day, into different camps of hatred.

You say you are astonished that I am able to go on producing literature, but I thank God for preserving my faculty for it, because a conscience which is pure and honest like mine, finds a moral purpose to pursue, outside all party questions. What should I do with myself if I abandoned my humble task? Join conspiracies? That is not my vocation; I have no talent for it at all. Write pamphlets? I have neither the malice nor the type of mind for that. Theories? There have been too many theories and thus we have become divided, which means the burial of all truth and all power. I am and always have been an

artist before all else; I know that all men who are politicians only,
have a great contempt for artists because they judge them by certain
idiotic types who are a dishonour to the name of art. But you, my friend,
must know that the true artist is as useful as the *priest* or *warrior*, and
that when the artist respects the *true* and the *good*, he is on a road
which God will bless without ceasing. Art is of all nationalities and of
all periods; its particular quality is precisely that of *being able to survive*
when all else must perish: It is for that reason that art is preserved
from mixing in passions which are either too personal or too general,
and has been given an organism of *patience* and *persistence* unknown
elsewhere; also durable sensibility and a contemplative outlook which
shelters an invincible faith. Now why and how should you think that
calmness of the will constitutes any kind of satisfaction of egoism?
To such a reproach I should have nothing to answer I admit, or at
least, only this: that I did not deserve the accusation. My heart is as
transparent as my life, and I do not discover any venomous fungi
growing therein, which I ought to try and extirpate. If it were the case,
I should put up a stout fight, I can promise you, before I would allow
myself to be invaded by Evil.

   Adieu, my friend. Never think me *changed* towards you or anything
else.

In the winter of 1860–61, MRS MARGARET OLIPHANT, a penniless,
undaunted little Scottish 'scribbling woman', called at the publishing
office of the brothers Blackwood.

It was a very severe winter, and it was severe on me too . . . I had not
been doing very well with my writing. I had sent several articles to
Blackwood's [Magazine] and they had been rejected. Why, this being
the case, I should have gone to them . . . I can't tell. But I was in
their debt, and had very little to go on with. . . . They shook their
heads, of course, and thought it would not be possible to take such a
story – both very kind, and truly sorry for me, I have no doubt. I think
I see their figures now against the light, standing up, John with his
shoulders hunched up, the Major with his soldierly air, and myself all
blackness and whiteness in my widow's dress, taking leave of them
as if it didn't matter, and oh! so much afraid that they would see the
tears in my eyes. I went home to my little ones, and as soon as I had

got them into bed, I sat down and wrote. . . . I sat up all night in a
passion of composition, stirred to the very bottom of my mind. The
story was successful, and my fortune, comparatively speaking, was
made.

MARGARET OLIPHANT

Colonel T. W. Higginson was the only professional critic to whom the
poet EMILY DICKINSON (1830–86) submitted her poems. He was
intrigued, but wrote advising against publication (he was later to co-edit
a posthumous selection). Here Emily describes a woman writer's problem
of loneliness.

                                                April 26 1862
Mr. Higginson,
Your kindness claimed earlier gratitude – but I was ill – and write
today, from my pillow.

Thank you for the surgery – it was not so painful as I supposed. I
bring you others – as you ask – though they might not differ –

While my thought is undressed – I can make no distinction, but
when I put them in the Gown – they look alike, and numb.

You asked me how old I was? I made no verse – but one or two –
until this winter – Sir –

I had a terror – since September – I could tell to none – and so I
sing, as the Boy does by the Burying Ground – because I am afraid
– You enquire my Books – For Poets – I have Keats – and Mr and
Mrs Browning. For Prose – Mr Ruskin – Sir Thomas Browne – and
the Revelations. I went to school – but in your manner of the phrase
– had no education. When a little Girl, I had a friend, who taught me
Immortality – but venturing too near, himself – he never returned –
Soon after, my Tutor, died – and for several years, my Lexicon – was
my only companion – Then I found I had one more – but he was not
contented I be his scholar – so he left the Land.

You ask of my Companions. Hills – Sir – and the Sundown – and
a Dog – large as myself, that my Father bought me – They are better
than Beings – because they know – but do not tell – and the noise in
the Pool, at Noon – excels my Piano. I have a Brother and Sister – My
Mother does not care for thought – and Father, too busy with his Briefs
– to notice what we do – He buys me many Books – but begs me not

to read them – because he fears they joggle the Mind. They are religious – except me – and address an Eclipse, every morning – whom they call their 'Father.' But I fear my story fatigues you – I would like to learn – Could you tell me how to grow – or is it unconveyed – like Melody – or Witchcraft?

Is this – Sir – what you asked me to tell you?
Your friend,
E – DICKINSON

How to earn money as a writer was a perennial problem. LOUISA MAY ALCOTT, best known for her novels about *Little Women*, was recently discovered to have written horror stories under a pseudonym. She obviously enjoyed the variety and the chance of earning more in order to support her family.

                                                                1869
I intend to illuminate the ledger with a blood and thunder tale as they are easy to compose and better paid than moral and elaborate works of Shakespeare. So don't be shocked if I send you a paper containing a picture of Indians, pirates, wolves, bears and distressed damsels, with a title like this: *The Maniac Bride* or *A Thrilling Tale of Passion*.

GEORGE ELIOT (1819–80) often claimed that fiction should represent 'real life', 'never lapse from the picture to the diagram'. However, when she felt strongly about causes, she allowed herself to use her work of fiction-writing as a means to explore an important moral issue. Here she explains some of her intentions to the American novelist Harriet Beecher Stowe, whose *Uncle Tom's Cabin* also aimed to help oppressed peoples. Mrs Stowe had written a 'generously appreciative' review of *Daniel Deronda*.

                                                          Sept. 1876
As to the Jewish element in 'Deronda', I expected from first to last in writing it, that it would create much stronger resistance and even repulsion than it has actually met with. But precisely because I felt that the usual attitude of Christians towards Jews is – I hardly know whether to say more impious or more stupid when viewed in the light

of their professed principles, I therefore felt urged to treat Jews with such sympathy and understanding as my nature and knowledge could attain to. Moreover, not only towards the Jews, but towards all oriental peoples with whom we English come in contact, a spirit of arrogance and contemptuous dictatorialness is observable which has become a national disgrace to us. There is nothing I should care more to do, if it were possible, than to rouse the imagination of men and women to a vision of human claims in those races of their fellow-men who most differ from them in customs and beliefs. But towards the Hebrews we western people who have been reared in Christianity, have a peculiar debt and, whether we acknowledge it or not, a peculiar thoroughness of fellowship in religious and moral sentiment. Can anything be more disgusting than to hear people called 'educated' making small jokes about eating ham, and showing themselves empty of any real knowledge as to the relation of their own social and religious life to the history of the people they think themselves witty in insulting? They hardly know that Christ was a Jew. And I find men educated at Rugby supposing that Christ spoke Greek. . . .

Yes, I expected more aversion than I have found. But I was happily independent in material things and felt no temptation to accommodate my writing to any standard except that of trying to do my best in what seemed to me most needful to be done, and I sum up with the writer of the Book of Maccabees – 'if I have done well, and as befits the subject, it is what I desired, but if I have done ill, it is what I could attain unto'.

The French writer COLETTE (1873–1954) joined a touring company to earn money to support herself and daughter. Here she describes some of the many problems to Charles Saglio.

Lyons, 12 December 1908

I'm coming back the 17th. May I see you Friday at the *Vie* offices? Let me have a word at the rue Torricelli address. Great success in every way except . . . I'm insufficiently paid. You aren't forgetting me, I hope? Because I still need . . . what you promised me. I'm bored here and pawing the ground with impatience to get home. Lyons is dark and it rains constantly. I'm nervous and disagreeable, though not to you. . . .

People in Baret's companies are used to touring and having to change the show every four days. They rehearse morning, noon, and night

without batting an eyebrow. It's a good school but a rough one. After
tonight's performance, I can rest up, but tomorrow morning the rest
of the company begins rehearsing the show which will follow me. And
they do that for six months at a time! I really admire them. Interesting
detail: the prompter disappeared this morning. He had drunk too much
and presumably gone somewhere to sleep it off. Since I know my lines,
it didn't bother me; but everyone was left dangling.

You were very kind to come with me to the station. All I can tell
you is that I am happy to have you as a friend.

COLETTE's first husband, Willy, put his *own* name to her early books, so
she could not claim royalties, as she explains to Lucien Solvay.

Brussels, February 1909

In the days when Willy did me the dubious honour of signing my
novels, he would occasionally insert into my texts a few words designed
to gratify his personal spite. He used to call this collaborating. In *Minne*,
this 'collaboration' consisted in giving to certain characters the names
of esteemed confrères, notably yours.

VIRGINIA WOOLF writes of her preoccupations and pleasures to her friend
Vita Sackville-West. 'Potto' was Vita's nickname for Virginia.

25 Tavistock Sq WC1
12 March 1928

. . . I fell in love with Noel Coward, and he's coming to tea. You cant
have all the love in Chelsea – Potto must have some: Noel Coward must
have some. I played a funny trick. I had no hat. Bought one for 7/11¾
at a shop in Oxford Street: green felt: the wrong coloured ribbon: all a
flop like a pancake in midair. Even I thought I looked odd. But I wanted
to see what happens among real women if one of them looks like a
pancake in mid air. In came the dashing vermeil-tinctured
red-stopper-bottle-looking Mrs Edwin Montagu. She started. She
positively deplored me. Then hid a smile. Looked again. Thought Ah
what a tragedy! Liked me even as she pitied. Overheard me flirting. Was
puzzled. Finally conquered. You see, women cant hold out against this
kind of flagrant disavowal of all womanliness. They open their arms as
to a flayed bird in a blast: whereas, the Mary's of this world, with every

feather in place, are pecked, stoned, often die, every feather stained with blood – at the bottom of the cage.

Darling, are you happy or unhappy? Writing? Loving? Please send me a long letter, on big paper, because Potto likes that best. . . .

VITA SACKVILLE-WEST replied:

> 24 Brücken-allee
> [Berlin] NW23
> 14 March

Here is the nice big paper that Potto likes – I have got some very smart blue paper with the address stamped on it, and telephone number Moabit 37–94, but if Potto likes this best he must have it. I have been coming to the not very original conclusion that Virginia is in every way the most charming person in the world – in fact I have spent the last three or four days thinking of very little else and being very happy in my absorption; it has been like living a little secret life that nobody knew anything about. And listen: I have got Bottome's story for you – and it will follow in a day or two. There must be this delay because the person who got it for me wants to read it again before I send it off. Bottome is so thrilled at the idea of your reading it that she rings up Berlin on the telephone out of Switzerland to know if it has yet been posted to you – and she wishes you to be told that 'the idea came to her in a dream'. You are called Avery Fleming in the story. You must return it when read.

I have been getting into a row with the Hogarth Press, as you will see by the enclosed bill, the reason being that I thought they would just knock it off my royalties if ever any became due to me; but I hurriedly and apologetically enclose a cheque now. I suppose making up our books means the final withdrawal of Angus. And more business before I go on to any more personal matter or geisterforschung: there's a woman here called Margaret Voigt-Goldsmith, who is a literary agent and who wrote to you some time ago to ask if she could deal with your books to get them translated into German. You referred her to Curtis-Brown, who sent her an answer which on investigation proved to be inaccurate; i.e. said that Fischer was doing your books here, which it seems he is not. Would there therefore be any chance of Margaret Voigt getting the handling of your books after all? She is extremely nice, and energetic and intelligent; and incidentally a bosom friend of mine. Though I would not recommend her if I were not sure that you would do well by her. Her address is: Mrs Voigt-Goldsmith, 7 Nürnberger-strasse. Really it seems a pity that you should not be translated in German, as they all know about you here; so if you can do anything about Margaret Voigt I think you should.

I disapprove violently of your driving yourself through France. I think it is extremely dangerous – and what's all that about flying? Am I to understand that you have left the ground and that that experience is over and need never be repeated? If so, I am thankful. Please write something about it, so that the anguish of terror which I expect you went through should not be wholly wasted. It *is* damnable about my not seeing you before you go, but you see there is Copenhagen, which was not my arrangement but Harold's. Send me your address at Cassis, and *please* don't stay there too long.

Your
V

The drama and tribulations of an impecunious writer in a bedsitting room in London: JEAN RHYS writes to her close friend Evelyn Scott.

Sunday, February 18th 1934
23 Brunswick Square
London WC1

My dear Evelyn,

Thank you for your letter (letters) more than I can say. You don't know how dam pleased I am when you write. My dear about the book (still Voyage in the Dark because I can't get another title tho I wish I could) it is still being typed. Leslie had an awful rush of work at Harpers end of last month and beginning of this.

I, of course, couldn't resist fiddling about and making alterations.

However it is really in its last stages. Leslie reckons to be able to finish the typing in ten days to a fortnight.

I don't know what I feel about the blessed thing. I had the horrors about it and about everything for a bit. I mean the complete futility. Nightmarish. But I expect that was my liver and lights giving way under the strain of two bottles of wine per day. Also the weather – more like hell than anything you can imagine – a yellow fog very cold. Blasted people wailing hymns outside.

You feel as if you're being slowly suffocated. At least I do.

Here I may say we still are in two Bloomsbury bed sitting rooms. And I don't see us getting away in a hurry either. Never mind. This morning (it was rather funny) a huge coloured lady presented herself while I was still in bed and demanded her rent. Very chic she was, pearl earrings and everything (and I believe a compatriot). Leslie was in the bathroom.

She wanted to be paid on the nail 'Can Mr Smith give me a cheque?' she said. 'No' I said, 'I shouldn't think so'. 'Why not?' she said.

There was no answer to that so I just looked vague.

'Perhaps', she said, 'Mr Smith could let me have so much.' 'Well' I said, 'it'll be a bit difficult today'. 'Why?' she said. A forthright creature. I said 'Well you see today is Sunday'. She said '*Why* should Sunday be different from any other day' and I looked very shocked. So she retreated.

Isn't it funny me upholding the Sabbath?

This is a rum house. The West Indian lady is the late owner. She's just sold the house to two German Jewish ladies (born in Wales and very sympathique.) I suppose she wanted to collect before departing . . . All for now,

JEAN

A woman writer used to have to work harder than most men to get published. Then and now she needs good reviews if her work is to be read. ANAÏS NIN (1903–77) wrote novels, erotica (to make money) and corresponded with many well-known writers. She chose a woman critic for whom she felt sympathy to review her novel *A Spy in the House of Love* (1954). Here she works to redress the poor opinion of the reviewer Frances Keene after her scathing review of *Spy*:

1954

I don't know how to thank you for spending all that time on rereading my work, but I must ask you to forgive me for having completely misunderstood you and your attitude towards my work, or I would never have even vaguely suggested you give time to a work which meant so little to you. When I first met you, you had indicated great feeling for *Four-Chambered Heart*, a response to Djuna, even a certain identification with her role. Then you struggled to get *Spy in the House of Love* published. Why? Your total estimate is not only negative, it is distorted too, by most unobjective attitudes. First you generously admit I have influenced the young, and then you cancel out the effect of such a statement by mentioning the one writer whose writing has no trace of my influence, who is the very opposite of what I believe in, Gore Vidal, who represents all that I dislike in writing. Which either means you have not read Gore or that you do not understand what I mean by the poetic novel. Then you proceed to say something positive: 'all the books . . . stem from a true searching inward eye. That's where the consistency lies.' But a few paragraphs later your puritanism writes this extraordinary phrase worthy of the most illiterate, uncultivated, Middle West reviewer: 'the story of Sabina, a would-be actress with all the instinct for miscellaneous coupling of an alley cat in heat. . . .' Dear Frances, that is rather unbelievable of anyone who has read *Madame Bovary*, or Proust, or Simenon, or even of someone who reads English pure and simple. Sabina is the story of the dissociation of the personality (the breakdown of integrity) which motivates Don Juanism, it is an attempt to go deeper into the classical Don Juan, or Madame Bovary. It is written with seriousness and dignity, psychological depth and poetry. Was it deliberate that you insisted on the rightness of a glaring proof error? Sabina herself could not say 'I have not loved yet,' [it was said by Djuna] since that truth is what she is seeking throughout the book, and if she had known this the book would never have been written.

Also I think it is completely unethical, and a grave fault of subjective criticism, to imply that all these women I describe are me and that I have used the diary undisguised. In the first place let me remind you, dear Frances, that to say this you would have had to read the diary, and also no woman could be the gallery of women I have portrayed. It is malice to leave out the portrait of Stella, when you know whose portrait it is, the portrait of Lillian, or the portrait of Hedja.

TRAVEL

Christian mythology represented the mother as staying at home, nursing children. Yet from the earliest wars, women were forced to travel, often to protect their offspring. We know that women like Saint Teresa of Avila travelled when she was reorganizing Spanish convents. Gradually humanism encouraged travellers to record their impressions and experiences in autobiographical style. Women, despite major cultural and physical impediments, such as social ostracism, tight corsetry and long heavy skirts, were among the least culturally inhibited commentators.

Virtually the first travel writer to tour all English counties was Celia Fiennes (1662–1741). Her lively *Journals* were at first unpretentiously intended for her family and not published till long after her death, in 1888. One of the first women to describe the customs of very different countries was Lady Mary Wortley Montagu, outstanding in her ability to examine another culture without too many preconceptions.

We have fascinating correspondence on Egypt from Florence Nightingale, Lucie Duff Gordon and Vita Sackville-West. We also hear from a wide range of more intrepid Victorian explorers, including Mary Kingsley in the Congo, Kate Marsden in Russia and Alexandra David-Néel, the first Western woman in the Forbidden City of Lhasa. Representative of the twentieth century is Freya Stark. When young, she travelled to the Middle East, fell in love with it and learned Arabic. Though she had very little money, she managed to support herself abroad until her unusually vivid letters home were published with a deserved financial reward. This is the longest section, a tribute to the adventurous spirit of women, which has only recently received public recognition. It is also a tribute to the remarkable writing skills of these travellers.

In 1717 MARY WORTLEY MONTAGU accompanied her husband to Turkey, where he had been appointed ambassador. From there she sent back

delighted descriptions of all she saw to her sister and friends. This letter
is to the Italian philosopher and poet Abbé Conti.

May 1717

The rest of our journey was through fine painted meadows by the side
of the Sea of Marmara, the ancient Propontis. We lay the next night
at Selivria, anciently a noble town. It is now a very good seaport, and
neatly built enough, and has a bridge of thirty-two arches. Here is a
famous ancient Greek church. I had given one of my coaches to a
Greek lady who desired the conveniency of travelling with me. She
designed to pay her devotions and I was glad of the opportunity of
going with her. I found it an ill built place, set out with the same sort
of ornaments but less rich than the Roman Catholic churches. They
showed me a saint's body, where I threw a piece of money, and a
picture of the Virgin Mary drawn by the hand of St Luke, very little
to the credit of his painting, but, however, the finest Madonna of Italy
is not more famous for her miracles. The Greeks have the most
monstrous taste in their pictures, which for more finery are always
drawn upon a gold ground. You may imagine what a good air this has,
but they have no notion either of shade or proportion. They have a
Bishop here, who officiated in his purple robe, and sent me a candle
almost as big as myself for a present when I was at my lodging.

We lay the next night at a town called Büjük Cekmege or Great
Bridge, and the night following at Küjük Cekmege, Little Bridge, in a
very pleasant lodging, formerly a monastery of dervishes, having before
it a large court encompassed with marble cloisters with a good fountain
in the middle. The prospect from this place and the gardens round it
are the most agreeable I have seen, and shows that monks of all religions
know how to choose their retirements. 'Tis now belonging to a *hogia*
or schoolmaster, who teaches boys here; and asking him to show me his
own apartment I was surprised to see him point to a tall cypress tree
in the garden, on the top of which was a place for a bed for himself,
and a little lower, one for his wife and two children, who slept there
every night. I was so much diverted with the fancy I resolved to
examine his nest nearer, but after going up fifty steps I found I had
still fifty to go and then I must climb from branch to branch with some
hazard of my neck. I thought it the best way to come down again.

We arrived the next evening at Constantinople, but I can tell you
very little of it, all my time having been taken up with receiving visits,
which are at least a very good entertainment to the eyes, the young

women being all beauties and their beauty highly improved by the
good taste of their dress. Our palace is in Pera, which is no more a
suburb of Constantinople then Westminster is a suburb to London. All
the Ambassadors are lodged very near each other. One part of our
house shows us the port, the city and the seraglio, and the distant hills
of Asia, perhaps altogether the most beautiful prospect in the world.
A certain French author says that Constantinople is twice as large as
Paris. Mr Wortley is unwilling to own 'tis bigger than London, though
I confess it appears to me to be so, but I don't believe 'tis so populous.
The burying fields about it are certainly much larger than the whole
city. 'Tis surprising what a vast deal of land is lost this way in Turkey.
Sometimes I have seen burying places of several miles belonging to
very inconsiderable villages which were formerly great towns and retain
no other mark of their ancient grandeur. On no occasion they remove
a stone that serves for a monument. Some of them are costly enough,
being of very fine marble. They set up a pillar with a carved turban on
the top of it to the memory of a man, and as the turbans by their different
shapes show the quality or profession, 'tis in a manner putting up the
arms of the deceased; besides, the pillar commonly bears a large
inscription in gold letters. The ladies have a simple pillar without other
ornament, except those that die unmarried, who have a rose on the
top of it. The sepulchres of particular families are railed in and planted
round with trees. Those of the Sultans and some great men have
lamps constantly burning in them.

In a letter to her sister Lady Mary comments on women's lives.

1717

I never saw in my life so many fine heads of hair. I have counted one
hundred and ten of these tresses of one lady's, all natural; but it must
be owned that every beauty is more common here than with us. 'Tis
surprising to see a young woman that is not very handsome. They have
naturally the most beautiful complexions in the world and generally large
black eyes. I can assure you with great truth that the Court of England
(though I believe it the fairest in Christendom) cannot show so many
beauties as are under our protection here. They generally shape their
eyebrows, and the Greeks and Turks have a custom of putting round
their eyes on the inside a black tincture that, at a distance or by
candlelight, adds very much to the blackness of them. I fancy many of
our ladies would be overjoyed to know this secret, but 'tis too visible by

day. They dye their nails rose colour; I own I cannot enough accustom myself to this fashion to find any beauty in it.

As to their morality or good conduct, I can say like Harlequin, ''Tis just as 'tis with you'; and the Turkish ladies don't commit one sin the less for not being Christians. Now I am a little acquainted with their ways, I cannot forbear admiring either the exemplary discretion or extreme stupidity of all the writers that have given accounts of 'em. 'Tis very easy to see they have more liberty than we have, no woman of what rank soever being permitted to go in the streets without two muslins, one that covers her face all but her eyes and another that hides the whole dress of her head and hangs half-way down her back; and their shapes are wholly concealed by a thing they call a *ferigée*, which no woman of any sort appears without. This has strait sleeves that reach to their fingers' ends and it laps all round 'em, not unlike a riding hood. In winter 'tis of cloth, and in summer, plain stuff or silk. You may guess how effectually this disguises them, that there is no distinguishing the great lady from her slave, and 'tis impossible for the most jealous husband to know his wife when he meets her, and no man dare either touch or follow a woman in the street.

This perpetual masquerade gives them entire liberty of following their inclinations without danger of discovery. The most usual method of intrigue is to send an appointment to the lover to meet the lady at a Jew's shop, which are as notoriously convenient as our Indian houses, and yet even those that don't make that use of 'em do not scruple to go to buy penn'orths and tumble over rich goods, which are chiefly to be found amongst that sort of people. The great ladies seldom let their gallants know who they are, and 'tis so difficult to find out that they can very seldom guess at her name they have corresponded with above half a year together.

You may easily imagine the number of faithful wives very small in a country where they have nothing to fear from their lovers' indiscretion, since we see so many that have the courage to expose themselves to that in this world and all the threatened punishment of the next, which is never preached to the Turkish damsels. Neither have they much to apprehend from the resentment of their husbands, those ladies that are rich having all their money in their own hands, which they take with 'em upon a divorce with an addition which he is obliged to give 'em. Upon the whole, I look upon the Turkish women as the only free people in the empire. The very Divan pays a respect to 'em, and the Grand Signior himself, when a pasha is executed, never violates the privileges of the harem (or women's apartment) which remains unsearched entire to the widow. They are queens of their slaves, which the husband has no permission so much as to look upon, except it be an old woman or two that his lady chooses. 'Tis true their law permits them four wives, but there is no instance of a man of quality that makes use of this liberty, or of a woman of rank that would suffer it. When a husband happens to be inconstant (as those things will happen) he keeps his mistress in a house apart and visits her as privately as he can, just as 'tis with you. Amongst all the great men here I only know the *tefterdar* (*i.e.* treasurer) that keeps a number of she slaves for his own use (that is, on his own side of the house, for a slave once given to serve a lady is entirely at her disposal), and he is spoke of as a libertine, or what we should call a rake, and his wife won't see him, though she continues to live in his house.

Thus you see, dear sister, the manners of mankind do not differ so widely as our voyage writers would make us believe. Perhaps it would be more entertaining to add a few surprising customs of my own invention, but nothing seems to me so agreeable as truth, and I believe nothing so acceptable to you.

In the following letter the nineteenth-century writer HARRIET MARTINEAU expresses a feminist's sympathy towards slaves.

1838

I could never get out of the way of the horrors of slavery in this region [New Orleans]. Under one form or another, they met me in every house, in every street; everywhere but in the intelligence pages of newspapers, where I might read on in perfect security of exemption from the subject. In the advertising columns there were offers of reward for runaways, restored dead or alive; and notices of the capture of a fugitive with so many brands on his limbs and shoulders, and so many scars on his back. But from the other half of the newspaper, the existence of slavery could be discovered only by inference. What I saw elsewhere was, however, dreadful enough. In one house, the girl who waited on me with singular officiousness was so white, with blue eyes and light hair, that it never occurred to me that she could be a slave. Her mistress told me afterwards that this girl of fourteen was such a depraved hussy that she must be sold.

Meantime you attempt to talk with the slaves. You ask how old that very aged man is, or that boy; they will give you no intelligible answer. Slaves never know, or never will tell their ages, and this is the reason why the census presents such extraordinary reports on this point, declaring a great number to be above a hundred years old. If they have a kind master, they will boast to you of how much he gave for each of them, and what sums he has refused for them. If they have a hard master, they will tell you that they would have more to eat and be less flogged, but that massa is busy, and has no time to come down and see that they have enough to eat. Your hostess is well known on this plantation, and her kind face has been recognised from a distance; and already a negro woman has come to her with seven or eight eggs, for which she knows she shall receive a quarter dollar. You follow her to the negro quarter, where you see a tidy woman knitting, while the little children who are left in her charge are basking in the sun, or playing all kinds of antics in the road; little shining, plump, cleareyed children, whose mirth makes you sad when you look round upon their parents, and see what these bright creatures are to come to. You enter one of the dwellings, where everything seems to be of the same dusky hue: the crib against the wall, the walls themselves, and the floor, all look one yellow. More children are crouched round the wood fire, lying almost in the embers. You see a woman pressing up against the wall like an idiot, with her shoulder turned towards you, and her apron held up to her face. You ask what is the matter with her, and are told that she is shy. You see a woman rolling herself about in a crib, with her head tied up. You ask if she is ill, and are told that she has not a good temper; that she struck at a girl she was jealous of with an axe, and the weapon being taken from her, she threw herself into the well, and was nearly drowned before she was taken out, with her head much hurt.

The overseer has, meantime, been telling your host about the fever having been more or less severe last season, and how well off he shall think himself if he has no more than so many days' illness this summer: how the vegetation has suffered from the late frosts, pointing out how many of the oranges have been cut off, but that the great magnolia in the centre of the court is safe. You are then invited to see the house, learning by the way the extent and value of the estate you are visiting, and of the 'force' upon it. You admire the lofty, cool rooms, with their green blinds, and the width of the piazzas on both sides the house, built to compensate for the want of shade from trees, which cannot be

allowed near the dwelling for fear of moschetoes. You visit the icehouse, and find it pretty full, the last winter having been a severe one. You learn that, for three or four seasons after this icehouse was built, there was not a spike of ice in the state, and a cargo had to be imported from Massachusetts. . . .
HARRIET MARTINEAU

GEORGE SAND took Chopin to the island of Majorca for his health, accompanied by her two children and a maid.

Palma, Mallorca
14th December 1838

Dear Friend,
You must be thinking me very idle. I too might complain of the scarcity of your letters, if I did not know by this time how business is carried on in this country. You people would never believe it. I laugh when I think of good old Manoël imagining that the post to Paris would only take a week. In the first place you must understand that the principal object of the steam-boat between Palma and Barcelona is the transportation of pigs. The passengers are a secondary consideration. The post does not count at all. What do politics or the arts matter to the Majorcans? The pig is the great, indeed the sole business of their lives. The steam-boat is supposed to run every week, but in reality it only goes when the weather is perfectly fine and the sea as smooth as glass. The slightest breeze makes the captain put back to port even if they are already half-way. Why? Not because they are not capable navigators, but because pigs have delicate digestions; they are afraid of seasickness. Now if a pig should die 'en route', the boat goes into mourning and sends papers, passengers, parcels and letters to the devil.

What is really fine here is the country, the sky, the mountains, Maurice's good health and Solange's *softening*. The good Chopin is not so brilliant in health. He misses his piano dreadfully. We have received news of it to-day at last. It has left Marseilles and we shall perhaps get it in a fortnight. My God! how rough, difficult and miserable sheer physical existence is made here. It is far beyond what anyone could have imagined.

By a stroke of luck I was able to buy some quite decent furniture

from a peasant who did not want it. I had incredible trouble in getting
hold of a saucepan, some firewood, some linen and anything else of
that nature. For quite a month I have been on the point of feeling
that we are really settled down but I never am. In this country a cart
takes three hours to go five miles, so you can judge by that, of the
rest. It takes two months to make a pair of tongs. There is no
exaggeration in what I tell you. You can guess everything else that I have
no time to go into. I laugh at it but I have indeed suffered a little from
fear of seeing my children suffer a great deal. . . .

FLORENCE NIGHTINGALE was twenty-nine when she first went to Egypt with
family friends, who were keen Hellenists. Interest in Egypt had developed
since Napoleon's campaign in 1798, and by 1849 many tourists, collectors
and scholars travelled there. Here she writes to her parents and sister.

                                        November 29th 1849
My Dearest People,
No one ever talks about the beauty of Cairo, ever gives you the least
idea of this surpassing city. I thought it was a place to buy stores at and
pass through on one's way to India, instead of its being the rose of
cities, the garden of the desert, the pearl of Moorish architecture, the
fairest, really the fairest, place of earth below. It reminds me always of
Sirius; I can't tell why, except that Sirius has the silveriest light in
heaven above, and Cairo has the same radiant look on earth below:
and I shall never look at Sirius in future years without thinking of
her. Oh, could I but describe those Moorish streets, in red and white
strips of marble; the latticed balconies, with little octagonal shrines, also
latticed, sticking out of them, for the ladies to look straight down
through; the innumerable mosques and minarets; the arcades in the
insides of houses you peep into, the first stories meeting almost
overhead, and yet the air with nothing but fragrance on it, in these
narrowest of narrow wynds! But there are no words to describe an
Arabian city, no European words at least: for that *one* day yesterday you
would have thought it worth while to make a voyage three times as
long, and ten times as disagreeable, as the one we made, and go back
again content, and well content.
    After threading these streets for miles, we came out upon the square
where stands the magnificent mosque of Sultan Hassan, and above it

the citadel, up which we wound, passing the palaces of Ibrahim Pacha, Nezleh Hanum, the widow of the Defterdar, till we came to the mosque built by Mehemet Ali, and not yet finished, though in it lie his bones. It is of splendid size, but tawdrily ornamented, and looks better now with the scaffolding supporting those lofty domes, than ever it will do when decorated like Drury Lane. The obnoxious female is still admitted. Mehemet Ali's tomb is covered with shawls and carpets. I have heard people express the wish that he had lived to see his mosque finished, so much do people's ideas get corrupted here: and within a stone's throw of his splendid tomb is the court where the Mamelukes died; he counted them at break of day, and when the sun set where were they? He sleeps now close to the murdered chiefs; and people can forget that murder, and laud Mehemet Ali!

Oh, if one could either forget, or believe, that the people here were one's fellow creatures, what a country this would be!

From the terrace of the mosque is what I should imagine the finest view in the whole world. Cairo, which is immense, lies at the feet, a forest of minarets and domes and towers. The Nile flows his solemn course beyond, the waters being still out (it is now high Nile), and the three Pyramids stand sharp against the sky. Here Osiris and his worshippers lived; here Abraham and Moses walked; here Aristotle came; here, later, Mahomet learnt the best of his religion and studied Christianity; here, people, our Saviour's mother brought her little son to open his eyes to the light. They are all gone from the body; but the Nile flows and the Pyramids stand there still.

We rode down again into the city, swarming with life, for the Arab is the busiest person in the world: you cannot imagine how you will get through the streets; you expect to run over every child, and to be run over by every camel, who, gigantic animals! loom round every sharp corner just as you are coming to it, and are the tallest creatures I ever saw: there does not appear standing room for a fly. You address your ass in the tenderest terms, and in the purest Arabic; you adjure him by all the names of friendship to stop: but he understands no Arabic except his driver's, and on he goes, full trot, while you are making hairbreadth 'scapes at every corner, yet receiving hardly a knock. Out of this city of noise and bustle and confusion you pass through the gate, and come, oh change! oh wondrous change! from the city of the living into the city of the dead. I never saw anything so wonderful as this: as far as the eye can reach you see nothing but tombs, and from these streets of tombs, all put on theirs which were white, sailed out of the cabin like a Juno in her majestic indignation, and actually went for the night on board the baggage steamer which followed us. She was the prettiest woman I ever saw, more like a sylph than a Juno, except on that occasion, and sat in her close jacket and trousers, with a sash round her waist, when with us. The women who *stood* the onset, were a bride from the island of Lemnos, a fat ugly woman, who had been married at eleven, and was being brought up by two duennas, rather nice old hags in turbans, to Cairo to her husband. The bride was magnificently dressed, and would have been handsome if she had not looked such an animal and so old. Her duennas always sat on either side of her, like tame elephants, and let her speak to none. She was covered with diamonds and pearls, had one jacket on of blue velvet trimmed with fur over another of yellow silk, &c. Most of the women crouched on the floor all night, and talked the whole time. They were amazingly puzzled by us, and I was asked some fifty times if I were married. This redoubled the difficulty; I could not conceive why one said to me so often, 'But you *did* go to the opera at Alexandria,' and would believe no denial. What we could be going to do in Upper Egypt was another difficulty; and that we should not travel by a caravan. At last we heard them settling in Greek that we were the singing people of the opera at Alexandria; but what could we be going to sing at Dongola for? Another woman was explaining her views on marriage. English, she said, married late, and fifteen *was* late. She never would marry her daughter later than ten or twelve; and when you *began* to think of it, the man ought not to be more than seven. (By the by, we saw a marriage at Alexandria; one horse bore the wedded couple, of six and seven, the lady riding behind her bridegroom.)

LUCIE DUFF GORDON also wrote from Egypt some thirteen years later.

Grand Cairo. Tues. 11 Nov. 1862

Dearest Mutter

Omar took Sally sightseeing all day while I was away, into several mosques; in one he begged her to wait a minute while he said a prayer. They compare notes about their respective countries and are great friends; but he is put out at my not having provided her with a husband long ago, as is one's duty towards a 'female servant,' which almost always here means a slave.

Of all the falsehoods I have heard about the East, that about women
being old hags at thirty is the biggest. Among the poor fellah women it
may be true enough, but not nearly as much as in Germany; and I
have now seen a considerable number of Levantine ladies looking
very handsome, or at least comely, till fifty. Sakna, the Arab Grisi, is
fifty-five – an ugly face, I am told (she was veiled and one only saw
the eyes and glimpses of her mouth when she drank water), but the
figure of a leopard, all grace and beauty, and a splendid voice of its
kind, harsh but thrilling like Malibran's. I guessed her about thirty, or
perhaps thirty-five. When she improvised, the finesse and grace of her
whole *Wesen* were ravishing. I was on the point of shouting out 'Wallah!'
as heartily as the natives. The eight younger Halmeh (*i.e.*, learned
women, which the English call Almeh and think is an improper word)
were ugly and screeched. Sakna was treated with great consideration
and quite as a friend by the Armenian ladies with whom she talked
between her songs. She is a Muslimeh and very rich and charitable;
she gets £50 for a night's singing at least.

It would be very easy to learn colloquial Arabic, as they all speak
with such perfect distinctness that one can follow the sentences and
catch the words one knows as they are repeated. I think I know
forty or fifty words already, besides my 'salaam aleikum' and
'backsheesh.'

The reverse of the brilliant side of the medal is sad enough: deserted
palaces, and crowded hovels scarce good enough for pigstyes. 'One day
man see his dinner, and one other day none at all,' as Omar observes;
and the children are shocking from bad food, dirt and overwork, but the
little pot-bellied, blear-eyed wretches grow up into noble young men
and women under all their difficulties. The faces are all sad and rather
what the Scotch call 'dour,' not *méchant* at all, but harsh, like their
voices. All the melody is in walk and gesture; they are as graceful as
cats, and the women have exactly the 'breasts like pomegranates' of
their poetry. A tall Bedaween woman came up to us in the field
yesterday to shake hands and look at us. She wore a white sackcloth
shift and veil, *und weiter nichts*, and asked Mrs. Hekekian a good
many questions about me, looked at my face and hands, but took no
notice of my rather smart gown which the village women admired
so much, shook hands again with the air of a princess, wished me
health and happiness, and strode off across the graveyard like a
stately ghost. She was on a journey all alone, and somehow it looked
very solemn and affecting to see her walking away towards the desert

in the setting sun like Hagar. All is so Scriptural in the country
here.

LUCIE DUFF GORDON showed great respect for other cultures. When she
was in Luxor, she met a physician whose wisdom she honoured, as she
reveals in this letter to her husband, Sir Alexander Duff Gordon.

Luxor,
April 19, 1867

Dearest Alick,

I have been much amused lately by a new acquaintance, who, in
romances of the last century, would be called an 'Arabian sage.'
Sheykh Abdurrachman lives in a village half a day's journey off, and
came over to visit me and to doctor me according to the science of Galen
and Avicenna. Fancy a tall, thin, graceful man, with a grey beard and
liquid eyes, absorbed in studies of the obsolete kind, a doctor of theology,
law, medicine and astronomy. We spent three days in arguing and
questioning; I consented to swallow a potion or two which he made
up before me, of very innocent materials. My friend is neither a quack
nor superstitious, and two hundred years ago would have been a better
physician than most in Europe. Indeed I would rather swallow his
physic now than that of many a M.D. I found him like all the learned
theologians I have known, extremely liberal and tolerant. You can
conceive nothing more interesting and curious than the conversation
of a man learned and intelligent, and utterly ignorant of all our modern
Western science. If I was pleased with him, he was enchanted with
me, and swore by God that I was a Mufti indeed, and that a man could
nowhere spend time so delightfully as in conversation with me. He said
he had been acquainted with two or three Englishmen who had pleased
him much, but that if all Englishwomen were like me the power must
necessarily be in our hands, for that my *akl* (brain, intellect) was far
above that of the men he had known. He objected to our medicine that
it seemed to consist in palliatives, which he rather scorned, and aimed
always at a radical cure. I told him that if he had studied anatomy he
would know that radical cures were difficult of performance, and he
ended by lamenting his ignorance of English or some European language,
and that he had not learned our *Ilm* (science) also. Then we plunged
into sympathies, mystic numbers, and the occult virtues of stones, etc.,

and I swallowed my mixture (consisting of liquorice, cummin and soda) just as the sun entered a particular house, and the moon was in some favourable aspect. He praised to me his friend, a learned Jew of Cairo. I could have fancied myself listening to Abu Suleyman of Cordova, in the days when we were the barbarians and the Arabs were the learned race. There is something very winning in the gentle, dignified manners of all the men of learning I have seen here, and their homely dress and habits make it still more striking.

ISABELLA BIRD wrote *Letters from the Rocky Mountains* in 1873.

Oct 23
Colorado

I set out upon the prairie alone. It is a dreary ride of thirty miles over the low brown plains to Denver, very little settled, and with trails going in all directions. My sailing orders were 'steer south, and keep to the best-beaten track,' and it seemed like embarking on the ocean without a compass. The rolling brown waves on which you see a horse a mile and a half off impress one strangely, and at noon the sky darkened up for another storm, the mountains swept down in blackness to the Plains, and the higher peaks took on a ghastly grimness horrid to behold. It was first very cold, then very hot, and finally settled down to a fierce east-windy cold, difficult to endure. It was free and breezy, however, and my horse was companionable. Sometimes herds of cattle were browsing on the sun-cured grass, then herds of horses. Occasionally I met a horseman with a rifle lying across his saddle, or a waggon of the ordinary sort, but oftener I saw a waggon with a white tilt, of the kind known as a 'Prairie Schooner,' labouring across the grass, or a train of them, accompanied by herds, mules, and horsemen, bearing emigrants and their household goods in dreary exodus from the Western States to the much-vaunted prairies of Colorado. The host and hostess of one of these waggons invited me to join their mid-day meal, I providing tea (which they had not tasted for four weeks) and they hominy. They had been three months on the journey from Illinois, and their oxen were so lean and weak that they expected to be another month in reaching Wet Mountain Valley. They had buried a child *en route*, had lost several oxen, and were rather out of heart. Owing to their long isolation and the monotony of the march they had lost count

of events, and seemed like people of another planet. They wanted me
to join them, but their rate of travel was too slow, so we parted with
mutual expressions of goodwill, and as their white tilt went 'hull down'
in the distance on the lonely prairie sea, I felt sadder than I often feel
on taking leave of old acquaintances. That night they must have been
nearly frozen, camping out in the deep snow in the fierce wind. I met
afterwards 2000 lean Texan cattle, herded by three wild-looking men
on horseback, followed by two waggons containing women, children,
and rifles. They had travelled 1000 miles. Then I saw two prairie
wolves, like jackals, with gray fur, cowardly creatures, which fled from
me with long leaps.

MARIANNE NORTH (1830–90) was born to a prosperous, intellectual
family. She knew the Director of Kew and met Charles Darwin. She
enjoyed travelling, first with her father in Europe, later on her own, to
make the flower paintings for which she is renowned. They are exhibited
in North Gallery at Kew. She travelled in Brazil and then Australia.
Here she describes a journey to redwood forests behind San Francisco.

1881

We reached the redwood forests all of a sudden, and the railway
followed the Russ river through them up to Guerneville, a pretty wooden
village with a big saw mill, all among the trees, or rather the stumps
of them, from which they have acquired the common name of
Stumptown. The noble trees were fast disappearing. Some of the finest
had been left standing, but they could not live solitary, and a little wind
soon blew them down. They had a peculiar way of shooting up from
the roots round the stumps, which soon became hidden by a dense mass
of greenery, forming natural arbours; and many of the large old trees
were found growing in circles which had begun that way: a habit peculiar
to that tree.

The little inn was capital; and all the gentlemen of the place dined
in their shirt-sleeves, and were much interested in my work. They told
me how to find the biggest trees, but everyone was busy, and not a boy
was willing to act as guide or to carry my easel. There was no difficulty
in finding the trees; only in choosing which to paint, and how to get
far enough away from such big objects as to see the whole of any one
. . . there was an undergrowth of laurel and oak, and many pretty

flowers: pink sorrel, trillium, aquilegia, blue iris, and a deep pink rose. I got back to Oaklands after the supper hour (8 o'clock); but the porter brought me a large plate of crackers and butter, a tumblerful of the most adorable iced mixture, and a straw to suck it through.

KATE MARSDEN (1859–1931) was born to a rural, middle-class family. When the father died, leaving eight children in relative poverty, Kate decided to train as a nurse. This career had only just been opened to women by Florence Nightingale. The hospital where she trained was run by Evangelicals, whose fervour inspired her. She decided to travel to Russia to nurse lepers. She arrived in Moscow in 1890, knowing no Russian. The journey was begun by train, but in Siberia Kate had to hire a local horse-drawn sleigh. She describes her experiences with unusual cheerfulness.

Feb. 1891

The horses dashed off full gallop, rushing through freshly formed snowdrifts. The snow soon found its way into every corner of the sledge, which, although covered at the top, was quite open in front. Then the snow had a way of settling down the collars of our coats, and, when melted by the heat of the body, trickling down the neck; and sometimes it flew up the sleeves unless we were careful to keep them closed at the wrists. Our good substantial boxes were all stowed away in the 'hold'; over them was a layer of straw, and on the straw we sat, or, rather reclined, with pillows at our backs. The word 'reclined' suggests ease and comfort; but when applied to sledge-travelling, under the circumstances that we travelled, it means 'Hobson's choice.' You are compelled to put yourself, or get put into that position; and in that position you must remain. . . .

For six hours all went well, with the normal amount of bumping and jolting. We had, this time, another youthful driver, a rare specimen of 'young Siberia'. As darkness fell it appeared to us that he was getting a little reckless; but we said nothing, attributing his daring exploits to vodka, or to the bitter cold, or to the faulty way of harnessing the horses. Anyhow, as midnight approached, it must be confessed that we became slightly nervous and irritable, having our recent nocturnal adventure vividly before our minds. We had a strong presentiment that something was going to happen. The harness, I must mention, is often responsible for accidents in sledge travelling. . . .

I was thinking of the two outer horses, and speculating how soon the horses' legs would get entangled in the odds and ends of rope that were supposed to help in keeping the horses together, when suddenly the second horse disappeared! The driver gave a lurch forward; the off-horse struggled; there was a bump and a thump against the sledge, and then the other horse also disappeared, and we came to a deadlock. We were both wide-awake in no time and we heard and felt an ominous knocking against the side; and on looking out we found both horses entangled in the ropes and on the ground, struggling frantically to get up.

The driver called 'Nichevo' (It is nothing). But no amount of 'nichevoeing' prevented my feeling uneasy. . . . I got my friend to translate a rather peremptory order to both men; and this woke them up to the fact that they must be doing something besides abusing each other. . . . The soldier quickly stood on one horse's neck, and the driver set the harness free. The other animal was treated in the same way; but the driver was evidently too angry with it to drive it any more; and so he just let it loose and away it trotted, looking such an odd creature in the half snowlight, with the harness dragging all around it. The oddity of the scene made us enjoy a hearty laugh, notwithstanding the discomfort of the occasion. After a little more hard tugging and painful compulsion, the three remaining horses were put, or rather tied, together, and away we started again.

MARY KINGSLEY (1862–1900) proved one of the most sensitive and intellectual of travellers. Yet she had lived uneventfully until the age of thirty, looking after her mother and ineffectual brothers. When she first travelled to West Africa, she immediately responded to the majestic wild forests. Her appreciation of the values of other cultures led to her writing pioneering studies in anthropology. In 1895 she journeyed to Calaban in the French Congo.

1895

On first entering the great grim twilight regions of the forest you hardly see anything but the vast column-like grey tree stems in their countless thousands around you, and the sparsely vegetated ground beneath. But day by day, as you get trained to your surroundings, you see more and more, and a whole world grows up gradually out of the gloom before

your eyes. Snakes, beetles, bats and beasts, people the region that at
first seemed lifeless. . . . There is the same difference also between
night and day in the forest. You may have got fairly used to it by day,
and then some catastrophe keeps you out in it all night, and again you
see another world. To my taste there is nothing so fascinating as
spending a night out in an African forest, or plantation; but I beg you
to note I do not advise any one to follow the practice. Nor indeed do I
recommend African forest life to any one. Unless you are interested
in it and fall under its charm, it is the most awful life in death
imaginable. It is like being shut up in a library whose books you cannot
read, all the while tormented, terrified, and bored. And if you do fall
under its spell, it takes all the colour out of other kinds of living.

The first foreign woman to enter the Forbidden City in Tibet was ALEX-
ANDRA DAVID-NEEL (1868–1969), who had left her husband soon after
her marriage in order to travel. She learned Tibetan and recounted her
adventures to him.

1914

We managed to reach Thana at night. We arranged it even too well
that time, it seems, for we were not able to find our way in the dark
and arrived near a temple where there were a number of watch-dogs,
who barked dreadfully at our approach. Happily, they were well shut in
and could not escape to attack us; but I feared that people would look
out to see who were causing the noise and make certain that they
were not thieves. Furthermore, the passage of mysterious strangers in
the night held the danger of enquiries about us and the risk of being
reported at the station. To avoid this, Yongden [her devoted Tibetan
helper, servant and friend] called aloud to the shrinekeeper, asking
shelter for the night for a tired *arjopa* who had hardly been able to
struggle through the last lap of his journey on account of a bad leg.
My companion's request was full of pathos and loud enough to be
heard all over the temple buildings. During his performance I had
hidden myself out of sight. We were practically convinced that the
shrinekeeper would not get up to receive a beggar at night. We knew
our Thibet and Thibetans well enough to risk the trick, being certain
of its result. When he had waited long enough, Yongden went away,
lamenting aloud: 'Oh, how unkind to leave a poor sick pilgrim out in

the cold! How pitiless!' and so on. His plaintive voice faded gradually away, as at the opera in songs of supposed passers-by behind the scenes. It was rather a pretty effect amidst natural scenery of standing rocks, along a path that led downward to a stream. I nearly applauded.

We had passed the shrine all right. Whoever might have been staying in it would not, on the morrow, give a single thought to the crying beggar of the previous night. But where was the village? In the pitch dark we could not see it and, had we caught sight of houses, we should not have dared to venture in their direction, lest we fall in with dogs of the same species as those who watched over the temple.

Yongden insisted on lying down on the road itself. I preferred to go farther from the temple and find a more comfortable place. Discerning, in the shallow water, some stepping-stones which crossed the stream, I went scouting on the other side, where I discovered two caves. We had a house for the rest of the night! What a blessing! We should sleep as if really at home. I ran to fetch my companion, and we installed ourselves in one of the caves, where we ate our supper with the clear, fresh water of the stream as beverage (cool, perhaps, even too cool), and slept the sound sleep of the tired yet happy Thibetan *neskorpas* [pilgrims].

In the morning, when putting on my upper dress, which I used at night as a blanket, I discovered that I had lost my small compass. This was a most distressing event! First, the compass was useful to me, and, although I had another, I should miss it. But the worst danger was in leaving a foreign object behind us. If it was found, that compass might be talked about all over the country and officials would quickly realize that a foreigner had been staying in that locality. . . .

VITA SACKVILLE-WEST (1892–1962) at first disliked Virginia Woolf's 'Gloomsbury' circle, but the two writers soon found they had a great deal in common. In 1925 her husband, Harold Nicolson was posted by the Foreign Office to the British Legation in Teheran. Vita accompanied him and wrote lively accounts of all she saw to her now beloved friend.

Luxor
29 January 1926

The only way I can deal with Egypt is as Molly MacCarthy did with Christmas: alphabetically. Amon, Americans, alabaster, Arabs;

bromides, buffaloes, beggars, Bronx; camels, crocodiles, colossi,
Cook's; donkeys, dust, dahabeeahs, dragomen, dervishes, desert;
Egyptians, Evian; fezzes, fellaheen, feluccas, flies, fleas; Germans,
goats, granite; hotels, hieroglyphics, hoopoes, Horus, hawkes; Isis, imshi,
irrigation, ignorance; jibbahs; kites, Kinemas, Kodaks; lavatories, lotus,
Levantines; mummies, mud, millionaires; Nubia, Nile; ophthalmia,
Osiris, obsidian, obelisks; palms, pyramids, parrokeets; quarries;
Rameses, ruins; sunsets, sarcophagi, steamers, soux, sand, shadoofs,
stinks, Sphinx; temples, tourists, trams, Tut-ankh-amen; Uganda;
vultures, Virginia; water-bullocks, warts; Xerxes, Xenophon; yaout; zest,
(my own). Having said this, there doesn't seem to be anything else to
say, except that Mr Robert Hichens is living in this hotel and that I met
him today riding a fiery Arab stallion. But indeed, and there is much
more to say, only I can't say it: there is the great untidy desolation of
Karnak, and the mountains-of-the-moon landscape of the Theban
hills, where I am going to build myself a brown mud house and end
my days. And I dined with some super-millionaire Americans, and
found The Common Reader in their sitting room. It gave me a shock.
There was your name sprawling on the table. They had just arrived
from Thibet, where they had dragged forty-seven Innovation trunks
and twenty-five pieces of smaller luggage over the spurs of the Himalaya
on yaks, an animal which hitherto I believed to exist only in Belloc.
The Common Reader had been to Thibet with them, and was
about to engender copies of all your other works. As they didn't and
still don't know that I knew you, this was a perfectly unsolicited
testimonial.

What else? I miss you horribly, and apart from that am permanently
infuriated by the thought of what you could make of this country if
only you could be got here. You see, you ought to. However, that
sounds too much like your own parody of my probable letters, so I'll
refrain from saying it.

What fills me with dismay is the idea that I cannot hear from you
till I get to Bombay, another fortnight at least. I wish I had given you
an address at Cairo. You may be ill or anything. It is an odd sensation
being so cut-off. And even the clock different. We kept dropping
half-hours at sea. What becomes of those poor waifs of one's existence
over which one has skipped? Mine are flotsam and jetsam now
somewhere on the Adriatic.

Do thin silk clothes and sunburn make you envious? No, you wretch,
you prefer your old misty Gloomsbury and your London squares.

The wish to steal Virginia overcomes me, – steal her, take her away,
and put her in the sun among the objects mentioned alphabetically above.
Damn that you're not here.
Your
V.

DAME FREYA STARK was born in 1893 and educated in London. She
decided she must travel and undertook many courageous expeditions on
her own. She fell in love with Syria, then stayed in Lebanon to learn
Arabic. Her six volumes of letters reveal her sense of place, her empathy
for other peoples. Her mother, Flora, she addressed as 'B'.

> Brumana,
> Lebanon
> 1 January 1928

Darling B.,
A Happy New Year to you! I was so pleased to get your letter when
home from Beirut last night. It is an hour's hairpins, quite amusing
with everyone jumbled into the cars: reminiscent of Mortola.

I had enough Arabic not to lunch in the hotel but found a ragout,
sweet, and coffee for five francs (French) cooked for me over a primus
stove in a lowdown little place without tablecloths. The gramophone
was set going for my amusement.

But this is a sad people. Neither Arab nor European. They could
not stand independently of Europe against the Moslems of the interior.
And if they hang on to Europe they are made the tool of every disgusting
politician. I believe there is nothing they can strive for with any hope
of success. They are a fine-looking people, too, magnificently built
men, and women with eyes like stars. And hardy they must be, or
they would all be dead. It seems a waste.

I think in April I shall get Venetia to join with a mule and walk
among the Druses. They are quite distinct; live in separate villages or
quarters of village, and wear white head-gear – the women not allowed
to show their hair.

They are all Christian here – about six different sorts. The Druses
come in from the hills, undistinguishable except by a white wrap round
their heads, and a fiercer look about them. I am trying to induce Venetia
to agree that our tramp should be through their country (quite safe, I

think, if we have a Druse guide and if only I can speak a little).
Meanwhile I shall do no sightseeing but work and save up. I live here
on 8s. 6d. a day including everything except postage stamps (my lessons
are included).

Oh, my dear, you can hardly imagine what a joy it is to be free all
day long to do my own work; this alone was worth travelling across the
world for. I sit in my little room and feel as if I were Queen of the
Universe, and the fact that I have to get up and do exercises every
half-hour to keep the circulation going makes no difference.

I have been received with great friendliness and the village is doing
its best to teach me – only too pleased to find someone who has come
neither to improve nor to rob, but with a genuine liking for their
language.

You will be amused at my Christmas Day. A Maronite mass at 8.30,
the ceremonial like the Latin, only set to the *wildest* Arab music, with
a fast fierce gaiety about it that made the oddest contrast with all
memories of masses I have ever heard.

Then our Quaker meeting, where we sing Syrian hymns to the tune
of 'God Save the King', and rows of scholars from the Quaker school
– Turks and Armenians side by side, Iraqis, Syrians, Greeks, Egyptians
– listen politely while someone tells them that the world is really one
harmonious family. This conglomeration of scholars is due to the motor
car, and I am wondering whether Mr. Ford has not done something
for the peace of the world after all.

Your loving

FREYA

The following letter was to Olivia Barker.

Brumana
1 January 1928

My dearest Olivia,
The very happiest of New Years to you and Ernest. What am I to begin
about now? I think I shall just tell you my good day in the country last
Thursday. Such a good day it was, and I thought of you, and W.P.,
and many many happy things, walking along under the Lebanon pines,
which looked for all the world like a gentleman's park, or perhaps like
the less cultivated corners of the Garden of Eden with the wild outer
world arranged as a background.

You should have seen the agitated circle of kind Syrians at Mlle.

Audi's tea party the day before, begging me not to go. Finally a
much-worried youth told me he would take his gun (for crows, not
Druses) and see me as far as the bridge in the valley.

It was very like Villatella country zigzagging down among myrtle,
pine, and oleander and an incredible variety of thorns. A good
well-marked track, stonier than anything in Italy, however. And, of
course, a mule harnessed with beads (blue, against the evil eye) and
cockleshells, and a driver in red sash and turban are more interesting
than our sober people.

When I left my guide I began climbing the other side in the shadow.
These valleys are so deep, the sun never gets at them I believe; you look
up and see a rim of sunny villages about 2,000 feet over your head,
and you walk in what looks like absolute solitude until the voices of
woodcutters shouting out to each other the news of one solitary female
wanderer make you feel painfully conspicuous – the sort of feeling
I remember in the war when being suddenly focused by a
searchlight.

When the track divided I was stymied, of course, and sat down to
consider; then Providence provided a young man, who afterwards told
me he had run over a half a mile to see my interesting person at close
quarters. He took me along through delicious woodland, his French
and my Arabic being equally bad – till we finally came to his village
and I had to be explained to the assembled relatives. I was invited into
the house, and sat on a long divan admiring the beautiful clean
whitewash and mats, and trying to answer questions about my clothes.
The sister sat beside me with her arm round my neck, and the mother
brought out their new dresses to show me. We then drank coffee,
and I was asked to stay a month, or ten months, or a year, or at least
a day; and finally I left with many kind words which I could not
understand. My language does not yet run to sentences, and I get
hopelessly tied up over the fifteen different ways of saying 'good-bye'
and 'thank you'.

After this adventure I found my way easily and got to the village (all
Druse) by lunch time, and was given a second lunch at the mission,
which is perched in an old Druse castle with all the hills of Lebanon
round it. Two Syrian boys accompanied me home, giving me scraps of
Arab poetry or playing on their reed pipes, joined with wax just as
Theocritus has it, and filling the wood with the wild sad sound as we
walked along.

I was home by four, and had not walked over six hours actually, but

it is hard walking for I must have been up and down over 10,000 feet, much of it like stairways. My heart went like a hammer all night.
Your
FREYA

In the 1930s the Irish writer KATE O'BRIEN revisited northern Spain, which she loved, having worked as a governess in Bilbao in 1922.

I have a soft spot for Bilbao, the Basque capital, but it's still nineteenth century, divided between the Carlists, who fought to have the brother of the Queen on the throne and the 'cristinos' who supported the Queen mother when Isabel was only three. They ostracize each other even today. Even more depressing is the misery of a typical Castilian village. It is a rubbish dump with a dog asleep on it. The village idiot, a cripple girl, a baby with ringworm, the other village idiot; they are unbearably sad places, if you carry a heart and not a blue book in your breast.

But in the slightly richer towns, I bristle at the signs of modernity: the Spanish girls in the paseo are dressed to kill, painted and waved, chattering and giggling; linked together in fives and sixes, they seem insipid. There are too many peroxide blondes in imitation of Hollywood sex goddesses. No race of women that I know of takes these matters of beauty culture with such unfortunate seriousness as does the Spanish. And the modest provincial hotels, which were gloriously unimproved when I stayed here before, have gone *moderno* with garish strip-lighting, a radio as big as a bathing hut & paintings of Sevillian ladies.

Kate O'Brien swings from the personal to the social reflection in one sentence, and each paragraph. This is a quality in one of the first women travel-writers on Spain, MADAME D'AULNOY. She published a book in 1691, which became a bestseller, using letters from her mother, who had fled to Madrid to avoid criminal prosecution.

Idleness breeds dissipation, even youths of quality begin at the age of 12 or 13 years to entertain a concubine. Syphilis is so common that it is taken for granted. Their children bring it into the world from their mother's womb or suck it from the nurse; a virgin may be justly suspected to have it; and they are hardly persuaded to be cured of it, they are so certain of falling again into the same condition. . . . At court, and amongst the women of the highest quality, they discourse of it as they do of a fever or the megrim.

A letter from a friend, the critic VALERIE GROSVENOR MYER, in Sierra Leone.

Freetown, 7 November 1991

Dear Olga,

Sierra Leone is brilliant green – Graham Greene: rust, rot, dilapidation. Wonderful wild flowers, tiny birds, scarlet, iridescent, blue-green, yellow. Vultures wheel high or sit hunched. Villagers who cook on fires of sticks between stones shake me by the hand. Everybody greets everybody else: 'Mawnin oh, aw debahdy?' This means 'Good morning, how's the body?' Only 40% of the children here go to school. Others sell sweets, batteries, medicines, anything they can get, from head-balanced baskets in the streets. Market women, in tie-dyed flounced dresses, babies at their backs, walk stately under their baskets, gently soliciting custom. 'I done buy 'em' one says tactfully. Prices are not always cheaper than in the air-conditioned Lebanese supermarket. . . . No driving tests nor MOTs here. Roads full of dangerous potholes. If you have an accident, you might get shovelled off the road. There isn't much public transport, as petrol has to be imported, and costs too much. President has just paid £250,000 for a private jet to a conference, yet people on the edge of starvation. Lacking a water supply, they use a waterfall nearby as public bath house. We had 2 hours of electricity today, the first for weeks, which produced the rare benison of hot water. Our drinking water has to be filtered *and* boiled. Ritual cannibalism is said to occur at elections, to ensure success. Young boys and pregnant girls preferred. This is denied, but when President Samuel Doe of Liberia was killed slowly, a video was made, which is now a bestseller in Freetown. His head was shaved with broken bottles, his toenails torn out, his penis cut off. His naked body was dragged round town like Hector's behind a Mercedes, a variant of Achilles' chariot.

PART FIVE

Surviving into one's fifties – Illness – Widowhood – Old age –
Confronting death

Before the end of the nineteenth century, few people lived beyond middle age, unless they were particularly strong, or wellfed. Ageing even if desired could be as frightening as today, bringing dependence on others, illness and physical decline.

Men who became widowers might be comforted with the image of the virile patriarch who remarried and produced more children, like Victor Hugo or Longfellow. Elderly males enjoyed status for their 'wisdom'. Women seldom lived as long as men because of the hazards of childbirth.

Even when they grow old in the West, they cannot expect the position of power of some Chinese or Japanese mothers-in-law. Here in the West, the adjectives 'young and beautiful' are coupled as frequently as 'old and ugly', making most women anxious about the time when they will be barren, financially constrained, even ridiculed by society. To redress the balance, I include two letters about women who fought social limitations for a brief time – by murder: Mary Queen of Scots and Madame de Brinvilliers.

The Church and moral tracts advised women over forty to behave and dress 'for the autumn of age'; Charlotte Brontë felt old at thirty! If widowed, few were expected to remarry, although the proportion of widows to widowers increased during the last century. Attitudes to widowhood varied widely as we see in the letters of Madame de Staël, Isabel Burton and Millicent Fawcett. The present situation, in which the majority of the aged are female, is very recent. Letters of women in the past, who have bravely faced illness and widowhood, are even more relevant now that our life expectancy has risen spectacularly.

Older women were allowed three main roles: grandmothering, philanthropy and religion. The model grandmother was to continue the selfless caring of the mother; society ignored the many mothers who lost their children in infancy, or remained childless. Those who were fortunate, such as George Sand and Queen Victoria, express real joy in their grandchildren.

Facing death is perhaps more terrifying today with our loss of belief in paradise, substituted by worship of quality of life on earth. These letters offer advice and comfort, while reminding us that 'there is no happiness without alloy' in the words of Lady Mary Wortley Montagu, the great eighteenth-century letter writer.

SURVIVING INTO ONE'S FIFTIES

From the Middle Ages until this century women in their fifties were relegated to unpaid grandchild-minding, too often reviled as nags or hags. Only recently have the media shown women as distinct as Toni Morrison, Jane Fonda and Simone Weill displaying elegance, ability and health after the menopause. To the end of the nineteenth century (and in much of the Third World today) life expectancy for fecund mothers was the low thirties. Fortunately for us, 'middle age' is now the fifties, extending the decades of physical capacity. Yet our culture still expects women to feel bereft when their offspring leave home, despite a survey in the *Guardian* stating that most enjoy renewed vigour and outside interests after the 'change'.

There is little research into the history of old age, even less into late middle age. Literature, dominated in the past by men, offered mainly deleterious images, from the Wife of Bath to Mrs Malaprop, a persecuted Woman in White, etc. Whatever course they chose might be ridiculed, either wishing to continue an active life or seeking comfort in religion. Even women novelists have not given us helpful role models, mainly the saintly, such as Mrs Ramsay in Virginia Woolf's *To the Lighthouse,* or the busybody, such as Mrs Norris in Jane Austen's *Mansfield Park.* Since the 1960s feminist novelists have rectified this, from Fay Weldon to Alison Lurie. Lurie's heroine Vinnie in the recent *Foreign Affairs,* in her fifties and unattractive, is given a passionate affair. The continuing ability of women to respond sexually is now stressed by feminists, overthrowing the ignorance of many cultures. My own father, a doctor, maintained that after the menopause women were 'extinct sexually'.

Until the Second World War medical textbooks, written by men, decreed that women suffer both physically from flushes and vaginitis and emotionally from depression, even hysteria. Neither I nor my friends have undergone any of these, though my stepmother and mother did.

These letters suggest that cultural conditioning, relegation to under-employment and scorn were more probable causes of distress.

In most cultures the 'natural' sphere of women has been hard work, while rearing children. Older women were expected to continue these functions from spinster aunts to the *babcia* (the grandmother), without whom many Slav families might not have survived emotionally. Society conveniently forgot the high mortality rate, which meant that many grand-mothers might face the pain of witnessing the deaths of daughters and even grandchildren. If sons left their community, forced to find work elsewhere, their mothers might never see them (or probable grand-children) again, due to distance, illiteracy and poverty.

Those who gained expertise in areas such as herbal medicine and midwifery could find themselves accused of witchcraft; more women were killed as witches in northern Europe than died at the hands of the Inquisition in the Renaissance. Gardening, child-minding, philanthropy and enforced inactivity horribly resemble openings for the middle aged today, but there are also study and sport, even paid work, slowly trans-forming societal stereotypes. The letters in this section reveal a wide range of attitudes, from Vera Brittain sharing her ideas to an impover-ished Irish mother of four feeling liberated after finally leaving her violent husband. As there is too little research on this decade, I asked friends to contribute ideas.

Those few women who analysed the ageing process in the nineteenth century lamented it: 'That careworn face, from which every soft line is blotted, those faded eyes, from which lonely tears have driven the flashes of fancy – at only forty years!' stressed Margaret Fuller in 1845 in her *Woman in the Nineteenth Century*. The courtesan Lola Montez recom-mended a reliable black hair dye for greying hair, but inveighed against 'paint and powder'. Too many pressurized women into supporting con-ventional male values: 'Women are not unhappy in growing old, except when they misunderstand their twofold role as mother, then grand-mother. Society at present, shaken to its very foundations, can only be re-established by means of the family, and the family cannot attain true elevation except by maternal influence,' wrote Louis Aimé-Martin, a professor at the Sorbonne in 1834.

Working-class women suffered most, movingly described by Mrs Gas-kell in her outstanding novels; Flora Tristan, in 1840 in Nîmes, was appalled to see a washerwoman, labouring in foul water, looking 'more like a slug and seventy, rather than fifty-one, with a daughter of nineteen, pale and weak' (*Le tour de France, journal inédit*).

The amazing resilience of some fifty-year-olds is testified in the diaries of various ordinary women, including the American Eleanor Knowlton, separated from her drunken husband, supporting her fourth child, born when she was in her forties. In 1883 she commented: 'I went to help a lady for a little while one day. She gave me one dollar. I commenced to repare my house and worked every day I could for a dollar and a half until 21 June. Then I went to take care of a lady in confinement. I got a good price and Olive's board. Came home 26 July. Home fully repared, all paid for' (*California Historical Society*).

VERA BRITTAIN, author of many books including *Testament of Youth*, to her daughter Shirley Williams, one of the founder members of the Social Democrat Party, who might have become an excellent Prime Minister.

1953

My dear daughter,
I owe you much gratitude for the title you were resourceful enough to suggest. You were right to propose *Lady into Woman*, a form of words which implies that the democratic movement described in this book has not been concerned exclusively with sex equality. Not only has the sheltered 'lady' of the Victorian epoch become the self-sufficient 'woman' of today; the political and social changes of the past half-century have brought her close in experience and understanding to the millions of women in all past ages who were never sheltered and always had to work . . .
When you were growing up you sometimes suggested, as you had every right to do, that certain aspects of your upbringing might have been better. But you have had three advantages: First the Chelsea Babies Club, which enabled you to show that the physical inferiority of women was a myth.
Second you have been free from the implanted sense of inferiority which handicaps so many women by undermining the self-confidence which is the basis of all achievement. You were desired as a *daughter*.
Third you belong to a household in which a woman's work with professional standards has been constantly in progress, though interrupted.
I could have written much better if interrupted much less, and should have proved altogether a more effective person if I had not been obliged – and not only in my youth – to spend time and energy in learning to believe in myself and my purposes, despite the enervating effects of an

Edwardian childhood. That you, who have been spared that particular battle, will live to see women ascend to heights of achievement hitherto undreamed of and make your own contribution to this future stage of a great revolution, is the constant and joyful hope of Your Mother

This Irish mother was one of ten children. Orphaned young, she went into service and married a man who took to drink. They had four daughters.

August 1978

Dear Kate,
Re our telephone conversation, I have 3 points to make. 1. I regret having married your father, but, having done so and being ever an optimist, always think things will be better tomorrow – they never were and by then it was too late to do anything about it and nowhere to go and no one to help. My second regret is not having had four kids, but having spoiled them so they grew up to be wayward, to go their own way, regardless of the pain or suffering they caused to the only person who cared – their mother. 3rd regret is that after 20 years of misery & hard work – no drip-dry clothes, washing machines, hoovers etc in those days; after 20 years of despair and worry with no light at the end of the tunnel, I took to the bottle, a degrading and shameful experience . . . The bottle, mental hospital or suicide, that's how low I was. For anything I may have said or done in drink that was offensive, I Sincerely Apologise. I've given up booze now and feel better for it.

December 1978

Dear Kate,
You said every child needs both parents. Don't you think every mother knows that; years you've been telling me to leave him and now you tell me what I already know . . . I've filed for a divorce, and rented a small room. A small electric cooker, a tiny washbasin. If I had visitors they were to be orderly and out by 11 pm. I stood there feeling like a little waif, spoken to like a child by people only as old as my own children. So there was me thinking this is what it comes to – I've brought up four kids, built up a home, worked hard all my life, to end up here. If only we could be hard, that would solve some problems . . .

(She started a new life, and the daughter felt released from guilt.)

This letter is from Anita, a teacher of yoga, still beautiful at fifty-six.

6 December 1993

Dear John,

Thanks for teaching meditation at my last yoga class. You asked me to tell you how women feel in their fifties. I hate writing letters, but as it's important men should understand more about women, I'll try. I suffered very little from the menopause, but a great deal when the two children left home. We live in an isolated farm house, and my husband wanted them to go to boarding school. For a time I felt bereft. But you've got to let them go, stop being trapped in hurts. For me the fifties have been positive, far fewer family duties, time to develop other parts of myself.

I told you that when I had asthma badly I took up yoga. Sometimes it's awful things which lead to new discoveries. I was gradually cured, so decided to teach it. Yoga classes have brought me into touch with a range of people, some of whom have become friends, like you. It's a creative physical activity, so for me the fifties are a most creative time, a new beginning – if you are lucky enough to have the strength, and be in a country where women are allowed to develop new interests.

Now my son is in a caring profession, my daughter in business, so we have a lot to talk about and share when we are together. Tomorrow I'm going to my son in hospital (he's had a slight accident), then on to a week's course in London. It's for doctors and mystics, like me. It's on 'How to use Energy', and includes hormonal balance in women, nutrition for M.E. I want to find out about the most recent thinking on these areas. I've started healing, by Reike, a Japanese way of working through the body, by touch. To heal, I need up-to-date information. Yoga is learning from yourself, listening to your body. Doctors are looking at us more holistically now, I'm keen to attend, though I can only afford a course like this once a year.

Yours, Anita.

Sophie was widowed young. Her husband died of a heart attack when she was five months pregnant with their only child. She looks back on

her relationship with her daughter from the vantage point of her fifties.
To her friend Janice:

8 November 1994
You asked me how I feel now Marina has gone to university. At times
lonely, as I'm the only person in the house at night; but since I've at last
found a full-time job, and it's almost too demanding, part of me is glad
not to have to talk, or cook or iron, when I get home.

Self-pity is easy to fall into, and you have to fight hard to avoid it.
Avoid it you must, not because it's undignified (and led to illness in
my mother) but simply because other people don't like it. It makes
them feel uncomfortable, and you will not survive in their company if
you give way to it. A useful lesson, and one that makes you tough.
However, 21 years later, I STILL hate shopping on a Saturday, because
that's when you see husbands and wives together, and the sight of them
sharing the small recurrent pleasures of everyday life produces a sense
of solitude, absent during the working week. It's a reminder that a
single woman, even at the end of the twentieth century, is an outsider
in society, something uncomprehended, to be folded up and put away
when not wanted.

This sense of the thinness of the crust on which we tread is balanced
by the warmth of real friends, and by the availability of the multifarious
interests, even for those of us with little money – music, fringe theatre,
the pursuit of knowledge in any direction. If you are not too tired.
From our sticky start, Marina and I lurched uneasily along, myself
having no heart for the business, as I'd only wanted a child for my
husband's sake. But I was determined to do the right thing; when I
realised I was coping inadequately, I took myself to the Child Guidance
Clinic. A crisp interview of 15 minutes was all I got; after all, I was a
middle-aged, middle-class mum, so many out there with worse problems.
Miraculously, those few unsentimental words, about the child missing
her unseen father, so I must be gentler, were all I needed.

The only child of a single parent, especially an unhappy, intelligent
and forceful single parent, is in danger of being swamped. Hard as I
tried, my daughter, now nearly 19, tells me she had to fight unceasingly
to retain her individuality. She recognises I did not shrink the difficult
bits, even the embarrassing facts of life. I tried to comfort and explain,
yet never came near to being a perfect mother; nor will she be that
impossible creature, though perhaps nearer?

While she laughs at my enthusiasms, and can't share my passion for

the theatre or chamber music, I think she's quite proud that my many
activities give me so much to talk to her about. She may even find some
of my experiences useful in assessing the difficult world the young live
in. I, in return, feel proud of this individual who does credit to all who
have an input, from her father's genes (his rationality and energy) to
friends and relations who taught her to feel warmth and sympathy (tho'
she sometimes disguises this quite well!) I hope, more than for
anything else, that she will achieve as much stability and happiness in
her future life as can be UNreasonably expected.

Pain and suffering are inevitable, the lucky cultivate stoicism,
knowing that disappointment is the eventual lot of most of us. A sense
of perspective helps: how can my situation compare to friends whose
children will never grow up to lead a normal life, or those who are
trying to survive civil wars and hunger? Identification with the rest of
humanity has helped my friendships too – they have deepened at
times of crisis, as I believe ours has. Anyway, it's a comfort to me, so
thanks and love,
Sophie.

Ruth has been a good friend of mine for thirty years. She is unique, not
only content with her lot, but still in love with her husband.

Stratford, 3 April 1995

Dear Olga,
You asked me to write to you about my experience of the menopause
and the post menopausal years. I was extremely fortunate in being
free of the usual physical discomforts and complaints which often
accompany the menopause. I also did not feel any regret that I could
not have any more children. As we had three, which we both wanted,
two girls and a boy, we were content. I might have felt some regret if
they had all been of the same sex?

This has been a time not of any regret, but of freedom and release.
It was good to be free of the discomfort and inconvenience of periods
and also to be free of the fear of unwanted pregnancies. When the
children began to leave the nest, I did not feel as some women do
that I had lost a role. Fortunately they did not all leave at the same
time, it was gradual. I did wonder whether I should return to teaching.
A daunting thought after such a long gap. The decision was made for

me as my mother died and my ninety-year-old father came to live
with us. He was very deaf, nearly blind and losing his memory. But we
did not want him to go into a home. During the six years he was with
us I was really tied to the house and my life was very limited. However
my husband, unusually co-operative, allowed me to employ carers to
look after him so that we could sometimes take holidays and have
evenings out together. He let me persuade him to come to language
classes with me. First we learned Spanish, then modern Greek, now
Russian, so that our holidays have always proved extremely interesting.

   That period of restriction made me appreciate, more than I otherwise
would have done, the freedom I have enjoyed since, able to travel to see
our grandchildren, often going to the theatre, etc.
Love to you,
Ruth

                                                              April 1995
Dear Reader,
Thank you for reading this far. I'm addressing you, like eighteenth-
and nineteenth-century novelists (and post-modernists) to offer you my
reactions to the post-menopausal fifties; and being an elderly parent,
because so little has been written on these topics.

   Though I never suffered from pre-menstrual tension, in my forties
I developed menorrhagia (excess), which left me weak each month from
loss of blood. The menopause was a real relief, with scarcely a flush.
The joy of no longer worrying each month whether I'd have to avoid
strenuous effort, even driving to work or taking the boys swimming. At
last I could pay less attention to my body, and I began a new activity:
writing. Five books in five years, I'd stored up so much to say.

   My two older boys took some time to leave home, like so many in
periods of recession. If they left, they came back whenever money or
jobs ended; for a time the house was even fuller, with live-in girlfriends.
To my amazement, I felt no jealousy of their sexual activity, rather relief
that my own stormy marriage had not undermined their ability to relate.

   When they finally left with their partners to live in their own tiny
flats, the peace (from Capital Radio) was bliss. My third is still at home,
a boy of nineteen, slightly 'special needs'. He does not seem too
ashamed of his elderly parents, he has made us into friends, since his
peers seldom appreciate his affectionate sensitivity, in view of his lack

of macho articulation. I'm torn between the desire to develop his talents, at word-processing, cooking, music, and leading my own life, studying Buddhism. I'm lucky to have a child who still needs me (sometimes) and an overwhelming interest, to deepen my knowledge of the Buddhist spiritual path. Despite back pain and poor eyesight, modern medicine has gives me a second chance. I hope it does as much for you.
With best wishes,
Olga

ILLNESS

This section contains some dignified examples of female endurance. Open-minded Lady Mary Wortley Montagu discovers vaccination. Fanny Burney, a lively novelist, though a shy woman, devoted her life to others. First her demanding father, then Queen Charlotte, as Lady-in-Waiting for five years; then her husband, French émigré General d'Arblay, with whom she went to France; and finally her none-too-easy son Alex. Queen Victoria, on the contrary, decides to put herself first in order to achieve comfort. Camille Claudel, a beautiful, gifted sculptress, fell in love with Rodin. He relegated her to an asylum, yet her moving protests at her fate reveal a balanced mind.

LADY MARY WORTLEY MONTAGU was impressed by the technique used in Turkey to control smallpox, and attempted to introduce it to Britain.

Adrianople, 1 April 1716

Dear S

A propos of distempers, I am going to tell you a thing that will make you wish yourself here. The small-pox, so fatal, and so general amongst us, is here entirely harmless by the invention of *ingrafting*, which is the term they give it. There is a set of old women who make it their business to perform the operation every autumn, in the month of September, when the great heat is abated. People send to one another to know if any of their family has a mind to have the small-pox: they make parties for this purpose, and when they are met (commonly fifteen or sixteen together), the old woman comes with a nut-shell full of the matter of the best sort of small-pox, and asks what vein you please to have opened. She immediately rips open that you offer to her with a large needle (which gives you no more pain than a common scratch), and puts into the vein as much matter as can lie upon the head of her needle, and after that binds up the little wound with a hollow bit of shell;

and in this manner opens four or five veins. The Grecians have commonly the superstition of opening one in the middle of the forehead, one in each arm, and one on the breast, to mark the sign of the cross; but this has a very ill effect, all these wounds leaving little scars, and is not done by those that are not superstitious, who choose to have them in the legs, or that part of the arm that is concealed. The children or young patients play together all the rest of the day, and are in perfect health to the eighth. Then the fever begins to seize them, and they keep their beds two days, very seldom three. They have very rarely above twenty or thirty in their faces, which never mark; and in eight days' time they are as well as before their illness. Where they are wounded, there remain running sores during the distemper, which I don't doubt is a great relief to it. Every year thousands undergo this operation; and the French ambassador says pleasantly, that they take the small-pox here by way of diversion, as they take the waters in other countries. There is no example of any one that has died in it; and you may believe I am well satisfied of the safety of this experiment, since I intend to try it on my dear little son.

I am patriot enough to take pains to bring this useful invention into fashion in England; and I should not fail to write to some of our doctors very particularly about it, if I knew any one of them that I thought had virtue enough to destroy such a considerable branch of their revenue for the good of mankind. But that distemper is too beneficial to them, not to expose to all their resentment the hardy wight [person] that should undertake to put an end to it. Perhaps, if I live to return, I may, however, have courage to war with them. Upon this occasion admire the heroism in the heart of your friend, etc, etc.

FANNY BURNEY faced illness with sense and courage. By 1823 she had suffered three 'seizures', possibly slight heart attacks. She describes the pain, and her method of dealing with weakness.

August 1823

I was seized with a giddiness, a glare of sparks before my eyes, and a torturing pain on one side of my head, that nearly disabled me from quitting my posture, and that was followed, when at last I rose, by an inability to stand or walk.

My second threat of seizure was at Eliot Vale, while Alex was at

Tunbridge. I have been suddenly taken a third time, in the middle of the night, with a seizure as if a hundred windmills were turning round in my head: in short, – I had now recourse to serious medical help, and, to come to the sum total, I am now so much better that I believe myself to be merely in the common road of such gentle, gradual decay as, I humbly trust, I have been prepared to meet with highest hope, though with deepest awe – for now many years back.

The chief changes, or reforms, from which I reap benefit are, 1st. Totally renouncing for the evenings all revision or indulgence in poring over those letters and papers whose contents come nearest to my heart, and work upon its bleeding regrets. Next, transferring to the evening, as far as is in my power, all of sociality, with Alex, or my few remaining friends, or the few he will present to me of new ones. 3rd. Constantly going out every day – either in brisk walks in the morning, or in brisk jumbles in the carriage of one of my three friends who send for me, to a tête-à-tête tea-converse. 4th. Strict attention to diet. . . .

I ought to have told you the medical sentence upon which I act. These were the words – 'You have a head over-worked, and a heart over-loaded.' This produces a disposition to fulness in both that causes stagnation, etc., with a consequent want of circulation at the extremities, that keeps them cold and aching. Knowing this, I now act upon it as warily as I am able.

The worst of all is, that I have lost, totally lost, my pleasure in reading! except when Alex [her son] is my lecturer, for whose sake my faculties are still alive to what – erst! gave them their greatest delight. But alone; I have no longer that resource! I have scarcely looked over a single sentence, but some word of it brings to my mind some mournful recollection, or acute regret, and takes from one all attention – my eyes thence glance vainly over pages that awaken no ideas. – This is melancholy in the extreme; yet I have tried every species of writing and writer – but all pass by me mechanically, instead of instructing or entertaining me intellectually. But for this sad deprivation of my original taste, my evenings might always be pleasing and reviving – but alas! . . .

CAMILLE CLAUDEL was a gifted sculptress, sister of the celebrated French poet Paul Claudel, who discussed many Christian dilemmas in his works. Camille fell in love with the sculptor Auguste Rodin and became his mistress. Rodin had many models and mistresses, and Camille suffered because of this. When she fell ill, Claudel and Rodin together put her into an asylum, where she spent the last *thirty-one* years of her life. Her pleas to be let out sound sane and reasonable.

Dear Brother,
Today, March 3rd 1920, is the seventh anniversary of my removal to this asylum. For seven years I've had to live among strangers. I've suffered the punishment of being with lunatics.

Having worked for most of my life, these years should have been of value! Rodin does not understand that, when he is dead, I shall take my place as an artist and become more successful than him. I'm sending you this drawing of myself, hobbling along wearing a threadbare old cloak and an old hat which comes over my nose. A mad old aunt of 55, that's how I shall appear in years to come.

How I long to be home again. I dream that from my poor studio all my sad pieces of furniture are being taken away and used by other people. My poor little household! How I wish I were there now. Above all I'd be warm, private and alone. Paul, it's really foolish of you to pay for me to live in such an asylum. My room is almost bare, no eiderdown, no slop pail, a revolting cracked chamber pot, a wretched iron bedstead which creaks all night and keeps me awake. I don't think you have any idea how dreadful this place is. The dining room is draughty, with small tables squeezed against each other. We all suffer from dysentery, the soup is vegetable water, the coffee is made from chick peas. And for all this you pay twenty francs a day. It is you who are mad.

Paul, Why must I continue here? How I long to be at home again. But sadly I don't believe I shall leave here. . . .
Your sister, Camille.

Not all the letter-writers I've studied faced illness with equal fortitude. The aged, crotchety QUEEN VICTORIA, a relentless correspondent, averaged about six letters a day, reflecting her changing, egocentric moods in her effusions. She had no intention of losing the comfort of the proximity of her personal physician, Sir James Reid, when he became engaged. Here she asserts her regal authority in insisting that when he marries her lady-in-waiting, he and his wife should continue to live at Court.

If I had been younger I would have let him go rather – but at my age it would be hazardous and disagreeable and so he remains living in my House wherever we are!! and she quite consents to it. But it is too tiresome and I can't conceal my annoyance. I have never said a word to her yet.

(Though she has been derided as foolish, even unintelligent, few people emerge more alive from their letters – of which I recommend the many volumes . . .)

WIDOWHOOD

Widowhood often meant being left financially and socially bereft. We read the sympathetic commiseration of Queens Elizabeth and Victoria for women they respected. I chose contrasting letters of two nineteenth-century women: Isabel Burton loved her husband the explorer and orientalist Richard Burton and was horrified to discover the extent of his collection of erotic Eastern writings. Millicent Fawcett, the feminist, had been fortunate in finding a husband who shared many of her aims and ideas. She considers 'what we should all feel, who have been privileged to live in constant companionship with an exceptionally noble nature from which we are now removed, is not how wretched we are to have lost them, but how blessed we are to have had them to light up our lives by their beautiful example'.

Muslim culture is represented by Mariama Ba's *So Long a Letter* (1982).

QUEEN ELIZABETH I could show kindness and compassion. Here she writes to Lady Hoby whose husband went as ambassador to France on 4 April 1566 and on 13 July died in Paris. His wife, heavily pregnant, brought his body back to England. She christened the child Posthumus. Compare this with Queen Victoria's letter on next page.

Madam
Although we heare that since the death of your husband, our late Ambassador, Sr Thomas Hoby, you have received, in France, great and comfortable courtesyes from the French King, the Queen Mother, the Queen of Navarre and sundry others, yet we made accompt that all these layd together cannot so satisfye you as some testimony and sparke of our favour, with the application of the late service of your Husband, and of your own demeanour there: wherefore though you shall receive it somewhat lately in time, yet we assure you the same proceedeth only of

the late knowledge of your return. And therefore we let you know that the service of your Husband was to us so acceptable, as next yourself and your children we have not the meanest loss of so able a Servant in that calling. And yet since it hath so pleased God to call him in the entry of this our Service, we take it in the better part, seeing it hath appeared to be Gods pleasure to call him away, so favourably to the service of him, especially in the constancy of his duty towards God, wherein, we hear say, he dyed very commendably.

And for your self, we cannot but let you know that we hear out of France such singular good reports of your duty well accomplished towards your husband, both living and dead, with other your sober, wise, and discreet behaviour in that Court and Country, that we think it a part of great contentation to us, and commendation of our Country, that such a Gentlewoman hath given so manifest a testimony of virtue in such hard times of adversity. And therefore though we thought very well of you before, yet shall we hereafter make a more assured account of your virtues and gifts, and wherein soever we may conveniantly do you pleasure, you may be thereof assured. And so we would have you to rest yourself in quietness, with a firm opinion of our especiall favour towards you. Given under our Signet at our City of Oxford the . . . of September 1566: the eight year of our Reign.
Your loving Friend
ELIZABETH R.

QUEEN VICTORIA's letter to Augusta, General Gordon's sister, shows that she was particularly upset by Gordon's death, for which she held Gladstone, whom she loathed, responsible.

Windsor Castle,
March 16, 1885.
Dear Miss Gordon,
It is most kind and good of you to give me this precious Bible, and I only hope that you are not depriving yourself and family of such a treasure, if you have no other. May I ask you during how many years your dear heroic Brother had it with him? I shall have a case made for it with an Inscription and place it in the Library here with your letter and the touching extract from his last to you.

I have ordered as you know a Marble Bust of your dear Brother to

be placed in the Corridor here, where so many Busts and Pictures of
our greatest Generals and Statesmen are, and hope that you will see
it before it is finished, to give your opinion as to the likeness.
Believe me always,
Yours very sincerely,
VICTORIA R. I.

When she accepted the proposal of her husband to be, GERMAINE DE
STAËL had written with equanimity.

... de Staël is a man whose conduct is perfectly correct, incapable of
saying or doing anything stupid, but sterile and inert; he will not make
me unhappy, for the simple reason that he cannot contribute to my
happiness, and not because he could trouble it. . . . Monsieur de
Staël is the only convenient choice for me.

He was much older than her and when he fell unpleasantly ill, she nursed
him dutifully. After his death on 8 May 1802 MME DE STAËL wrote the
following.

It is true that I felt much more pain than I would have felt in any
different circumstances. I had found real happiness in making up through
my care for the sentiments I had been unable to give him. I had spent
six weeks doing nothing but putting his affairs in order, and I was going
to present him, as a result, with his pension from Sweden and with
ours, i.e., 10,000 pounds a year, without any deductions. I shall continue
to make every effort and sacrifice to see his debts paid, but I shall find
no more pleasure in this duty. Also I am very much affected by this
death, and I shall never find any consolation for my inability to make
him happy for a little while when he had abandoned himself to me.
Besides this feeling, there was the horror of being alone with him,
alone with his sad remains. I never had seen death from so close, and
for twenty-four hours I experienced the most painful and, at the same
time, the most fantastic impressions.

After the death of explorer Richard Burton, his adoring wife ISABEL BURTON discovered his private journals and collection of erotic Oriental literature. She was shocked, and though offered 6,000 guineas, decided to burn all his manuscripts. She wrote explaining:

1858

Is God offended? My heart said, 'You can have six thousand guineas; your husband worked for you, kept you in a happy home with honour and respect for thirty years. How are you going to reward him? That your wretched body may be fed and clothed and warmed for a few miserable months or years, will you let that soul *which is part of your soul* be left out in cold and darkness till the end of time, till all those sins which may have been committed on account of reading those writings have been expiated, or passed away, perhaps for ever? Why, it would be just parallel with the original thirty pieces of silver.

I fetched the manuscript and laid it on the ground before me, two large volumes.... Still my thoughts were, Was it sacrilege? It was his *magnum opus*, his last work that he was so proud of, that was to have been finished on that awful morrow – that never came. Will he rise up to curse or bless me? The thought will haunt me till death.... Sorrowfully, reverently, and in fear and trembling I burnt sheet after sheet, until the whole of the volumes were consumed.

Isabel wrote to the *Morning Post* to exonerate her destruction.

My husband had been collecting for fourteen years, information on a certain subject ... *The Scented Garden* ... treated of a certain passion. Do not let anyone suppose for a moment that Richard Burton ever wrote a thing from the impure point of view. He dissected a passion as a doctor may dissect a body, showing its source, its origin, its evil and its good.

Burton had written to a friend, his co-translator of *Catallus*, describing it in these terms: 'It will be a marvellous repertory of Eastern wisdom; how Eunuchs are made, and are married; what they do in marriage; female circumcision, the Fellahs copulating with crocodiles, etc. Mrs. Grundy will howl till she almost bursts and will read every word with an intense enjoyment....'

(In Isabel's defence, it should be remembered that Ruskin took a similar action when he discovered 'shameful, inexcusable paintings' by Turner. 'I took the hundreds of scrofulous sketches and paintings and burnt all of them.')

When QUEEN VICTORIA lost Albert she felt she had lost not only a friend, adviser and husband, but love itself, as she reveals in this letter to Earl Canning.

Osborne, 10th January 1862

Lord Canning little thought when he wrote his kind and touching letter on the 22nd November, that it would only reach the Queen when *she* was *smitten* and *bowed* down to the earth by an event similar to the one which he describes – and, strange to say, by a disease greatly analogous to the one which took from him *all* that he loved best. In the case of her adored, precious, perfect, and great husband, her dear lord and master, to whom this Nation owed more than it ever can truly know, however, the fever went on most favourably till the day previous to the awful calamity, and then it was congestion of the lungs and want of strength of circulation (the beloved Prince had always a weak and feeble pulse), which at the critical moment, indeed only two hours before God took him, caused this awful result. To lose one's partner in life is, as Lord Canning knows, like losing *half* of one's *body* and *soul*, torn forcibly away – and dear Lady Canning was such a dear, worthy, devoted wife! But to the Queen – to a poor helpless woman – it is not that only – it is the stay, support and comfort which is lost! To the Queen it is like *death* in life! Great and small – *nothing* was done without his loving advice and help – and she feels *alone* in the wide world, with many helpless children (except the Princess Royal) to look to her – and the whole nation to look to her – *now* when she can barely struggle with her wretched existence! Her misery – her utter despair – she *cannot* describe! Her *only* support – the *only* ray of comfort she gets for *a moment*, is in the *firm conviction* and certainty of his nearness, his undying love, and of their eternal reunion! Only she prays always, and pines for the latter with an anxiety she cannot describe. Like dear Lady Canning, the Queen's darling is to rest in a garden – at Frogmore, in a Mausoleum the Queen is going to build for him and herself.

Though ill, the Queen was able to tell her precious angel of Lord Canning's bereavement, and he was deeply grieved, recurring to it several times, and saying, 'What a loss! She was such a distinguished person!'

May God comfort and support Lord Canning, and may he think in his sorrow of his widowed and broken hearted Sovereign – bowed to the earth, with the greatest of human sufferings and misfortunes! She lived but *for* her husband!

The sympathy of the many thousands of her subjects, but above all their sorrow and their admiration for him, are soothing to her bleeding, pierced heart!

The Queen's precious husband, though wandering occasionally, was conscious till nearly the last, and knew her and kissed her an hour before his pure spirit fled to its worthy and fit eternal Home!

MILLICENT FAWCETT was extremely fond and proud of her half-paralysed husband, who had worked hard with her to promote women's rights. After his death in 1887 she wrote to a Newnham friend, Clotilda Bayne.

I do not think constancy and fidelity to dead friends consist in any strain to keep up the great pain of the time when you first know you have lost them, but rather in trying to be and to do what they wished and what they thought you capable of doing and being. One can't feel anything at first but a sort of numbness and then pain; but later there comes a most blessed and even happy feeling about it all. 'Blessed are they that mourn' has a meaning in this sense too. I do not know if I am quite clear, but what I mean is that the widow or widower who does not feel keen anguish is much more really to be pitied than the one who does; because it shows that he has never had what the other is mourning the loss of.

This is consistent with the view expressed to another student friend, Miss Barton, in 1885, about her husband and his work.

What you say about my dear husband's example helping you to persevere with your work, and not give way to feelings of discouragement, helps me more than anything else. The worst is when it seems as though people forgot him and that his great good influence is gone. I do not really believe that it is so, but it is not easy always to keep alive a firm conviction of the reverse; and it is a great help to be told, from the outside as it were, that courage and goodness have been made easier by his example.

A year later she was able to write again to Clotilda Bayne.

I think what we should all feel, who have been privileged to live in constant companionship with an exceptionally noble nature from which we are now removed, is not how wretched we are to have lost them, but how blessed we are to have had them to lift up our lives by their beautiful example.

When a Muslim widow prepared for her husband's funeral she had to sit beside the younger, preferred wife. In her epistolary novel *So Long a Letter*, MARIAMA BA describes the indignities which some wives suffer when polygamy is allowed.

1982

Dear Aissatou,

Yesterday you were divorced. Today I am a widow. Modou is dead: a heart attack suddenly, in his office. . . .

Women, close relatives, are busy. The presence of my co-wife beside me irritates me. She has been installed in my house, in accordance with tradition, for the funeral. With each passing hour her cheeks become more deeply hollowed, acquire ever more rings, those big and beautiful eyes which open and close on their secrets, perhaps their regrets. At the age of love and freedom from care, this child is dogged by sadness.

While the men, in a long, irregular file of official and private cars, public buses, lorries and mopeds, accompany Modou to his last rest (people were for a long time to talk of the crowd which followed the funeral procession), our sisters-in-law undo our hair. My co-wife and myself are put inside a rough and ready tent made of a wrapper pulled taut above our heads and set up for the occasion. While our sisters-in-law are constructing it, the women present, informed of the work in hand, get up and throw some coins on to the fluttering canopy so as to ward off evil spirits.

This is the moment dreaded by every Senegalese woman, the moment when she sacrifices her possessions as gifts to her family-in-law; and, worse still, beyond her possessions she gives up her personality, her dignity, becoming a thing in the service of the man who has married her, his grandfather, his grandmother, his father, his mother, his brother, his sister, his uncle, his aunt, his male and female cousins, his friends. Her behaviour is conditioned: no sister-in-law will touch the head of any wife who has been stingy, unfaithful or inhospitable.

As for ourselves, we have been deserving, and our sisters-in-law sing a chorus of praises chanted at the top of their voices. Our patience before all trials, the frequency of our gifts find their justification and reward today. Our sisters-in-law give equal consideration to thirty years and five years of married life. With the same ease and the same words, they celebrate twelve maternities and three. I note with outrage this desire to level out, in which Modou's new mother-in-law rejoices.

Having washed their hands in a bowl of water placed at the entrance to the house, the men, back from the cemetery, file past the family grouped around us, the widows. They offer their condolences punctuated with praises of the deceased.

'Modou, friend of the young as of the old. . . .'
'Modou, the lion-hearted, champion of the oppressed. . . .'
'Modou, at ease as much in a suit as in a caftan. . . .'
'Modou, good brother, good husband, good Muslim. . . .'
'May God forgive him. . . .'

OLD AGE

Many women, despite their loss of looks, and ailments, have, in old age, been determined to make the best of things, as can be seen in Lady Mary Wortley Montagu's witty description of the ladies of Vienna. Almost fifty years later, when she herself was old, she faced her situation with the same wit. George Sand too found wisdom and happiness, and time to cheer her aging, hypochondriacal friend Flaubert.

Old age need not be the end of the world. How women in Vienna spent their time is described in this letter from LADY MARY WORTLEY MONTAGU to her friend, Lady Rich, considered vain by her contemporaries.

Vienna, 20 September 1716

I can assure you that wrinkles or a small stoop in the shoulders, nay, grey hair itself, is no objection to the making new conquests. I know you can't easily figure to yourself a young fellow of five and twenty ogling my Lady Suffolk with passion, or pressing to lead the Countess of Oxford from an opera, but such are the sights I see every day, and I don't perceive anybody surprised at 'em but myself. A woman till five and thirty is only looked upon as a raw girl and can possibly make no noise in the world till about forty. I don't know what your Ladyship may think of this matter, but 'tis a considerable comfort to me to know there is upon earth such a paradise for old women, and I am content to be insignificant at present in the design of returning when I am fit to appear nowhere else.

I cannot help lamenting upon this occasion the pitiful case of so many good English ladies long since retired to prudery and ratafia, whom, if their stars had luckily conducted them hither, would still shine in the first rank of beauties; and then that perplexing word reputation has quite another meaning here than what you give it at London, and getting a lover is so far from losing, that 'tis properly getting reputation, ladies being much more respected in regard to the rank of their lovers than that of their husbands. But what you'll think very odd, the two sects that divide our whole nation of petticoats are utterly unknown. Here are neither coquettes nor prudes. No woman dares appear coquette enough to encourage two lovers at a time, and I have not seen any such prudes as to pretend fidelity to their husbands, who are certainly the best natured set of people in the world, and they look upon their wives' gallants as favourably as men do upon their deputies that take the troublesome part of their business off of their hands, though they have not the less to do, for they are generally deputies in another place themselves. In one word, 'tis the established custom for every lady to have two husbands, one that bears the name, and another that performs the duties; and these engagements are so well known, that it would be a downright affront and publicly resented if you invited a woman of quality to dinner without at the same time inviting her two attendants of lover and husband, between whom she always sits in state with great gravity.

These sub-marriages generally last twenty year together, and the lady often commands the poor lover's estate even to the utter ruin of his family, though they are as seldom begun by any passion as other matches. But a man makes but an ill figure that is not in some commerce of this nature, and a woman looks out for a lover as soon as she's married as part of her equipage, without which she could not be genteel; and the first article of the treaty is establishing the pension, which remains to the lady though the gallant should prove inconstant, and this chargeable point of honour I look upon as the real foundation of so many wonderful instances of constancy. I really know several women of the first quality whose pensions are as well known as their annual rents, and yet nobody esteems them the less. On the contrary, their discretion would be called in question if they should be suspected to be mistresses for nothing, and a great part of their emulation consists in trying who shall get most; thus you see, my dear, gallantry and courting are as different as morality.
Yours, etc

LADY MARY WORTLEY MONTAGU was a lively correspondent. Even when old and ill she writes with wit and warmth, to cheer elderly friend James Stuart Mackenzie, who had just been recalled from his post as ambassador in Turin.

Venice, 6 June 1761

Your Excellency is dead, but as I do not doubt it is only a removal to a better life I ought rather to congratulate than condole. I wish you would take Venice in your way when you make your journey. I almost despair of being able to undertake mine; the infirmities of age come fast upon me, and sometimes I am inclined to think with Shakespeare, 'tis better to endure the ills I have, than fly to others that I know not of.

I will not trouble you with a long letter; you are in a hurry sufficient to tire any spirits but yours. I only beg you to be assured that while I exist you will have a sincere and faithful friend.

M. W. MONTAGU

To Sir James and Lady Frances Steuart

Rotterdam, 20 November 1761

Sir,

I received yesterday your obliging and welcome letter by the hands of Mr Simpson. I tried in vain to find you at Amsterdam; I began to think we resembled two parallel lines, destined to be always near and never to meet. You know there is no fighting (at least no overcoming) destiny. So far I am a confirmed Calvinist, according to the notions of the country where I now exist.

I am dragging my ragged remnant of life to England. The wind and tide are against me; how far I have strength to struggle against both I know not. That I am arrived here is as much a miracle as any in the Golden Legend; and if I had foreseen half the difficulties I have met with I should not certainly have had courage enough to undertake it. I have scrambled through more dangers than his Majesty of Prussia, or even my well-beloved cousin (not counsellor) Marquis Granby; but my spirits fail me when I think of my friends risking either health or happiness. I will write to Lady Fanny to hinder your coming to Rotterdam, and will sooner make one jump more myself to wait on you at Antwerp. I am glad poor D. has sold his medals; I confess I thought his buying them a very bold stroke. I supposed that he had already left London, but am told that he has been prevented by the machinations of that excellent politician and truly great man, Murray, and his ministry.

My dear Lady Fanny, I am persuaded that you are more nearly concerned for the health of Sir James than he is himself; I address myself

to you to insist on it to him not to undertake a winter progress in the
beginning of a fit of the gout. I am nailed down here by a severe
illness of my poor Marianne, who has not been able to endure the
frights and fatigues that we have passed. If I live to see Great Britain,
you will have there a sincere and faithful servant that will omit no
occasion of serving you; and I think it almost impossible I should not
succeed. You must be loved and esteemed wherever you are known.

Give me leave however, dear madam, to combat some of your
notions, or more properly speaking, your passions. Mr Steuart is in a
situation that opens the fairest prospect of honour and advancement.
We mothers are all apt to regret the absence of children we love. Solomon
advises the sluggard to go to the ant and be wise; we should take the
example of the innocent inhabitants of the air: when their young are
fledged they are delighted to see them fly and peck for themselves.
Forgive this freedom. I have no other receipt for maternal fondness, a
distemper which has long afflicted your ladyship's obliged and obedient
humble servant,

M. W. MONTAGU

The French novelist GEORGE SAND kept up a voluminous correspondence
with Gustave Flaubert. He felt the loneliness and pain of old age bitterly.
Though she suffered from haemorrhages and fatigue, she used her
female caring to comfort him, and sustain a supportive intellectual
friendship.

Dec. 8, 1874. Nohant

Poor dear friend, I love you all the more because you are growing more
unhappy. How you torment yourself, and how you disturb yourself
about life! for all of which you complain, is life; it has never been better
for anyone or in any time. One feels it more or less, one understands
it more or less, one suffers with it more or less, and the more one is
in advance of the age one lives in, the more one suffers. We pass like
shadows on a background of clouds which the sun seldom pierces, and
we cry ceaselessly for the sun which can do no more for us. It is for
us to clear away our clouds.

You love literature too much; it will destroy you and you will not
destroy the imbecility of the human race. Poor dear imbecility, that,
for my part, I do not hate, that I regard with maternal eyes: for it is a

childhood and all childhood is sacred. What hatred you have devoted to it! what warfare you wage on it!

You have too much knowledge and intelligence, you forget that there is something above art: namely, wisdom, of which art at its apogee is only the expression. Wisdom comprehends all: beauty, truth, goodness, enthusiasm, in consequence. It teaches us to see outside of ourselves, something more elevated than is in ourselves, and to assimilate it little by little, through contemplation and admiration.

But I shall not succeed in changing you. I shall not even succeed in making you understand how I envisage and how I lay hold upon *happiness*, that is to say, the acceptation of life whatever it may be! There is one person who could change you and save you, that is father Hugo; for he has one side on which he is a great philosopher, while at the same time he is the great artist that you require and that I am not. You must see him often. I believe that he will quiet you: I have not enough tempest in me now for you to understand me. As for him, I think that he has kept his thunderbolts and that he has all the same acquired the gentleness and the compassion of age.

See him, see him often and tell him your troubles, which are great, I see that, and which turn too much to *spleen*. You think too much of the dead, you think that they have too soon reached their rest. They have not. They are like us, they are searching. They labour in the search.

Every one is well, and embraces you. As for me, I do not get well, but I have hopes, well or not, to keep on still so as to bring up my grandchildren, and to love you as long as I have a breath left.

Their correspondence shows a contrast between an ageing male writer and an ageing woman. First Flaubert to Sand; then Sand to Flaubert.

July 12, 1872, Bagnères de Luchon
I have been here since Sunday evening, dear master, and am no happier than at Croisset, even a little less so, for I am very idle. They make so much noise in the house where we are, that it is impossible to work. Moreover, the sight of the bourgeois who surround us is unendurable. I am not made for travelling. The least inconvenience disturbs me. Your old troubadour is very old, decidedly! Doctor Lambron, the physician of this place, attributes my nervous tendencies to the excessive use of tobacco. To be agreeable I am going to smoke less; but I doubt very much if my virtue will cure me! . . .

This letter is stupid. But they are making such a noise over my head that it is not clear (my head).

In the midst of my bewilderment, I embrace you and yours also. Your old blockhead who loves you.

Aug. 31, 1872, Nohant

My old troubadour, here we are back again at home, after a month passed, just as you said, at Cabourg, where chance more than intention placed us. We all took wonderful sea baths. . . . We have returned in splendid health, and we are glad to see our old Nohant again, after having been glad to leave it for a little change of air.

I have resumed my usual work, and I continue my river baths, but no one will accompany me, it is too cold. As for me, I found fault with the sea for being too warm. Who would think that, with my appearance and tranquil old age, I would still love *excess*? My dominant passion on the whole is my [granddaughter] Aurore. My life depends on hers. She was so lovely on the trip, so gay, so appreciative of the amusement that we gave her, so attentive to what she saw, and curious about everything with so much intelligence, that she is real and sympathetic company at every hour. Ah! how *unliterary* I am! Scorn me, but still love me.

I don't know if I shall find you in Paris when I go there for my play. I have not arranged with the Odéon for the date of its performance.

CONFRONTING DEATH

From a culture where there was little letter-writing, I feel the right to include this poem written by SANGHA, a Buddhist woman, 3,000 years ago. She waited until after her husband's death, then left the world to prepare for her own.

> Home have I left, for I have left my world!
> Child have I left, and all my cherished herds.
> Lust have I left, and Ill-will, too is gone,
> And Ignorance have I put far from me;
> Craving and root of craving overpowered,
> Cool am I now, knowing Nirvana's peace.

The translation is pedestrian, but the thought worth transmitting.

ISABEL THE CATHOLIC, mother of Catherine of Aragon, ruled a rebellious Spain till she imposed order and a certain amount of justice. To maintain order she needed a male heir. Yet when her only son lay dying, in late adolescence, she was able to think of his needs for comfort rather than her own despair.

July 1497

Very beloved son, be patient since God has called you, Who is the greatest King of any, and has other realms and lordships greater and better than this which would have been yours and for which you were prepared. He will give them to you and they shall endure for ever. And have heart to accept death, which each man must of necessity once accept, in the hope of going forever to immortality and the life of glory.

The last letter of CATHERINE OF ARAGON to King Henry VIII reveals her enduring love for him in spite of his contemptuous treatment.

1535

My Lord and Dear Husband,
I commend me unto you. The hour of my death draweth fast on, and my case being such, the tender love I owe you forceth me, with a few words, to put you in remembrance of the health and safeguard of your soul, which you ought to prefer before all worldly matters, and before the care and tendering of your own body, for the which you have cast me into many miseries and yourself into many cares.

For my part I do pardon you all, yea, I do wish and devoutly pray God that He will also pardon you.

For the rest I commend unto you Mary, our daughter, beseeching you to be a good father unto her, as I heretofore desired. I entreat you also, on behalf of my maids, to give them marriage-portions, which is not much, they being but three. For all my other servants, I solicit a year's pay more than their due, lest they should be unprovided for.

Lastly, do I vow, that mine eyes desire you above all things.

Murder most foul: the body of Mary Queen of Scots' second husband, Darnley, was found in their garden. Beside him were a dagger, rope and his dead servant. The bold lord Bothwell was suspected of the assassination. QUEEN ELIZABETH was appalled and urged Mary to hold a public enquiry.

Westminster, 24 February 1567

Madam,
My ears have been so astounded and my heart so frightened to hear of the horrible and abominable murder of your former husband, our mutual cousin, that I have scarcely spirit to write; yet I cannot conceal that I grieve more for you than for him. I should not do the office of a faithful cousin and friend, if I did not urge you to preserve your honour, rather than look through your fingers at revenge on those who have done you that pleasure as most people say. I advise you so to take this matter to heart, that you may show the world what a noble Princess and loyal woman you are. I write thus vehemently not that I doubt, but for affection. As for the three matters communicated by Melville, I

understand your wish to please me, and that you will grant the request
by Lord Bedford in my name to ratify the treaty made six or seven
years ago. I will not trouble you about other matters, referring you to
the report of this gentleman.

Madame de Brinvilliers used poison to kill her father, her brothers and
several others. Hers was a notorious case, at the time of Louis XIV.
MADAME DE SÉVIGNÉ's description of Brinvilliers' final hours in a letter
to Madame de Grignan is so vivid it is often quoted.

Paris, Friday 17 July 1676

Well, it's all over and done with, Brinvilliers is in the air. Her poor
little body was thrown after the execution into a very big fire and the
ashes to the winds, so that we shall breathe her, and through the
communication of the subtle spirits we shall develop some poisoning
urge which will astonish us all. She was tried yesterday and this
morning the sentence was read to her; it was to make a public
confession at Notre-Dame and to have her head cut off, her body burnt
and the ashes scattered to the winds. She was taken to the torture but
she said there was no need and that she would tell all. And indeed
until five in the evening she recounted her life, even more appalling than
people thought. She poisoned her father ten times running (she
couldn't finish it off), her brothers and several others, and always love
and confidential matters mixed up with it. She said nothing against
Pennautier. This confession notwithstanding, they put her to the torture
first thing in the morning, both ordinary and extraordinary, but she
said nothing more. She asked to speak to the Public Prosecutor and
was with him for an hour, but so far nobody knows the subject of this
conversation. At six o'clock she was taken, with only a shift on and a
rope round her neck, to make the public confession at Notre-Dame.
Then she was put back into the tumbril in which I saw her, thrown
on her back on to the straw, wearing a low cornet and her shift, having
on one side a priest and on the other the executioner; it really made me
shudder. Those who saw the execution say that she mounted the
scaffold with great courage. As for me, I was on the Pont Notre-Dame
with the good d'Escars; never has such a crowd been seen, nor Paris
so excited and attentive. If you ask me what I saw, it was nothing but

a cornet, but the day was given up to this tragedy. I shall know more tomorrow and it will reach you.

EMILY BRONTË nursed Branwell devotedly during his final illness. It is possible that some of his violence was transmuted into Heathcliff of *Wuthering Heights*. Charlotte was horrified by the ways he succumbed to misery, and brought suffering to the family, as she shows in this letter to Mr Williams, soon after the funeral:

The removal of our only brother must necessarily be regarded by us rather in the light of a mercy than a chastisement. Branwell was his father's and his sisters' pride and hope in boyhood, but since manhood the case has been otherwise. It has been our lot to see him take a wrong bent; to hope, expect, wait his return to the right path; to know the sickness of hope deferred, the dismay of prayer baffled; to experience despair at last – and now to behold the sudden early obscure close of what might have been a noble career.

I do not weep from a sense of bereavement – there is no prop withdrawn, no consolation torn away, no dear companion lost – but for the wreck of talent, the ruin of promise, the untimely dreary extinction of what might have been a burning and a shining light. My brother was a year my junior. I had aspirations and ambitions for him once, long ago – they have perished mournfully. Nothing remains of him but a memory of errors and sufferings. There is such a bitterness of pity for his life and death, such a yearning for the emptiness of his whole existence as I cannot describe. I trust time will allay these feelings.

My unhappy brother never knew what his sisters had done in literature – he was not aware that they had ever published a line. We could not tell him of our efforts for fear of causing him too deep a pang of remorse for his own time mis-spent, and talents misapplied. Now he will *never* know. I cannot dwell longer on the subject at present – it is too painful. . . .

After Emily Brontë had nursed her difficult and demanding brother Branwell during his final months, she herself had to face death from galloping tuberculosis.

Shortly before she died, in October that year, a review of the Brontës' novels appeared in *The North American Review*. The novels were first published under the male pseudonyms of Currer, Ellis and Acton Bell (Charlotte, Emily and Anne). CHARLOTTE BRONTË wrote to Mr Williams, who sent her a copy of the review.

> 22 November 1848
>
> To-day, as Emily appeared a little better, I thought the Review would amuse her, so I read it aloud to her and Anne. As I sat between them at our quiet but now somewhat melancholy fireside, I studied the two ferocious authors. Ellis the 'man of uncommon parts, but dogged, brutal, and morose,' sat leaning back in his easy chair drawing his impeded breath as he best could, and looking, alas!, piteously pale and wasted; it is not his wont to laugh, but he smiled half amused and half in scorn as he listened. Acton was sewing, no emotion ever stirs him to loquacity, so he only smiled too, dropping at the same time a single word of calm amazement to hear his character so darkly portrayed. I wonder what the reviewer would have thought of his own sagacity could he have beheld the pair as I did.

CHARLOTTE BRONTË testifies to Emily's spiritual strength.

> November 1848
>
> While physically she perished, mentally she grew stronger than we had yet known her. Day by day, when I saw with what a front she met suffering, I looked on her with an anguish of wonder and love. I have never seen anything like it; but indeed, I have never seen her parallel in anything. . . . The awful point was, that while full of ruth for others, on herself she had no pity; the spirit was inexorable to the flesh; from the trembling hand, the unnerved limbs, the faded eyes, the same service was extracted as they had rendered in health. To stand by and witness this, and not dare to remonstrate, was a pain no words can render.

Marian Evans, who was later to adopt the pen name GEORGE ELIOT, adored her father. Though she knew that he had left many prized possessions in his will, such as Scott's Waverley novels and her dead mother's silver forks, to her sisters and brother, she nursed him devotedly, often going without sleep. Here her friend Cara Bray describes the scene with perspicacity to their mutual friend Sara Hennell.

May 1849

Dear friend,
The doctors expect his death to take place suddenly, by a suffusion of
water on the chest; and poor Mary Ann, alone with him, has the
whole care and fatigue of nursing him day and night with this constant
nervous expectation. She keeps up wonderfully mentally, but looks
like a ghost. It is a great comfort that he is now quite aware of his
situation, and was not in the least discomposed when Isaac told him he
might die suddenly. It was quite a pleasure to see him sitting in his
chair looking so calm just after he had known this; and he takes
opportunities now of saying kind things to Mary Ann, contrary to his
wont. Poor girl, it shows how rare they are by the gratitude with which
she repeats the commonest expressions of kindness.

MRS OLIPHANT supported her parents, then her brother's family, as well
as her own. She describes the suffering caused by the death of one's
children which many people had to bear in the past, and in Third World
today.

1888

My child's birth made a momentary gleam of joy soon lost in clouds.
    My mother became ailing and concealed it, and kept alive – or at
least kept her last illness off by sheer stress of will until my second
child was born a year and a day after the first. She was with me, but
sank next day into an illness from which she never rose. She died in
September 1854, suffering no attendance but mine, though she
concealed from me how ill she was for a long time. I remember the first
moment in which I had any real fear, speaking to the doctor with a
sudden impulse, in the front of her door, all in a green shade with the
waving trees, demanding his real opinion. I do not think I had any
understanding of the gravity of the circumstances. He shook his head,
and I knew – the idea having never entered my mind before that she
was to die. I recollect going away, walking home as in a dream, not able
to go to her, to look at her, from whom I had never had a secret, with
this secret in my soul that must be told least of all to her: and the
sensation that here was something which would not lighten after a while
as all my troubles had always done, and pass away. I had never come
face to face with the inevitable before. But there was no daylight here
– no hope – no getting over it. Then there followed a struggle of a

month or two, much suffering on her part, and a long troubled watch and nursing on mine. At the very end I remember the struggle against overwhelming sleep, after nights and days in incessant anxiety, which made me so bitterly ashamed of the limits of wretched nature. To want to sleep while she was dying seemed so unnatural and horrible. I never had come within sight of death before. And, oh me! when all was over, mingled with my grief there was – how can I say it? – something like a dreadful relief.

Within a few months after, my little Marjorie, my second child, died on the 8th February: and then with deep shame and anguish I felt what I suppose was another wretched limit of nature. My dearest mother, who had been everything to me all my life, and to whom I was everything; the companion, friend, counsellor, minstrel, story-teller, with whom I had never wanted for constant interest, entertainment, and fellowship, – did not give, when she died, a pang so deep as the loss of the little helpless baby, eight months old. I miss my mother till this moment when I am near as old as she was (sixty, 10th June 1888); I think instinctively still of asking her something, referring to her for information, and I dream constantly of being a girl with her at home. But at that moment her loss was nothing to me in comparison with the loss of my little child.

I lost another infant after that, a day old. My spirit sank completely under it. I used to go about saying to myself, 'A little while and ye shall not see me,' with a longing to get to the end and have all safe – for my one remaining, my eldest, my Maggie seemed as if she too must be taken out of my arms. People will say it was an animal instinct perhaps. Neither of these little ones could speak to me or exchange an idea or show love, and yet their withdrawal was like the sun going out from the sky.

HARRIET MARTINEAU in this letter to her close friend Henry Atkinson shows philosophical resignation in facing death. Atkinson was, like her, an agnostic and a believer in mesmerism.

19 May 1876

Dear Friend, – My niece J – and also my sister have been observing that you ought to be hearing from us, and have offered to write to you. You will see at once what this means; and it is quite true that I have become so much worse lately that we ought to guard against

your being surprised, some day soon, by news of my life being closed. I feel uncertain about how long I *may* live in my present state. I can only follow the judgment of unprejudiced observers; and I see that my household believe the end to be not far off. I will not trouble you with disagreeable details. It is enough to say that I am in no respect better, while all the ailments are on the increase. The imperfect heart-action immediately affects the brain, causing the suffering which is worse than all other evils together, – the horrid sensation of not being quite myself. This strange, dreamy *non-recognition of myself* comes on every evening, and all else is a trifle in comparison. But there is a good deal more. Cramps in the hands prevent writing, and most other employment, except at intervals. Indications of dropsy have lately appeared: and after this, I need not again tell you that I see how fully my household believe that the end is not far off. Meantime I have no cares or troubles beyond the bodily uneasiness, (which, however, I don't deny to be an evil). I cannot think of any future as at all probable, except the 'annihilation' from which some people recoil with so much horror. I find myself here in the universe, – I know not how, whence, or why. I see every thing in the universe go out and disappear, and I see no reason for supposing that it is not an actual and entire death. And for *my* part, I have no objection to such an extinction. I well remember the passion with which W. E. Forster said to me, 'I had rather be damned than annihilated.' If he once felt five minutes' damnation, he would be thankful for extinction in preference. The truth is, I care little about it any way. Now that the event draws near, and that I see how fully my household expect my death pretty soon, the universe opens so widely before my view, and I see the old notions of death and scenes to follow to be so merely human, – so impossible to be true, when one glances through the range of science, – that I see nothing to be done but to wait, without fear or hope or ignorant prejudice . . . So goodbye for today, dear friend!
Yours ever HM

VIRGINIA WOOLF had contradictory reactions to her rival, New Zealand writer Katherine Mansfield. Here she uses a letter to Vita Sackville-West to come to terms with her feelings, after Mansfield's death from tuberculosis, at only thirty-three.

Summer 1931

We did not ever coalesce; but I was fascinated, and she respectful, only
I thought her cheap, and she thought me priggish; and yet we were
both compelled to meet simply in order to talk about writing. This we
did by the hour. Only then she came out with a swarm of little stories,
and I was jealous, no doubt; because they were so praised; but gave
up reading them not on that account, but because of their cheap sharp
sentimentality, which was all the worse, I thought, because she had, as
you say, the zest and the resonance – I mean she could permeate one
with her quality; and if one felt this cheap scent in it, it reeked in ones
nostrils. But I must read her some day. Also, she was forever pursued
by her dying; and had to press on through stages that should have
taken years in ten minutes – so that our relationship became unreal
also. And there was Murry squirming and oozing a sort of thick motor
oil in the background – dinners with them were about the most
unpleasant exhibitions, humanly speaking, I've ever been to. But the
fact remains – I mean, that she had a quality I adored, and needed; I
think her sharpness and reality – her having knocked about with
prostitutes and so on, whereas I had always been respectable – was
the thing I wanted then. I dream of her often – now thats an odd
reflection – how one's relation with a person seems to be continued after
death in dreams, and with some odd reality too.

VIRGINIA WOOLF herself committed suicide. This is her last letter to her
husband, Leonard Woolf, who had looked after her lovingly, though
perhaps too protectively, since the first days of their relatively compatible
marriage.

28 March 1941 (Monk's House, Rodmell)

I have the feeling that I shall go mad and cannot go on any longer in
these terrible times. I hear voices and cannot concentrate on my work.
I have fought against it and cannot fight any more. I owe all my
happiness to you. You have been so perfectly good. I cannot go on
and spoil your life.

Note the amazing directness and simplicity from a novelist who explored
ambiguity and complexity of language. Anaïs Nin commented 'Her

writing was so abstract and mysterious and labyrinthian. Here it's simple, direct, as all true suffering.'

VITA SACKVILLE-WEST had loved Virginia, with whom she had an affair which began and ended in friendship and novelistic correspondence. She wrote to her husband Harold Nicolson on 31 March:

I've just had the most awful shock: Virginia has killed herself. It is not in the papers, but I got letters from Leonard and also from Vanessa [Virginia's sister] telling me. He says she had not been well for the last few weeks and was terrified of going mad again. I simply can't take it in. That lovely mind, that lovely spirit. And she seemed so well when I last saw her.

A few years later, in another letter to her husband she wrote:

I still think that I might have saved her if only I had been there and had known the state of mind she was getting into.

Vita was possibly right.

BRIEF BIOGRAPHIES OF THE MAJOR
LETTER-WRITERS

LOUISA MAY ALCOTT (1832–88). Born Pennsylvania, one of four daughters of an idealistic, improvident philosopher. Today she is remembered for her novel *Little Women* (1868), which drew on her family experiences. In the Civil War she worked as an army nurse, for the Union, described in *Hospital Sketches* (1863). Under a pseudonym she wrote blood-and-thunder stories, earning enough to write two feminist novels.

KATE AMBERLEY (1842–74), mother of Bertrand Russell. When he was only two, she died, followed soon by the husband she adored, Lord Amberley. Their two small sons were brought up by grandparents. Russell collected his parents' letters in *The Amberley Papers*.

MARIAMA BA (1929–81). Born Dakar, Senegal. Her father, a civil servant, became the first Minister of Health after decolonization in 1956. After the early death of her mother she was brought up as a Muslim by maternal grandparents. She learnt fluent French which she used in her two novels, became a teacher, and active in the feminist movement in Senegal and abroad. She married the Minister of Information, and had nine children, but divorced, like the unhappy heroine of her brilliant short epistolary novel *So Long a Letter*.

DJUNA BARNES (1892–1982). Born in New York State. A poet, novelist and playwright, best known for her novel *Nightwood* (1936) about five unusual people living in Paris, where she spent many years. T.S. Eliot praised it for its Jacobean sense of doom and treatment of lesbianism.

APHRA BEHN. Probably born in 1640, near Canterbury, Kent. During her childhood, her family went to Surinam, Guiana, where her father was to take up the post of Lieutenant-General. He died on the voyage, but she lived there long enough to see how the Indian slaves were treated, which inspired her novel *Oroonoko*, the first in the English language. Behn returned to London in 1664, and probably married a Dutchman, Mr Behn, in 1666. It is believed that he died in the Great Plague, and to earn some money she agreed to act as a spy in the Dutch wars. Her instructions were to find William Scot, son of a regicide, and pump him for information about Dutch naval and military activities. For this work the government failed even to pay her expenses. She turned to writing for the Restoration stage and soon won popularity with her lively comedies about sexual mores, such as *The Rover*, successfully revived recently. One of her most moving prose works is *Love Letters from a Nobleman to his Sister*, based on an aristocratic scandal, it nevertheless contains much of her own passion – and suffering caused by loving Hoyle, who was profligate, cruel and bisexual. She was unjustly ignored for centuries, but has been 'rediscovered' recently.

ISABELLA BIRD (1831–1904) was a churchman's frail child, expected to entertain in their Victorian vicarage. She rejected conventional life, in order to travel on foot, horseback, elephant and even yak. She visited Japan, Korea, Kurdestan, Persia and the Rocky Mountains. Her books earned her election to the Royal Geographical Society, the first woman there.

BRYHER (1894–1983), daughter of a wealthy English shipowner, Sir John Ellerman. As a child she found herself in a constant struggle with her parents' repressive, constricting expectations. She discovered a new world in modern poetry, and a meeting with H.D. (American poet Hilda Doolittle, born 1886) in 1918 was a decisive event in her life. Abandoned by her husband, ill and pregnant, H.D. was in need of the care which the wealthy young woman was eager to provide. The two women became lifelong friends and companions.

FANNY BURNEY. Born in 1752. Her father was a celebrated musicologist, a talented man with a powerful character, which she admired and respected. Feminists maintain that she was too subservient to his wishes; she often allowed him to sway her judgment; nevertheless her letters to him reveal a warm reciprocal relationship.

She received no formal education, at eight could scarcely recognize the alphabet, but taught herself to read; soon she roamed her father's impressive library – a freedom which also aided the Brontë sisters, at Haworth. His collections of sermons, moral tracts and history gave her the firm ethical concepts which appealed to readers of her novels.

The Burney household was large and lively. Though her mother died when Fanny was ten (most of her heroines lack a mother's guidance), her father remarried an attractive widow with three children, and invited many well-known intellectuals home, including the actor Garrick. Fanny used to ask her step-mother to re-enact his parts for them, which she loved to imitate. Nevertheless Fanny suffered from painful timidity, which often inhibited her. In 1768 she began a diary in which we learn that she burned her first attempt at a novel, as she thought she ought to fight this 'propensity to degradation'. Her desire to write was so compelling that her father harnessed it into his *General History of Music* which occupied them both for hours each day. But her need to invent found outlet in journals and imaginary letters – which became her first novel *Evelina*, from which I have selected three letters. It is so lively and fresh that it gained immediate acclaim when it was published in 1778.

She worked for five years as Keeper of Robes for Queen Charlotte and at forty married a French immigré, General d'Arblay. They had one son.

MRS PATRICK CAMPBELL. Born in 1865 she became one of the best-known actresses of her era. She was thirty-four when she met George Bernard Shaw. He was forty-two and making his name, as opera and theatre critic, and pamphleteer, but only just beginning his career as playwright. Mrs Campbell was at the height of her career, praised for her beauty, her actor-managing and the creation of roles such as Mrs Tanqueray, Melisande and soon Eliza Doolittle in *Pygmalion*. Her popularity waned, while his increased, but their friendship continued, mainly through letters. Their correspondence reveals the strength of her personality, and wit and warmth as marked as Shaw's. She died in relative poverty.

ALEXANDRA DAVID-NEEL (1868–1969) was born in Paris. Her father was a radical journalist, forced to live in exile in Belgium, and his marriage was an unhappy one. The young Alexandra often ran away from home and from school, longing to travel and for solitude.

She began to study eastern religions, with a particular interest in Buddhism, in Paris, worked for a time as a journalist, and then toured the Middle East and North Africa as an opera singer. In 1904 she married a distant cousin, Philippe Néel, but she felt trapped by marriage, and they separated within a matter of days. Nevertheless, they continued to correspond, and he supported her financially, enabling her to study and travel abroad.

The Dalai Lama was in exile in Darjeeling in 1911 when Alexandra David-Néel became the first Western woman to interview him. Her meeting with him inspired her to concentrate on Tibetan Buddhism in her studies. Illegally entering Tibet in 1914, she spent time in a monastery, lived as a hermit in a cave, and became a Lama herself. In 1923, disguised as a Tibetan beggar on pilgrimage with her adopted son, Alexandra David-Néel became the first Western woman to enter the 'Forbidden City' of Lhasa, where she remained for two months before her identity was discovered.

Returning to France after fourteen years in Asia she found herself received as an honoured celebrity. Her last Asian journey ended in 1944, but she went on to write many books about her travels and about Buddhism. She died in 1969, shortly before her one hundred and first birthday.

MADAME DE SÉVIGNÉ (1626–96) was born in Paris, and married at eighteen to the Marquis de Sévigné, who left her a widow at twenty-five. She lived near the brilliant court of Louis XIV at Versailles, learning of the happenings and scandals directly, from friends. These she recounted with unusual vivacity and wit, mainly for her beloved daughter, who had to follow her husband to a post in the south. She was a friend of the outstanding woman novelist, Madame de la Fayette, and appreciated the plays of Corneille, Molière and Racine. Her letters provide an invaluable chronicle of the long reign of Louis XIV, and his centralizing of power in the Court.

HILDA DOOLITTLE (1886–1961), known by her pen-name H.D. Born in Pennsylvania in 1911, she preferred to live in Europe, like many American writers of her generation. She was briefly engaged to Ezra Pound, then married the English novelist Richard Aldington. Her first poems were inspired by Greek writers, from Sappho to Euripides. They reveal her ability to use natural objects to symbolize emotions. When her marriage was dissolved, she formed a lifelong relationship with the English novelist and patron Bryher (Winifred Ellerman). Her prose fiction including *Palimpsest* (1926) analyses sexual betrayal and a woman's attempt to find personal fulfilment through love and art. Her explicitly lesbian writing was not published until after her death (*Hermione*, 1981).

She wrote prolifically and is now being revalued, especially for *Trilogy*, a long poem on her experience of analysis under Freud and London in the Second World War.

LUCIE DUFF GORDON (1821–69) was the only child of a privileged intellectual couple, whose radical friends included Jeremy Bentham and John Stuart Mill. At eighteen she fell in love with Sir Alexander Duff Gordon, a civil servant. They knew many writers, Dickens, Caroline Norton, Meredith and Tennyson, who respected Lucie's independent mind, her dislike of snobbery, and her wit.

The couple had three children. In the 1850s when Lucie began to suffer from tuberculosis, the doctor advised her to go to South Africa, where she wrote *Letters from the Cape* (1864). Then she went to Upper Egypt for seven years, a longer stay than any other European. Her sympathy for the Arabs contrasts to many English attitudes of the time; she proved the only contemporary witness to the disastrous governments of Ismail (praised as Viceroy by English male politicians). She died in Cairo in 1869. Her *Letters from Egypt* (1865) were reprinted three times in their first year. They remain a valuable historical document and a lively account of one remarkable individual's view of another culture.

GEORGE ELIOT (1819–80) was born Mary Ann (or Marian) Evans in Warwickshire, the daughter of an estate agent. She took charge of the household after her mother's death in 1836, and still managed to continue her studies, but growing religious doubts led to a serious quarrel with her father. In 1843 she embarked on a career which was usually unpaid and often anonymous, as an editor, essayist, critic and translator. She translated Strauss's *Life of Jesus*, Spinoza's *Tractatus Theologico-Politicus*, and Feuerbach's *Essence of Christianity*.

Her father died in 1849. In 1851 Mary Ann Evans moved to London to become the assistant editor of *The Westminster Review*. She met and fell in love with George Henry Lewes. At first they travelled abroad, but the need to earn a living brought them back to London, where she knew she would face social disapproval and ostracism as a fallen woman. Although they considered themselves husband and wife, Lewes already had a wife, who had left him for another writer. He was unable to obtain a divorce, because of restrictive laws. However their life together is an example of a close, tender, supportive, passionate friendship. Lewes, well-known for his encouragement of other women writers, now suggested to Mary Ann that she should try her hand at fiction. The result was the well-received *Scenes from Clerical Life* (1858).

This first book was followed by *Adam Bede* (1859), *Mill on the Floss* (1860), *Silas Marner* (1861), *Middlemarch* (1871), *Daniel Deronda* (1876) and others. Lewes died in 1878. George Eliot married John Cross in 1880, but died later that same year. Highly successful in her own day, George Eliot continues to be considered one of the greatest of all English novelists. However she had to use a male pseudonym to gain publication.

ELIZABETH I (1533–1603), Queen of England and Ireland from 1558. Neglected for a short time, after the divorce of her father Henry VIII, then declared illegitimate, her place in the succession was restored by Parliament. She grew up during civil disturbance and political intrigue, forced young to develop skill in dealing with those powerful enough to destroy her. She was unusually well educated, and learned Greek and Latin from the age of five. Her court became a centre of culture.

Under her long rule England became a prominent European power. To bolster her initially shaky position, after her brother's Protestant persecutions and the Catholic intolerance of her sister Mary, she imposed a 'middle way', insisting that no religious group should outrage its opponents in public. She cleverly encouraged propaganda of the 'virgin queen' partly to take the place of the icon of the Virgin Mary, partly for political reasons. She cunningly balanced some of England's diplomatic relations in Europe with the possibility of alliance through marriage. Spain refrained from attacking, until the time of the 'Invincible Armada'. Just before her death she named James I as heir, to avoid open conflict over the succession.

MILLICENT FAWCETT (1847–1929) was born in Cambridge. As a young woman, she watched John Stuart Mill introduce the first women's suffrage bill in Parliament. For the next fifty years, she worked with the leaders of the English suffrage movement. One of the most capable and energetic women of her generation, she helped in a variety of ways to limit prostitution, and to make higher education available to women.

Fawcett believed women would only be listened to once they gained the vote. She was fortunate to live to see this granted in 1918 – though only to married women over thirty. She died in 1929. Her sister Elizabeth Garrett Anderson was the first woman doctor. They had the joy of caring, committed parents and in finding men whom they could love and who shared their ideals.

ELIZABETH GASKELL (1810–65) was a mother of five children. Her husband, a Unitarian minister in Manchester, suggested she turn to writing to find solace after the death of their only son. Her income helped supplement the modest earnings of her husband (of course her earnings were in his name, since a woman then had no right to her own money). She became famous for her novels which give a skilful, detailed picture of life in the middle and the working class. She was better acquainted with workers than most, since she helped her husband distribute food and comfort in the poorest streets of Manchester, and describes the dignity, intelligence and potential of the underpaid factory workers. After a long period of virtual neglect, like many women writers, her novels have recently been studied again. Her remarkable creative and political capacities are revealed in *North and South* (1855), *Mary Barton* (1848) and *Ruth* (1853).

HÉLOÏSE, (1101–63(4?)) was born in France, and soon lost her parents. Although it was rare at that time for women to be educated, she had an uncle in the church who encouraged her studies. He allowed her to be tutored by Abélard, the leading philosopher at the University of Paris.

Abélard and Héloïse fell passionately in love. She had a son by him, and, in an attempt to appease her relations, married Abélard in secret. But in a fury her uncle sent his servants to castrate Abélard. Subsequently Abélard entered a monastery, and persuaded Héloïse to become a nun, although she felt strongly that she had no vocation for a religious life. She wrote letters to Abélard revealing her despair and her continual longing for him. In response, he wrote as her religious adviser, and gradually their correspondence became more concerned with questions of faith, morality and religious discipline.

Héloïse became the abbess of the Paraclete, and under her charge it became one of the most distinguished religious houses in France. She died as one of the great abbesses of the Church, admired for her skills, her sanctity and her intellect.

Eight letters between Héloïse and Abélard written in Latin survive. These date from 1128–34. In the first Abélard recounts the details and conflicts of his relations with Héloïse. When this came into the hands of Héloïse, she wrote reproaching him for his neglect, entreating him to answer. He replied coldly at first, then more comfortingly. The correspondence ends with two long letters of spiritual advice from him.

HILDEGARD OF BINGEN (1098–1179) was born in a German prov-
ince bordering the Rhine, where her family owned estates. She was their
tenth child, offered to the local Benedictine monastery as a gift at the
age of eight. She lived immured with an anchoress till she was fifteen,
learning the liturgy, and to pray in Latin. She wrote in Latin, though
she was never taught it officially. Like many at the time, she dictated
her books to the provost, a man called Volmar, who encouraged her
spiritual development.

From childhood she experienced frequent religious visions, and felt
called to preach. To gain male support she wrote to Bernard of Clairvaux;
once he had answered approvingly she gained confidence and became
well-known both for her visions and her preaching. Her learning was
wide, almost miraculous in one who had received so little formal education. She believed that it came from God. Her writings include three
visionary books: *Know the Ways* (1141–51), *The Book of Life's Merits*, a
moral treatise (1158–63); her most mature is her last, *The Book of Divine
Works*, which links science, our psyche and the cosmos. She also wrote
a book on *Medicine* based on her knowledge of healing herbs, and analysis
of the four elements, dating back to the Greeks. Her science offers
remedies for many ailments, combining medicine with recommendations
for calmer, more spiritual ways of living. Furthermore she was an outstanding composer of plainsong (which should no longer be called Greg-
orian chant, since her compositions for her nuns to sing are so beautiful)
and wrote what may be termed the first opera. Her sermons were well
attended in her time, and attracted many requests for spiritual guidance.
One hundred and forty-five of her letters, from 1147 to 1179 survive.
They show us a mystic in action, as preacher, counsellor and religious
thinker.

LADY HONOR LISLE (1490?–1566) was the second wife of Lord
Lisle, illegitimate son of King Edward IV, a Plantagenet. He was easy-
going, but she was ambitious and hoped to produce a Plantagenet heir.
She was disappointed in this, but enlarged her ample estates in Devon,
and ensured the worldly success of the children by her first marriage
to Basset. Her husband was appointed Lord Deputy of Calais, where
she accompanied him. Their correspondence with England gives us
an unusual, virtually unique insight into the way such a family lived,
running their many households, finding homes for their daughters to
be trained in the habits of court, supervising their sons' tutors. The
letters span the years 1533–40, a turbulent period under Henry VIII,

when even the well-born had to be skilful to avoid his arbitrary decisions.

MADAME (1652–1722) was the daughter of the Elector Palatine, and a cousin of George I. She married the only brother of Louis XIV, known as 'Monsieur' and lived at Versailles for much of her life. Her letters contain the intimate history of the French court, not intended for publication. They were addressed to close friends, including the Princess of Wales. They are notable for their first-hand knowledge, vivacity and honesty. Her early letters reveal a Louis XIV seldom seen now in history books – considerate, just, and a loving father. After the deaths of the many heirs of Louis XIV, her son Philippe became Regent to the young Louis XV. In that position Madame had to perform many public duties, while keeping an eye on her son's numerous legitimate and illegitimate children. She died of dropsy in 1722, followed by her son only one year later. Unfortunately during that year he had requested the return of her letters from many correspondents, and destroyed them.

KATHERINE MANSFIELD (1888–1923) was born in Wellington, New Zealand. She came to London to study at Queens College, 1903–6. In 1908, in Bavaria, she wrote her first published volume of short stories *In a German Pension* (1911). She had married in 1909, but that first marriage lasted only a few days. She became pregnant, but by another man. The child was stillborn, in fact she never had a child which survived. In 1911 she fell in love with the writer and editor John Middleton Murry. Her letters to him are passionate and moving, longing for his presence which he denied somewhat frequently, because he had to earn a living. They married in 1918, staying occasionally with Frieda and D.H. Lawrence, who recreated them as the protagonists of *Women in Love*. After the collection *Bliss and Other Stories* in 1920, she produced *The Garden Party and Other Stories* in 1922. The following year she died of tuberculosis, then incurable.

MARIA THERESA (1717–80) was Austrian Empress and Queen, by marriage, of Bohemia. She was born in Vienna, the eldest of three daughters of the Holy Roman Emperor Charles VI and his wife. At eighteen she married the then Duke of Tuscany, who became Emperor of Austria. Their union was described as a marriage of love rather than convenience and they had sixteen children, ten of whom survived to adulthood, including Marie Antoinette.

After Charles' unexpected death in 1740, the twenty-three-year-old Maria Theresa, then expecting her fourth child, immediately assumed control. Her initial impetuosity and love of frivolity gave way to a stern, autocratic and rather puritanical style. She ensured that her husband was crowned Emperor in 1745 and instituted severe taxes and levies to pay for an army to defend her right to the throne, which was challenged by Frederick the Great of Prussia in the War of the Austrian Succession. To do so she limited the power of the nobles, enlarged the central administration, reformed the treasury, implemented sweeping changes in the civil service and the universities, and, despite her piety, brought the Church more strictly under state control.

Towards the end of her life she was often ill, but remained an able far-seeing ruler, who had re-united many areas of the Austro-Hungarian Empire.

HARRIET MARTINEAU (1802–76). English novelist, political economist, and children's writer. She was born into a Huguenot family which had settled in Norwich in the seventeenth century; her father was a textile manufacturer. She had a strict puritanical upbringing, and her good education was marred by her nervousness and increasing deafness. In 1819, after a visit to a school-mistress aunt in Bristol, she became intensely religious and her first works were *Devotional Exercises for the use of Young Persons* (1823) and *Addresses for the Use of Families* (1826). In 1826 her father went bankrupt and within a short space of time her father, brother and fiancé all died; from then on she was determined to become independent as a professional writer.

In 1831, after winning prizes for essays in the *Unitarian Journal*, she visited her brother in Dublin. On her return, influenced by the work of Jane Marcet, she decided to write a series of stories illustrating principles of political economy, which was then a new subject. She began publishing her *Illustrations of Political Economy* (1832–4) in which ideas taken from Mill, James and Ricardo formed the basis of short tales. The series was an instant success. Similar series on reform issues were *Poor Laws and Paupers Illustrated* (1833–4) and *Forest and Game-Law Tales* (1845–6). Harriet now established herself as a London journalist. She visited the USA (1834–6) where she attended abolitionist meetings, publishing *Society in America* in 1837.

She was a contributor to the *London Daily News* from 1852 to 1866, her radical articles covering diverse subjects, from agricultural economics to the evils of licensed prostitution. She also supported the Married

Women's Property Bill in 1857 and wrote a critical article on women's employment, *Female Industry*, in 1859. In 1849 she had become Secretary of Bedford College for Women, London. In 1851 she described her rationalist philosophy in *Letters on the Laws of Man's Nature and Development* (with H.G. Atkinson) and in 1853 published a translation, *The Philosophy of Comte*.

In 1854 she was told she was incurably ill, and she was prompted to write her brilliant and courageous *Autobiography*, which was not published until after her death in 1876.

MARY I (Mary Tudor; Bloody Mary) (1516–58). Queen of England. The daughter of Henry VIII and Catherine of Aragon, she was born at Greenwich Palace, and was given a superb education by her mother and by scholars such as Linacre and Vives, but even as a child she was a political pawn, with bids for her hand coming from France, Austria and other sources. Eventually she was betrothed to Charles V, the Holy Roman Emperor and King of Spain, though she did not marry him. When she became Queen, she returned England to Catholicism. Philip II of Spain, an ardent Catholic, married her in order to unite their Kingdoms. She longed to have a child and heir, but was unable to do so, possibly because of the syphilis of her father.

MARY, QUEEN OF SCOTS (1542–87). Scottish queen, claimant to the English throne. Born at Linlithgow, West Lothian, she was the only child of James V of Scotland and the French Mary of Guise. She became Queen when she was six days old, and her mother betrothed her to the French dauphin (later Francis II) and sent her to France at the age of five to be brought up at the court of Henry II and Catherine de Medici. Her childhood was happy and she received an excellent education, learning Latin, Italian and Spanish, and a little Greek, and speaking French as a first language. She married Francis under a treaty whereby a male heir would unite the two thrones. In the same year Elizabeth I's succession to the English throne was challenged by Mary's Catholic supporters. Francis was crowned in 1559, but died in 1560, and the young widow returned to Scotland in 1561.

Diplomatic and charming, she took pro-English counsellors, her illegitimate brother James and William Maitland, and overcame hostility to her Catholicism by her policy of tolerance, accepting the Presbyterian Church but continuing to attend Mass herself. Her marriage in 1565 to Henry Stewart, Earl of Darnley, an equal claimant to the English throne, caused a political crisis, and his jealous murder in her presence of her confidential secretary Rizzio made life intolerable. After the birth of their son James she became involved with James Hepburn, Earl of Bothwell, and when Darnley was found murdered in January 1565, he was suspected but acquitted. Three months later Bothwell abducted Mary, rapidly divorced his wife and married her. The Scots rebelled, and by June Bothwell was exiled (he died in prison in 1587). Mary was banished to Lochleven Castle and deposed in favour of James. She was executed at Fotheringay at the age of forty-four. She has remained a potent and mysterious figure in history and literature.

FLORENCE NIGHTINGALE (1820–1910) was born into a wealthy English family, trapped by the conventions of the times into a restricted existence as a dutiful, enforcedly idle, daughter. At the age of twenty-four, she asked permission to take a three-month course in nursing. Her mother responded with hysterical convulsions and her father called her a spoiled, ungrateful child. Florence obeyed her parents, but the need she felt to be of use did not vanish. By studying governmental reports on social conditions she became a self-taught expert on social statistics. A visit to a Lutheran hospital in Germany further inspired her, and then, in 1853, when she was thirty-three, Florence was invited to become the Superintendent of the Institute for Sick Gentlewomen in Distressed Circumstances. Her father decided to give her the yearly allowance which would make her independent, and allow her to work.

In her new role Florence Nightingale learnt much about organization, but little about practical nursing. However in 1854 there was a cholera epidemic in London, and Florence went to the Middlesex Hospital as a volunteer. Here she set new, high standards for nursing, and her work was so impressive that the government formally invited her to lead a party of nurses to improve conditions at the barrack hospital in Scutari during the Crimean War.

It was there, leading a party of thirty-eight nurses, that Florence Nightingale came into her own, reforming the medical organization within the British Army, raising the standard of hygiene, reorganizing the supply system, and reducing the death rate by nearly forty per cent in a matter of months. By the time she returned to England in 1856 she was a national heroine, 'the Lady with the Lamp'.

She founded the Nightingale School of Nursing at St Thomas' Hospital in 1860, and nursing began to be seen as a respectable and highly respected profession for women. In 1907 Florence Nightingale became the first woman to be awarded the Order of Merit.

ANAÏS NIN (1903–77). Her father was the Spanish composer, Joaquin Nin, her mother was half French and she was born in Paris. In 1914 they went to New York, and she later took American citizenship. However she returned to Paris with her husband, a banker, in 1923, had a long affair with Henry Miller and was a friend of Lawrence Durrell. She worked briefly as a model, and for a while practised as a psychoanalyst under Otto Bank. In her time she was best known for her erotic writings including *Delta of Venus and Erotica* (1977). She wrote novels, criticism (*The Novel of the Future* [1968]) and short stories; I consider her most interesting writing to be her renowned *Diary* in ten volumes.

CAROLINE NORTON (1808–77). Granddaughter of Sheridan, she married a barrister and Member of Parliament. He became brutal, often beat her, and in 1832 left her, taking their three sons. Against friends' advice, she attempted to regain her children by legal means. After careful study of the law she wrote *The Separation of Mother and Child by the Law of Custody* (1837), which led to the passage of the first Infants Custody Bill allowing children up to the age of seven to remain with their mothers. Sadly, Norton had already taken the boys to Scotland, where one died in a riding accident. She later wrote *English Laws for Women in the Nineteenth Century* (1854) which was influential in the Reform of Marriage and Divorce Laws, passed in 1857.

DOROTHY OSBORNE (1627–95). Her father, Sir Peter, governed Guernsey for Charles I. She fell in love with William Temple, later to become Archbishop of Canterbury. He was the eldest son of Sir John Temple, a member of the Long Parliament. As Sir John wanted a more advantageous marriage for his son, for seven years they were forced to maintain their relationship through correspondence. Her letters are unusually lively, well crafted and witty – and prove that she could well have written an epistolary novel if her family had allowed her some ambition. We learn of the interests and daily life of a Cavalier family; and gain precious insights into the mind and feelings of a remarkably caring and isolated woman in the seventeenth century, whose letters deserve wider readership.

MARGARET PASTON (*c.*1420–84) inherited property from her father John Mautby of Caister. She had an arranged marriage with John Paston, whose father made money by studying law and buying up property near the small Norfolk village of Paston, where he was born. John worked in London, an absence which has provided us with one of the most fascinating collections of letters to survive the Wars of the Roses. Margaret's first letters to him when he was studying in Cambridge are formal, but soon become warmer in tone. They all include details about the daily life and requirements of a large estate, and give us unique knowledge of the duties and skills of a lady of the manor, in peacetime, and under siege.

EMMELINE PANKHURST (1858–1922). Often simply referred to as Mrs Pankhurst, she came from Manchester to London in 1905 and led the militant Women's Social and Political Union before the First World War. Her three daughters, Christabel, Sylvia and Adela, were born in Manchester and initially educated at home and at Manchester High School. They all joined their mother in the early activities of the Women's Social and Political Union (WSPU) but their lives took increasingly divergent paths after 1910.

CHRISTINE DE PISAN (*c.* 1364–*c.* 1430) was born in Venice. She was the daughter of an Italian physician in the service of Charles V, and brought up in Paris. At twenty-five she was left a widow with three small children and an elderly mother to support. She did this from her home, successfully, with her pen. In fact she is the first professional woman writer. She was a woman of intelligence and education (a 'blue-stocking' in the opinion of some), and wrote both in prose and verse. Her prose works include *La Cité des dames* and *Le Livre des trois vertus* (a treatise on women's education). In her *Epître au dieu d'amour* (1399) and *Dit de la rose* (1400) she ardently took up the defence of her sex against the strictures of Jean de Meung. Her poetry comprised *ballades* and longer poems on themes of love, also a *Ditié en l'honneur de Jeanne d'Arc* (whose early successes she witnessed), showing her devotion to the country of her adoption. Of this and her other patriotic tales an English translation was printed by Caxton (*The Fayttes of Arms*, 1489). Another translation, *The City of Ladies*, was probably printed originally by Wynkyn de Worde. A recent translation of this remarkable book was made by E. V. Richards and published in New York in 1982 by Persea Books.

JEAN RHYS, pseudonym of Gwen Williams (1894–1970), was the daughter of a doctor in Dominica and educated at a convent there. In 1910 she accompanied an aunt to England, where she briefly went to school in Cambridge, and then to Tree's Academy, and later to the Royal Academy of Dramatic Art. After the death of her father, she had to earn her own living, and she changed her name to Jean Rhys and went into vaudeville. In 1919 she married Max Hamer, a Dutch poet and translator, and went to live in Vienna, Budapest and finally Paris. There she met James Joyce, Ernest Hemingway, the poet H.D., Djuna Barnes, and, most important, Ford Madox Ford, who became her literary mentor. Her relationship with Ford and his wife is portrayed in her first novel, *Quartet* (1928). She wrote three more novels before the Second World War, all depicting women duped or betrayed by the men they love or struggling to survive alone, as in *Good Morning, Midnight* (1939). During this period she also worked as a translator, a tutor and a fashion model. She divorced and returned to England in 1934, and later remarried. She then lapsed into obscurity until the publication of her last novel, *The Wide Sargasso Sea* (1966), which told the story of Mr Rochester's first wife, Bertha, in Charlotte Brontë's *Jane Eyre*, and which was partly set in the Caribbean of her childhood. At the end of her life she divided her time between a remote cottage in Devon and London. Her autobiography, *Smile Please*, was unfinished, but was published posthumously in 1980.

GEORGE SAND, pseudonym of Amandine Aurore Lucile Dupin, Baronne Dudevant (1804–76). An illegitimate daughter of the Maréchal de Saxe, she spent her early childhood with her grandmother at the château of Nohant. She was educated at a convent and returned to Nohant in 1820, marrying Baron Dudevant two years later. She found Nohant and married life stifling and in 1831 she left her husband, taking her two children with her to Paris. There she outraged bourgeois society by her unconventional ways. She not only wore trousers and smoked cigars in public, but had various love affairs: with Jules Sandeau, with whom she collaborated on newspaper articles and a novel, and from whose name her pseudonym was derived, and later with the Romantic poet, Alfred de Musset. Her literary output was prolific and her novels defend both sensual and idealistic love: *Indiana* (1832); *Valentine* (1832); *Lélia* (1833); *Mauprat* (1838). *Lélia* created a sensation for its erotic candour. From the time of her relationship with Chopin, which lasted ten years, her private life became quieter and she turned her interest to politics. In *Le meunier d'Angibault* (1845) she exalts the working man, while in *Consuelo* (1842) she preaches a pantheistic religion. In 1848 she supported the Revolution and wrote *Lettres au peuple* but retreated to Nohant at the time of the June insurrection. Here she wrote a series of pastoral novels including *La petite Fadette* (1849). Under the Second Empire, George Sand became a *grande dame* in the village of Nohant – entertaining writers and artists, presiding over village fêtes and bestowing alms. In 1854 her autobiography, *L'histoire de ma vie*, was published. Although her exalted style and outspoken views on conventional marriage now seem dated she was hailed as a great writer by many contemporary critics and writers, even the exacting Flaubert, author of *Madame Bovary*.

SEI SHONAGON (*c.* 965–?) was born in Japan. She served as lady-in-waiting to the cultured Empress, a brief, enlightened reign in the last decade of the tenth century. Her father was a provincial official, known for his poetry and scholarship. She may have married a government official, and she may have had a son. Once her court service ended we know nothing more about her, and she probably died in lonely poverty. Our knowledge of her comes from her skilful, subtle *Pillow Book*, an extraordinarily sensitive, poetic and intelligent account of her life and acquaintances in tenth-century Japan.

STEVIE SMITH (1902–71). Born in Hull, she moved to an aunt's house in Palmer's Green, London, where she lived till her death. Her lifelong employment was with magazine publishers, which she mentions in her first book, *Novel on Yellow Paper* (1936). She is best known for her poems, now in eight slim volumes, often illustrated with her own line drawings. These recall the naïve humour of Edward Lear, whose love life was not unlike hers – sad, yet irrepressible. Her witty, wry poems reached a wide audience thanks to her distinctive public readings and recordings.

GERMAINE DE STAËL (1766–1817) was a French novelist, literary critic, political writer and philosopher of history. Her mother was a strict Calvinist and her father, whom she greatly admired, was an eminent figure in French financial and political life and he encouraged her interest in politics. She received an intellectually rigorous education and her interest in literature was stimulated by her mother's famous literary salon. In 1786 her parents arranged for her to marry Baron Eric Magnus de Staël-Holstein, the Swedish ambassador in Paris. The marriage was an unhappy one and Madame de Staël had many love affairs, including a long-standing one with the Comte de Narbonne and a turbulent one with the writer, Benjamin Constant. Before the French Revolution she opened a salon which became a meeting place for the liberal aristocracy. However her initial sympathy for the ideals of the Revolution soured and she escaped from Paris. She returned in 1795 and re-opened her salon which during the Consulat became a centre for opposition to Napoleon, who saw her influence as so dangerous that in 1804 he refused to allow her to live in France. She retreated to the family estate, Coppet, by Lake Geneva in Switzerland, and her home became a meeting-place for leading intellectuals. During the years in exile she travelled widely. She returned to Paris in 1814 after Napoleon's abdication and continued to be an influential figure in European politics until her death.

A pioneer of French Romanticism, her principal works include *De l'influence des passions sur le bonheur des individuels et des nations* (1796), in which she developed one of the favourite themes, the impossibility of separating ideas from feelings; *De la littérature considérée dans ses rapports avec les institutions sociales* (1800); *De l'Allemagne* (suppressed by Napoleon in 1810 but published in London in 1813); and her two novels *Delphine* (1803) and *Corinne ou l'Italie* (1807), which contain self-portraits and relate to her liaison with Constant.

SAINT TERESA (1515–82) was born in Avila to a devout Catholic family. This small town, high in the Castilian mountains, walled to protect it from Moorish attack, still contains many impressive churches and convents. When young, she and her brother set off one day to convert the Moors, but were soon recaptured. This religious enthusiasm inspired her whole life, dedicated to the reform of Carmelite convents. With the Pope's permission she set up many new convents, where she took full share of the work, alongside less nobly born nuns. She often quoted the proverb 'God is also in the kitchen'. In spite of ill health, arduous travelling and organizing, she found time for writing. Her books include *Las Moradas* (*In My Father's House There are Many Mansions*) and some of the most direct mystic poetry in Spanish, including the well-known 'Que muero porque no muero' (I'm dying of longing for death). Her *Autobiography* is virtually the first to appear in Spain. Yet eminently practical at the same time, she raised funds for her new institutions, a lasting memorial to her faith.

FLORA TRISTAN (Célestine Thérèse) (1803–44). Flora Tristan's father was a Peruvian Spanish colonel and her uncle was President of

Peru, yet she was brought up in poverty in Paris by her widowed French mother. In 1821 she married her employer, the painter and engraver André Chazel, but left him in 1824, initiating a long battle over custody of their children. From 1825 to 1830 she worked as governess to an English family. In 1830 she went to Peru, in a vain attempt to persuade her uncle to support the family. Eight years later the frank revelations in her autobiography, *Pérégrinations d'une paria*, provoked her husband to attempt murder, for which he was sentenced to twenty-two years' hard labour. Their grandson was Paul Gauguin. On returning to France in 1834 she wrote various feminist tracts. A great admirer of Mary Wollstonecraft, she was first influenced by the libertarian philosophy of Fourier, and then by the social reformism of Robert Owen, whom she met in 1837. She continued to write, publishing the novel *Mephis* in 1838. During a long visit to England she studied Chartism and made a detailed analysis of social conditions which resulted in her *Promenades de Londres* (1840). Her travels had crystallized her strong socialist and feminist views and in 1843 she published her *Union ouvrière*. This is the first proposal for a Socialist International, advocating the uniting of all artisan clubs into a single international union, and the establishment of educational and welfare centres on a co-operative basis, as 'Workers' Palaces'. She died of typhoid in Bordeaux while travelling around France to publicize her ideas. The workers of the city collected funds for her tombstone, which is inscribed *Liberté-Egalité-Fraternité-Solidarité*.

NELLIE WEETON (1776–1844) was one of the few governesses whose letters were preserved by friends and relatives. We learn of her support for a sick mother, an improvident brother, a brutal husband; above all we read of her varied experiences in middle-class homes, in *Miss Weeton: Journal of a Governess* published in 1936 by E. Day.

DAME REBECCA WEST (1892–1983) was the adopted name of Cicily Fairfield, of an Anglo-Irish family. The father died young, leaving a widow with four daughters, in straitened circumstances. Rebecca adopted this name after the heroine of Ibsen's *Rosmersholm*, at nineteen. She trained briefly for the stage, then turned to journalism. When she met the Pankhursts she became an ardent supporter of women's rights. From 1911 she wrote for the *Freewoman*. Many of her witty polemical articles have been collected in *The Young Rebecca*: this includes her outspoken review of H. G. Wells' *Marriage* (1912), which led to a ten-year love affair and the birth of a son, Anthony. Her first novel, *The Return of the Soldier* (1918), describes the return of a shell-shocked soldier. Two of her best known are *The Fountain Overflows* (1957) and *The Birds Fall Down* (1966). In 1930 she married a banker, Henry Maxwell Andrews. She was present at the Nuremberg trials and her *Meaning of Treason* grew out of articles she wrote then.

MARY WOLLSTONECRAFT (Godwin) (1759–97). She was born in Hoxton near London of Irish parents. Largely self-educated, in 1778 she began work as a companion in Bath. After her mother's death in 1782 she started a school in Newington Green with her friend Fanny Blood and met many liberal non-conformists; the school failed and Fanny left and later died in childbirth in Lisbon, while Mary was hurrying to nurse her. In 1787 she published *Thoughts on the Education of Daughters*, and took a post as governess to Lord Kingsborough's family, but by 1790 she was back in London, working for the publisher Johnson, reading manuscripts, writing articles and translating. She became a member of a radical intellectual group which included Tom Paine, William Godwin and Fuseli, to whom she was deeply attached. In 1792 she went to Paris and began her love affair with the American Gilbert Imlay, following him to Le Havre, where their daughter Fanny was born in 1794. She returned with him to England and travelled on business to Norway for him, but, unable to accept his infidelity, attempted suicide at Putney Bridge in 1795. During 1796 she worked for Johnson again and met William Godwin, and despite objections of principle they married when she became pregnant. She died of puerperal fever ten days after the birth of their daughter Mary (later Mary Shelley). Her *Vindication of the Rights of Women* challenges Rousseau's notions of female inferiority, arguing for equality of education, employment for single women, and companionship with men. It caused a scandal, linked by critics to her own unconventional life, but has become a seminal work in the tradition of liberal feminism.

LADY MARY WORTLEY MONTAGU (1689–1762) was the eldest child of the Earl of Kingston. She married in 1712, against her father's wishes, after a long courtship. While courting, she wrote her future husband, a government employee, letters that were witty, teasing, passionate and sensible, yet at times aimed to provoke jealousy. Lytton Strachey declared them 'strange love-letters, of the deepest interest' in 1907.

Her children were a rebellious son and much-loved daughter. Soon marriage became difficult, since her husband proved somewhat cold, hard-headed and with far fewer interests than his wife. Nevertheless she accompanied him to Turkey for two years when he was made ambassador there, and her letters home give us invaluable glimpses of other societies. Back in England she soon gained a reputation for her learning and wit, and was counted, rightly, among the great letter-writers, including Lord Chesterfield, Johnson, Alexander Pope and Walpole. She has other claims to distinction, as travel-writer, educationist and above all as an outspoken feminist who concerned herself with women's education and rights.

SOURCES AND ACKNOWLEDGEMENTS

The editor and publisher gratefully acknowledge permission to include brief extracts. We have assiduously contacted every source and apologise if a letter is not correctly attributed, because a request went unanswered.

(All books are published in London, unless otherwise stated)

Adams, Carol and Bartley, Paula (eds), *From Workshop to Warfare* (C.U.P. 1983)

Aitken, James, *English Letters of the XVIII Century* (Pelican 1946)

Austen, Jane, *Letters*, R.W. Chapman (ed.) (OUP 1932)

Bâ, Mariama, *So Long a Letter*, M. Bodé-Thomas (trans.) (Virago 1982)

Barbera, Jack and McBrien, W., *Stevie: A Biography of Stevie Smith* (Macmillan 1985)

Behn, Aphra, *Love Letters between a Nobleman and his Sister* (Virago 1987. First published in 3 vols, probably 1684–7)

Bell, Lady (ed.), *The Letters of Gertrude Bell* (Benn 1930)

Benstock, Shari (ed.), *Women of the Left Bank* (Virago 1988)

Bird, Isabella, *A Lady's Life in the Rocky Mountains* (Virago 1982)

Blanch, Lesley, *The Wilder Shores of Love* (Murray 1954)

Brittain, Vera, *Lady into Women* (A. Dakers 1953)
      Selected Letters of Winifred Holtby and Vera Brittain 1920–35 (A. Brown 1960)

Burney, Fanny, *Diary and Letters* 7 vols ed. by her niece, Charlotte Frances Barratt (Henty Colburn 1842–6)

Cahiers Balzaciens, *Lettres de femmes adressées à Honoré de Balzac 1832–6* (Paris 1924 pp 43–4)

Carlyle, Jane, *Letters and Memorials*, J. Froude (ed) (1883)

Chapple, J.A.V. (ed), *The Letters of Elizabeth Gaskell* (Manchester University Press 1967)

Coghill, Mrs Harry, *The Autobiography and Letters of Mrs Oliphant* (Blackwood 1899)

Crankshaw, E., *Maria Theresa* (Longman 1969)

David-Néel, A., *My Journey to Lhasa* (Souvenir Press 1983)

Davidoff, L., and Hall, C., *Family Fortunes: Men and Women of the English Middle Class 1780–1850* (Hutchinson 1987)

Dent, A. (ed), *Bernard Shaw and Mrs Patrick Campbell: Their Correspondence* (Gollancz 1952)

De Saho, L., and Leaska, M. (eds), *The Letters of Vita Sackville-West and Virginia Woolf* (Macmillan 1984)

Duff Gordon, L., *Letters from Egypt* (reprinted Virago 1988)

Eden, Emily, *Up the Country: Letters from India* (E. Eden 1872)

Edgeworth, Maria, *Letters for Literary Ladies* (Edgeworth 1795)

Elizabeth, Queen, *Letters* 1558–1570, G. Harrison (ed.) (Greenwood Press 1935). Her letters are all in the Fawcett Library, London E.1.

Fernandez-Arnesto, F., *Ferdinand and Isabella* (Weidenfeld 1975)

Fox, M., *Letters of Hildegard of Bingen* (Bear, USA 1987)

Fraser, Antonia, *Love Letters* (Penguin 1953)
    Mary Queen of Scots (Weidenfeld 1969)

Fyrth, Jim, with Sally Alexander, *Women's Voices from the Spanish Civil War* (Lawrence & Wishart 1991)

Gerin, Winifred, *Branwell Bronte* (Hutchinson 1961)
    Charlotte Bronte (O.U.P. 1967)

Glendinning, Victoria, *Rebecca West* (Weidenfeld 1985)

Grosvenor Myer, Valerie, *A Victorian Lady in Africa; Mary Kingsley* (Ashford Press 1989)

Haight, Gordon, *George Eliot: A Biography* (O.U.P. 1968)
    Selections from George Eliot's Letters (Yale University Press 1954)

Halsband, R., *The Complete Letters of Lady Mary Wortley Montagu* (Oxford, Clarendon Press 1965)

Hanscombe, G., and Smyers, V.L., *Writing for Their Lives* (Women's Press 1987)

Hawkes, Jean (trans), *The London Journal of Flora Tristan* (Virago 1982)

Hellerstein, Erna, Olafson, Hume, Parker, Leslie, and Offen, Karen, *Victorian Women* (Stanford University Press 1981)

Heloise, *Epistola* vols i–clxxviii (in libraries under Abelard!)

Hill, Bridget, *Eighteenth Century Women* (Allen & Unwin 1984)

Honan, Park, *Jane Austen: Her Life* (Weidenfeld 1987)

Hutchinson, Lucy, *Memoirs of the Life of Colonel Hutchinson*, R. Child (ed) (Everyman 1904)

Keay, Julia (ed), *With Passport and Parasol* (BBC Books 1989)

Kenyon, Olga, *800 Years of Women's Letters* (A. Sutton 1992)

Labanoff, *Lettres, etc., de Marie Stuart* vol. 6 (1852)

Lefkowitz, Mary R., and Fant, M.B., *Women's Life in Greece and Rome* (Duckworth 1982)

Martineau, Harriet, *Harriet Martineau's Autobiography* (Boston 1877)

Mavor, Elizabeth, *The Ladies of Llangollen: A Study in Romantic Friendship* (Michael Joseph 1971)

Merriman, Marion, and Leruda, W., *American Commander In Spain* (University of Nevada Press 1986)

Mitchell, David, *The Fighting Pankhursts* (Cape 1967)

Moriarty, Catherine, *The Voice of the Middle Ages* (Oxford, Lennard 1989)

Morris, Mary (ed), *Women Travellers* (Virago 1994)

Nin, Anaïs, *Journals* (Peter Owen 1970)

Osborne, Dorothy, *The Letters of Dorothy Osborne to Sir William Temple* (Everyman 1914)

Pali Text Society, *Elders Verses* 11, K. Norman (ed) (1977)

Pastons: *The Paston Letters* (ed. J. Gairdner Library 1904)

Payne, Karen, *Between Ourselves: Letters Between Mothers and Daughters* (Virago 1994)

Peers, A. (trans), *The Autobiography of St Teresa of Avila* (Sheed 1946)

Perry, Maria, *The Word of a Prince: A Life of Queen Elizabeth* (Boydell & Brewer, Woodbridge, Suffolk 1990)

Pisan, Christine de, *The City of Ladies* (Persea Books, N.Y., 1982)

Rhys, Jean, *Letters 1931–66*, F. Wyndham and D. Melly (eds) (Penguin 1985)

Sand, George (trans and ed. Leclos de Beaufort) 3 vols 1885 (Ward & Downey 1885–6)

Spender, Dale, and Todd, Janet (eds), *Anthology of British Women Writers* (Pandora 1989)

Strachey, Ray, *Millicent Fawcett* (Murray 1931)

Tancock, L. (trans), *Madame de Sévigné: Selected Letters* (Penguin 1982)

Teresa of Avila, *The Complete Works of Saint Teresa of Avila* (trans Allison Peers) (Sheed 1946)

Tomalin, Claire, *The Life and Death of Mary Wollstonecraft* (Weidenfeld 1974)
   Katherine Mansfield: A Secret Life (Viking 1987)

Victoria, Queen, *Letters* 3 vols (John Murray 1907)

Wardle, R. (ed), *Collected Letters of Mary Wollstonecraft* (1979)

Weeton, Nellie, *Miss Weeton: Journal of a Governess*, E. Hall (ed) (1936)

Weldon, Fay, *Letters to Alice, on first reading Jane Austen* (Michael Joseph 1984)

White, C., *Treatise on the Management of Pregnant and Lying-in Women*
   (1777)

I should also like to thank the librarians of Fawcett Library, Morley
College and Bradford University for their help. The many friends who
lovingly read parts of this manuscript and gave me feedback have been
immensely supportive, as have the friends who allowed me to include
their own precious letters to me.

FURTHER READING

Glendinning, Victoria, *Trollope* (Hutchinson 1992) (Her best biography)

Grosvenor Myer, Valerie, *Charlotte Bronte: Truculent Spirit* (Vision 1987)

Howe, Bea, *A Galaxy of Governesses* (Verschoyle 1954)

Kenyon, O., *Introduction to Black Women Novelists* (Bradford University Print Unit 1994)

Power, E., and Postan, M., *Medieval Women* (C.U.P. 1975)

Read, C. *Bibliography of British History* (Clarendon Press 1959)

Roe, Sue (ed), *Women Reading Women's Writing* (Harvester 1988)

Shahar, S. *The Fourth Estate: Women in the Middle Ages* (Methuen 1983)

Simons, Judy, *Fanny Burney* (Macmillan 1987)

Spender, Dale, *Mothers of the Novel: 100 Great Women Novelists Before Jane Austen* (Pandora 1986)

Taplin, G.B., *The Life of Elizabeth Barrett Browning* (1957)

Warner, Marina, *Joan of Arc* (Penguin 1983)

Warrack, G. (ed), *Revelations of Divine Love of Julian of Norwich* (1901)

Wharton, Edith, *The Letters of Edith Wharton*, Lewis (eds) (Simon and Schuster 1988)

Wollstonecraft, Mary, *A Vindication of the Rights of Woman* (London 1792) (New York: Norton 1975, ed. C. Poston)

Wortley Montagu, Lady Mary, *Selected Letters* (St Martins Press, New York 1971. Pelican, London 1986)

HELPFUL BACKGROUND BOOKS

(All published in London, unless otherwise indicated)

Aries, Philippe, *Centuries of Childhood* (trans) R. Baldick (New York 1962)

Bowie, Fiona, and Davies, Oliver, *Hildegard of Bingen: An Anthology* (SPCK, Marylebone Rd, London NW1 4DU 1990)

Chapple, J.A.V. (ed), *Elizabeth Gaskell: A Portrait in Letters* (Manchester University Press 1980)

Clark, Alice, *Working Life of Women in The Seventeenth Century* (Chaytor 1982)

David, Deirdre, *Intellectual Women and Victorian Patriarchy* (1987)

Davidoff, L., and Hall, C., *Family Fortunes: Men and Women of the English Middle Class 1780–1850* (Hutchinson 1987)

Dyson, H., and Tennyson, C., *Dear and Honoured Lady: The Correspondence of Queen Victoria and Tennyson* (Murray 1969)

Feinstein, Elaine, *Marina Tsvetayeva* (Penguin 1989)

Feuillâtre, E. (ed), *Lettres Choisies de Madame de Sévigné* (Larousse, Paris 1965)

Figes, Eva (ed), *Women's Letters in Wartime* (Pandora 1993)

Glendinning, Victoria, *The Life of Vita Sackville-West* (Weidenfeld 1983)

Goldsmith, Elizabeth, *Writing Female Voices: Essays on the Epistolary Novel* (Pinter Press 1989)

Haight, Gordon (ed), *The Portable Victorian Reader* (Penguin 1972)

Harrison, G., *The Letters of Queen Elizabeth I* (Greenwood Press 1935)

Hildegard of Bingen's *Book of Divine Works*, M. Fox (ed) (Bear, New Mexico 1987)

Longford, Elizabeth, *Victoria R.I* (Weidenfeld 1989)

Navor, Elizabeth, *The Ladies of Llangollen: A Study in Romantic Friendship* (Michael Joseph 1971)

McCleod, M., *The Order of the Rose: Life and Ideas of Christine de Pisan*

Middleton, D., *Victorian Lady Travellers* (Routledge 1965)

Mitchell, David, *Queen Christabel* (Cape 1965)

Newton, J., Ryan, M.P., Walkowitz, J.R. (eds), *Sex and Class in Women's History* (Routledge & Kegan Paul 1983)

Oakley, Ann, *Women's Work: A History of the Housewife* (New York 1974)

Ostriker, A.S., *Stealing the Language* (Beacon Press, Boston USA 1986)

Palser, H.C., *This Grand Beyond: The Travels of Isabella Bird* (Century 1984)

Power, E., and Postan, M., *Medieval Women* (C.U.P. 1975)

Radice, B. (trans), *Letters of Abelard and Heloise* (1974)

Raymond, J. (ed), *The Early Letters of Queen Victoria* (Murray 1963)

Read, C., *Bibliography of British History* (Clarendon Press 1959)

Simons, Judy, *Fanny Burney* (Macmillan 1987)

Spender, Dale, *Mothers of the Novel* (Pandora 1986)

Stanley, Arthur, *Madame de Sévigné, her Letters and her World* (Eyre & Spottiswoode 1946)

Stoddart, A., *The Life of Isabella Bird* (John Murray 1906)

Taplin, G.B., *The Life of Elizabeth Barrett Browning* (1957)

Tillotson, K., *Novels of the 1840s* (Oxford Paperback 1961)

Todd, Janet, *Women's Friendship in Literature* (Pandora 1980)

Tong, Rosemarie, *Feminist Thought* (Unwin Hyman 1989)

Trollope, Frances, *Domestic Manners of Americans* (ed) van Thal (Folio Society 1974)

Vicinus, M., *Independent Women: Work and Community for Single Women 1850-1920* (1985)

Walker, Alice, *The Color Purple* (Women's Press 1983)

Warner, Marina, *Alone of All Her Sex* (Pan 1985)

Warnock, Kitty, *Mary Wollstonecraft* (Hamish Hamilton 1988)

Wolff, C.G., *Classic American Women Writers* (Harper & Row, New York 1980)

Wollstonecraft, Mary, and Godwin, W., *A Short Residence in Sweden* and *Memoirs of The Author of 'The Rights of Woman'*, R. Holmes (ed) (Penguin 1987)

Wood, Nigel, *Dr Johnson and Fanny Burney* (Bristol Classical Press 1989)

INDEX

Note: page references for the letters reproduced in this book are given following the appearance of author's names in **bold**.